A GUIDE TO

SACRED

SHAMBHALA WARRIORSHIP

WORLD

IN DAILY LIFE

JEREMY HAYWARD

December '95

Sacred World

For, Mom, Dad & Michael.

I work closely with the author. I would like to share this with you.

Love Lesley

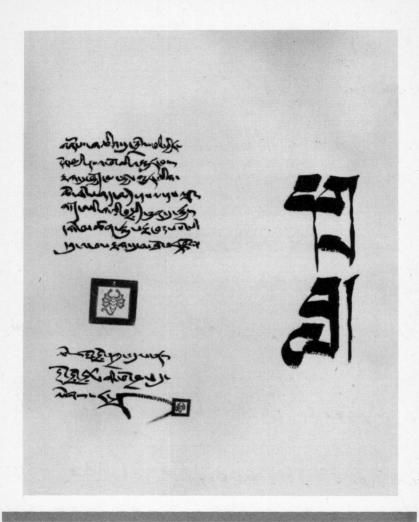

A gift to the author from the Dorje Dradul, July 1979.

DRALA

In order that you may join heaven and earth
May the unchanging ultimate Warrior
Ever protect you.
May you possess long life, freedom from sickness, glory
And ever-increasing primordial dignity.
May your good virtuous windhorse
Be glorified eternally higher and higher.

Written by the Dorje Dradul
at the palace of Dorje Dzong

Sacred World

A Guide to Shambhala Warriorship in Daily Life

Jeremy Hayward

with

Karen Hayward

Bantam Books
New York Toronto London Sydney Auckland

SACRED WORLD

A Bantam Book / June 1995

All rights reserved.

For Permissions, please see page 263.

Book design by Maria Carella

Library of Congress Cataloging-in-Publication Data

Hayward, Jeremy W.
Sacred world: a guide to Shambala warriorship in daily life / Jeremy Hayward
p.   cm.
Includes bibliographical references and index.
ISBN 0-553-37195-9
1. Spiritual life.   I. Title.
BL624.H378   1995
294.3'444—dc20   94-41949
                                           CIP

Published simultaneously in the United States and Canada

Bantam Books are published by Bantam Books, a division of Bantam Doubleday Dell Publishing Group, Inc. Its trademark, consisting of the words "Bantam Books" and the portrayal of a
rooster, is Registered in U.S. Patent and Trademark Office and in other countries. Marca
Registrada. Bantam Books, 1540 Broadway, New York, New York 10036.

PRINTED IN THE UNITED STATES OF AMERICA

BVG   10 9 8 7 6 5 4 3 2 1

Contents

Part One
A Vision of Sacredness

Part Two
The Practice of Warriorship

x

Contents

Part Three
Authentic Action in the World

Acknowledgments

Many friends and fellow Shambhala warriors read the manuscript at various stages along the way, and offered encouraging advice and precise criticism. Among these I particularly want to thank Sam Bercholz, David Brown, Jan Cressman, Ken Friedman, Bill Gordon, Andrew Holecek, Lodro Dorje Holm, Carol Hyman, Sherab Chodzin Kohn, Peter Lieberson, Mark Matthews, Jill Morley, Douglas Penick, Shelley Pierce, David Rome, and Alan Sloan. Thanks also to Leslie Meredith, my editor at Bantam, for her gentle and insightful suggestions.

I received many letters from Shambhala warriors telling personal stories that illustrated their own journeys and that they felt could help others. Thanks to all of you who responded for your generosity and openness. I have changed the names of the storytellers, since some of them preferred to remain unknown.

Emily Hilburn Sell helped to get this project off the ground, and together we spent several months preparing a proposal with the encouragement and insight of our agent Jeff Stone. I am grateful to Emily for her help and support in this phase of the writing.

Karen worked closely with me in the actual writing of the book, discussing every detail with patience and insight. She contributed directly to the writing, bringing genuine heart and the inspiration of the dralas.

Introduction

There are many ways to discover and rediscover the sacredness and magic of human life. At heart, all of these ways are much the same, revealing human life as a journey and an adventure that has no end. This journey is a quest for joining inner and outer experience, mind and body, and waking up to the reality of being genuinely human. The path that I will be describing in this book is called the Shambhala path of the warrior. The Shambhala teachings describe ordinary human life, lived fully and completely, as a path of warriorship. To be a warrior, whether you are male or female, is to dare to live genuinely, even in the face of obstacles like fear, doubt, depression, and external aggression. Being a warrior has nothing to do with waging war. Being a warrior means having the courage to know who you are, through and through. Whether you believe yourself to be good or bad, whether you are happy or depressed, young or old, neurotic or sane, as an authentic warrior you recognize the inherent basic goodness that is more profound and enduring than all these ephemeral ups and downs. When you are authentic, genuinely being just who you are, you can be open to that basic goodness in yourself and others, even when it seems obscure or buried altogether. Warriors never give up on anyone, including themselves.

The life of the Shambhala warrior is a life with heart—not the superficial heart of romance or emotionalism, although that could be where the discovery of heart begins. Unfortunately, for many people superficial emotionalism is where the realization of heart ends. Heart goes much deeper than this. Living with heart is being not sentimental or woolly-minded but very precise and intelligent. The heart feels the qualities of everything in its own uniqueness. It is the capability to value, to cherish deeply, whatever we come in contact with.

The name *Shambhala* refers to an ancient kingdom where ordinary people practiced the path of warriorship. As Edwin Bernbaum says in *The Way to Shambhala,* "Rather than renounce worldly activities and interests for the asceticism of a hermit or monk, the people of Shambhala use everything, even the distractions of luxury and family life, as a means of attaining enlightenment. They strive to free themselves from illusion through the very things that bind others to it."

The Kingdom of Shambhala is believed to have been an actual kingdom on earth, but it is also an inner vision. The Kingdom of Shambhala is the purity and clarity, the inherent basic goodness that everyone possesses. In this sense, the search for the Kingdom of Shambhala is the search to live genuinely in a world experienced as sacred. Shambhala is not some heavenly realm altogether separate from the ordinary world we inhabit. It is a sacred world that is none other than the ordinary world seen with pure eyes and heart. Bernbaum says of the inner vision with which we can perceive this world, "At times . . . some people become aware of a hidden, almost luminous depth in the most ordinary objects, such as flowers and stones. A fresh feeling of wonder, reminiscent of childhood, comes over them, and they sense what seems to be a deeper reality permeating their surrounding world."

In the Shambhala teachings, the vision of human life and society based on genuineness and the sacredness of the world is symbolized by the *Great Eastern Sun.* The physical *sun* always arises, is a constant source of warmth and brilliance, and is always there—we just have to open our eyes to see it. The symbolic sun—basic goodness and the sacredness of the world—is a fathomless source of creativity; they too are always available if only we open our minds and look. The vision of this sun is called *great* because it goes far beyond narrow human prejudices. It is a primordial vision found in all cultures throughout history. It is not dependent on dogma or moralistic judgments of "good" and "bad." Finally, like the *eastern* sky at dawn, this vision inspires wakefulness, freshness, and delight. Just as we feel like facing toward the sun when we awaken in morning, so the vision of the Great Eastern Sun shows us how to go forward in our lives on the path of warriorship. The vision of the Great Eastern Sun is contrasted with an attitude that inspires sleep, symbolized by the setting sun.

Introduction

The setting-sun vision is the attitude of degradation, despair, and meaninglessness that pervades so much of our world today—an attitude that can hardly be called a vision at all.

The Shambhala teachings are guided by this vision of the possibility of an enlightened society. Shambhala warriors aspire to create a society that acknowledges the basic goodness of humans, of all living beings, and of the earth that supports us and the space that surrounds us. The society is organized so that its people can aspire to nourish this goodness rather than to hide from it and deny it. After describing his search for Shambhala through history, geography, oral accounts, personal journeys, and inner practice, Bernbaum concludes:

> The prophecy [of Shambhala] speaks of much more [than the awakening of the individual]: it predicts the coming of a golden age in which everyone will make great progress toward enlightenment. This makes it clear that the purpose of the inner journey is not to withdraw from the world, but to make it a place more conducive to the attainment of liberation by all. In seeking to awaken the deeper mind, we seek a new awareness that will enable us to help others to free themselves from the bondage of their illusions. . . . As we become aware of the sacred nature of all that surrounds us, we cease to see people and things as objects to be abused and exploited. We come, instead, to cherish them for what they are—and to treat them with the utmost care and respect. If we can awaken this sense of the sacred in the world around us, then we may have a chance of bringing about the golden age of so many myths and dreams.

Attaining such a society is a real practical possibility. It has happened on this earth many times before, and it can happen again. A growing number of people today now see the urgent need for such a society and are working both individually and in groups toward bringing it about, each in their own way. The Shambhala teachings are a path that links these individuals and lets everyone join this worldwide community.

The Shambhala path of the warrior was first taught by Chogyam Trungpa, one of the first and most senior Tibetan teachers to bring Tibetan Buddhist practice to the West. In the context of the Shambhala teachings, he was known by his secular Shambhala title, the Dorje Dradul, "Indestructible (or Master) Warrior."

The Dorje Dradul was born in Tibet as a tulku. In the Tibetan Buddhist tradition, the *tulkus* are the successive rebirths of a person who has no ego in the ordinary sense of self-centeredness, but who makes a vow to return continually to work on earth for the sake of all beings. The Dorje Dradul was the eleventh rebirth in the Trungpa line. The Trungpa tulku was one of the oldest known tulkus in Tibet—the first Trungpa having been born in the fourteenth century. The eleventh Trungpa, the Dorje Dradul, was trained from an early age as a scholar and meditation master to the level of khenpo—the equivalent of a Western doctorate. Not only was he an important figure in Tibetan Buddhism, he was enthroned as secular governor of the Kham region of eastern Tibet and trained in governing according to classical Chinese and Tibetan traditions of rulership.

In 1959, the Dorje Dradul was forced out of Tibet by the Chinese Communist invasion. He escaped over the Himalaya Mountains, leading his friends and followers in the extraordinary adventure of danger and companionship that he describes in his autobiography, *Born in Tibet*. He traveled to England in 1963 and studied Western philosophy and comparative religion at Oxford University. There he learned to speak English as fluently as a native and developed a firsthand understanding of Western culture. While he was in England, he also studied and mastered ikebana, the Japanese art and meditative practice of flower placement. During this time, he established a Buddhist meditation center in Eskdalemuir, Scotland.

In 1969, the Dorje Dradul had an automobile accident that profoundly affected his teaching. In the epilogue to *Born in Tibet,* he describes what happened. Before the accident, he says:

There remained some hesitation as to how to throw myself completely into proclaiming the Dharma to the Western world, uprooting spiritual materialism and developing further confidence and affection. I went through several months of ambivalence, of feeling pushed forward and pulled back simultaneously, unable to respond clearly in spite of a series of small warnings. Then driving one day in Northumberland, I blacked out at the wheel of my car, ran off the road and smashed through the front of a joke shop . . . finally the real message had got through—I felt a sense of relief and even humor.

When plunging completely and genuinely into the teachings, one is not allowed to bring along one's deceptions. I realized that I could no longer preserve any privacy for myself, any special identity or legitimacy. I should not hide behind the robes of a monk, creating an impression of inscrutability, which, for me, turned out to be only an obstacle. With a

sense of further involving myself with the sangha [community of Bud-
dhists], I determined to give up my monastic vows. More than ever I felt
myself given over to serving the cause of Buddhism.

At this time, the Dorje Dradul married a young Englishwoman, Diana
Pybus. A few months later, in early 1970, he was invited to the United States
to teach and took up residence there. He taught and traveled throughout the
world until his death in 1987.

The Dorje Dradul saw that many people in North America and Europe
had a great hunger to discover an inner path of development in their lives but
were cut off from that possibility because of their prior experience of "religion"
or their belief that the modern scientific worldview no longer accommodates
spiritual insights. He yearned to teach in a way that could genuinely benefit
people living in the modern world, a world increasingly marked by speed and
hatred. In 1977 he began to teach a secular training in how to live ordinary life in
a profound and enriching way, without reliance on a religious belief in an
external savior or on religious dogma. This teaching was later systematized in
the Shambhala Training Program.

The Shambhala Training Program introduces participants to a simple
practice of mindfulness and awareness. This basic practice derives from the
Buddhist practice of meditation and is compatible with Buddhism but is not
identified with it. A closely similar practice is found at the basis of all living
sacred tradition. Aspects of Shambhala training come from the pre-Buddhist
culture of Tibet and China. In addition to mindfulness and awareness practice,
participants are taught warrior practices that empower them to cut through the
obstacles that make us feel separate from the sacred world. These practices were
discovered by the Dorje Dradul through his training in Tibetan shamanistic
methods. They arose out of his deeply compassionate understanding of the
courage, the fearlessness, and the sense of greater family bond that are needed to
restore balance and harmony on earth, as human societies look toward the next
five hundred years. Shambhala training is unusual in that it joins the grounded
sanity of mindfulness and awareness practice with the kind of training more
common among native traditions that is designed to open us and connect us to
the energy and power of the sacred world.

This book is a course in how to discover basic goodness and how to live
in the profound, ordinary, and magical sacred world. As we start out on the
Shambhala path, there are some basic things we need to learn. It is like taking
baby steps or learning to sing scales. We need to first sit and look at what

actually goes on with us in detail—what we think and feel when we aren't being distracted by action and entertainment. We need to learn to experience the claustrophobia of our own minds—the jailor that prevents us from seeing sacredness. Then we need to learn how to feel the actual unlimited space—in our own minds and bodies and environment. We will first see how we trap ourselves in a cocoon world of our own making, which cuts off our fresh air and stifles our energy and relationships; then we will see how to free ourselves into a true experience of ourselves and the world. Mindfulness and awareness are the tools we learn to use to pay attention to ourselves and our world.

Then we become warriors, taking bigger steps. Warriors in Shambhala are not afraid of their own fear. They have the courage to face their fear and so become fearless. Warriors know how to stop making war on themselves and others, with gentleness. Having become warriors—humble but energetic—we can then take a giant leap into a world that cowards who crawl in a degraded world can never see. We can discover the power and magic of being present in the timeless space of now—and the path of authentic warriorship, of living and dying with dignity and gallantry, unfolds.

I am not offering an "orthodox" version of the Shambhala Training Program or the Shambhala path—fortunately, such a narrow path does not exist. Without doubt, the Shambhala teachings could be presented in many other ways. This book is a personal view of the path of Shambhala warriorship, based on my own experience and the experiences that colleagues and students have shared with me.

I would like to say a little about how I came to write this book. From my early teenage years I had felt a need to awaken my personal understanding as well as to further my conceptual knowledge of the world. When I was seventeen, I fell in love with physics after reading James Jeans's *The Mysterious Universe*. Jeans's description of physics opened a world to me in which body, mind, and spirit seemed not to be separate. However, as I went on to study physics and then to do research in molecular biology in college, I became disappointed and lost heart. University studies in the early 1960s had little or nothing to say about the direct experience of reality and seemed almost to deliberately put that experience out of reach. Academic studies had so little to do with my intuitions of the fullness and beauty of the world or with the anxiety and stress that so many people felt at that time and still feel.

I felt an increasingly desperate need to find something real in my life, to discover real heart and real humanity. I spent some years with a group studying and practicing the work of G. I. Gurdjieff. Gurdjieff was a Russian spiritual teacher who taught the Way of the Householder—how to practice spirituality in daily life—through a variety of methods that he gleaned from his travels in the East. He put these together into a system to meet the needs of modern men and women and to help us wake up from the constant hypnosis or waking sleep in which he saw us trapped.

When I looked into the origin of Gurdjieff's teachings, I discovered that the parts that spoke to me most directly, especially the practice of mindfulness, came from Buddhism. I met the Dorje Dradul in 1970 and immediately began to study Buddhism and practice under his guidance. For the next several years I helped to establish Karme Choling, a Buddhist contemplative center in Vermont. The Dorje Dradul spoke in such a simple but profound way about the activities of daily life—work, sex, money, and mindfulness—that as I listened to him in those early talks, I kept wondering, "Why didn't *anyone* else tell me this before?" Tibetan Buddhism, according to the Dorje Dradul, promises no final answer, but it did show me how to *look for myself*. One of the key phrases I heard from him was, "The question *is* the answer." Openness and longing contain within themselves the seed of their own resolution—and of further opening in an endless journey of heart and mind.

In 1974, guided by the Dorje Dradul, I and other students of his who had lost heart with traditional university training established the Naropa Institute— a degree-granting college that understands learning as a personal journey of opening, of awakening heart as well as intellect. From 1975 until his death, I was the Dorje Dradul's personal representative to the Naropa Institute. Karen and I met at the Naropa Institute, where she was student adviser. Karen had also been a student of the Dorje Dradul since 1971. Later, she taught in the Shambhala Training Program and was the first director of Kalapa Ikebana, a new school of Japanese flower arranging founded by the Dorje Dradul.

In 1982, the possibility of publishing a book of talks by the Dorje Dradul on the teachings of Shambhala was being discussed. He gave his assent to the publication of these talks, which were edited as *Shambhala: The Sacred Path of the Warrior*. At the same time, he asked that another book be written about the Shambhala path from a student's perspective. From 1977, when the Dorje Dradul first began to teach the Shambhala path of warriorship, I had worked closely with him on developing and teaching Shambhala training, and he asked me to write the book on the student's path.

I actually wrote a first draft of that book in the winter of 1983, but at that time I lacked sufficient confidence in my understanding of these teachings to complete the task. I also needed to work out the particular path of my own life: joining science with spiritual insight harmoniously in the same bodymind. That first draft resulted in my book *Perceiving Ordinary Magic: Science and Intuitive Wisdom*. Though inspired by the Shambhala teachings, it was primarily a book about how belief in science conditions the perceptions and consciousness of us all, and how in turn the study of science can help us see through that conditioning.

In May 1991 I was again asked, by the Dorje Dradul's editors, to write the book he had requested on the Shambhala student warrior's journey. The result is this book. In the text I tell many stories of warrior students and practitioners. These stories will help to make the path a living reality for you and help you understand the nature of both the subtle and dramatic changes that warriorship makes possible. I have seen, in my own life and in the lives of many of my friends and students, how effective these teachings are and how they have helped people in sudden as well as gradual ways to change their lives.

The path that leads our journey has been traveled many times before. It is well trampled and strewn with thick skins and stuck minds. It is adorned with open hearts.

Part One offers a view of the sacred world from the perspective of the Shambhala teachings. Here I introduce the concept of the basic energy-awareness of the cosmos within which everything arises, has its being, and returns. I also introduce the dralas, the patternings within energy-awareness that are known to some as "the gods," through which we can communicate with and celebrate with the cosmos. The dralas are an ancient idea, part of the pre-Buddhist Tibetan universe, and common to indigenous cultures throughout the world. Part Two points out the obstacles, all based in fear, to discovering our own as well as universal basic goodness. Here I give practical instructions on how you can train yourself to open to the sacred world, let your life be illuminated by the peaceful confidence of the Great Eastern Sun, and invite the dralas into your world. In Part Two I also give suggestions at the end of each chapter, as well as within the text. Please try these suggestions with a light touch, experiment with them—and enjoy them. They suggest how you could investigate the topic of each chapter for yourself. I hope they will help you to make the teachings more personal. But take your time with them, there is no hurry. Some things you may understand in a flash; others can take years. Your path will unfold gradually over time and in the context of mindfulness and awareness practice.

Please remember the common teaching of sages of all time: Don't rely on authority or on hearing the teachings of others; experience the truth for yourself. Wang Yangming was one of the most learned and influential thinkers in Chinese history who combined Taoism, Zen Buddhism, and Confucianism in his teaching. He was also a highly successful leader both in civil administration and in military campaigns. The school of neo-Confucianism, which brought new life to Confucianism in the great period of the early Ming dynasty, arose largely out of his teaching. Yet Wang Yangming reminded people, "Sincere belief [in the teaching of the sages] is certainly right, but it is not as cogent as verifying the truth within yourself. If at present you have not found the truth in your mind, then how can you dogmatically follow what you have heard in the past, without seeking to find out if it is correct? The great chaos in the world is due to the triumph of empty words and the decline of genuine practice."

Part Three deals with the warrior's action in the world, dedicated to creating enlightened society. Genuine warriors long to create a society enlightened by trust and straightforwardness, by loving care and appreciation of basic goodness. This sacred journey of warriorship is much more than discovering personal confidence and joy or trying to become a spiritual person. When you discover your genuine heart, you naturally want to act in the world with decency and work with others to create a genuinely good society. So Shambhala warriorship is authentic action to benefit the world. You can do it—if you have the desire and courage to wake up in a world different from the one you are used to, a world that might seem strange to the fearful mind. It is hard work, but it is neither solemn nor grim. Actually, it can be a lot of fun. It is magic. It is the sacred journey.

Sacred World

PART ONE

A Vision
of Sacredness

CHAPTER 1
Sacred World

The ordinary world already is and always has been sacred. This means that the world is complete in itself and is basically pure—uncorrupted by good and bad. Everything is alive and connected to everything else in a way that is vital to the world's existence. Our earth hangs in the sky and turns and moves. The sky rains on the earth, and trees grow. Trees help make air, and animals breathe. Birds fly in the air, flowers attract bees. Bodies have livers and hearts, brains and nerves and muscles, teeth and claws, and all the rest. Hurricanes have their own power and energy, as do tulips and mosquitoes. We have perceptions and awareness, so that all of this beautiful and powerful world comes within our experience. Everything works together. It is so ordinary, we usually don't think twice about it. But that ordinary world is sacred and magical when we look again, when we feel it, see it, hear it, open all our senses to its profundity.

We cannot control or conquer this sacred world, although we spend much of our life trying to do just that. We *can* connect with it and feel that we, too, are a sacred part of it. When we relax all of our ideas about the world, all of our interpretations, and just let ourselves see and hear it as it is, we connect ourselves directly to it. This experience of direct connection might seem extremely simple, but it is profound. It is a glimpse of the sacred world.

Glimpses of sacredness happen frequently throughout our daily lives, but we usually ignore them in our rush to achieve goals that seem more important.

The sun peeks through an overcast sky and momentarily cheers us up; we see a brightly colored bird; we hear strange music; we suddenly get a whiff of fresh manure; we are shocked by the power and energy of a thunderstorm; someone touches us affectionately. It is the sharpness or suddenness of a loud sound, a flash of color, or a bitter smell, and not *necessarily* its beauty, that penetrates our thoughts and calls us from our daily rush. Such glimpses hold our attention and, like a fresh breeze, wake us up to what is happening in the sacred world *at that very moment*. We have to be awake to experience beauty in ordinary things, but we do not have to turn away from our own world to find the sacred. As Christian contemplative Neal Donner says, "To seek ultimate reality . . . there is no need to reject the mundane to turn toward the saintly."

We are all capable of experiencing in this way. Such moments have varying degrees of intensity, from the merest flash to the deeply affecting. Yet we all do experience moments that point toward the sacredness of our world. When our habitual anxieties are quiet for a moment, we can feel the living energy of the world of which we are part. We discover a sense of value as well as humor in our lives that gives our lives meaning and wholeness.

People often have memories of childhood that still have the power to recall for them the flavor of sacredness. Frederick Franck, painter and Zen drawing teacher, tells of a childhood experience in this way:

> On the dark afternoon—I was ten or eleven—I was walking on a country road; on my left a patch of curly kale, on my right some yellowed Brussels sprouts. I felt a snowflake on my cheek, and from far away in the charcoal-gray sky I saw the slow approach of a snowstorm. I stood still.
>
> Some flakes were now falling around my feet. A few melted as they hit the ground. Others stayed intact. Then I heard the falling of the snow, with the softest hissing sound.
>
> I stood transfixed, listening . . . and knew what can never be expressed: that the natural is supernatural . . . that what is outside happens in me, that outside and inside are inseparable.

Often our rediscovery of sacredness as adults reminds us that as young children we were immersed in the sacred world. Once, early in my experience of the Shambhala teachings, I was taking a week off to practice sitting meditation and staying in a tiny cabin in a meadow. I was having many mixed thoughts and feelings—of anger and resentment, of sexual desire and passion, of longing and eager anticipation—as I sat there. I would occasionally remind myself that I had not taken the week off just to go over my past or plan my future. I would return to trying to be in the present mindfully, doing the technique. On one of these days, I went out for a walk in the meadow. My perception of that meadow was transformed. The tall grass and the white and red and yellow wildflowers were glowing with their own life. The difference between this perception and how I normally saw the world was like the difference between a black and white photograph of a cornfield and a Van Gogh painting of it. At the same time, I had a feeling of crystal clarity and joy. The meadow began to quiver and vibrate with life, as if it were a photograph that had been still and were suddenly set in motion like a movie, or as if it had been flat and were now three-dimensional.

This perception sparked the memory of an occasion that I had forgotten for twenty years. As a small boy, I had had a similar change of perception. I was lying in bed, just having recovered from a fever. As I looked at the cross-hatched pattern on my orange-pink knitted blanket, it suddenly seemed to stand out and glow. An extraordinarily strong feeling of love for that blanket extended out to the whole room. I thought that this must be how the world *really* is. I had other similar experiences as a child, but as I entered my teens, I forgot them. They had lain dormant until, taking that walk in the meadow two decades later, I rediscovered them.

This sacred world is ordinary, but our experience of the ordinary can be magical. We can catch a glimpse of sacredness when we come across our ordinary familiar world freshly, as if for the first time. Photographer Freeman Patterson describes this beautifully:

Have you ever noticed, on returning home from a holiday your increased sensitivity to the details of your home? You glance around when you step in the door, and some things in the house may actually seem unfamiliar for a few minutes. You notice that the English ivy looks spectacular in the west window, that the living room walls are more cream than ivory. You notice the light of the evening spilling across the little rug at the foot of the stairs, something you can't recall seeing before. But these moments pass quickly, familiarity is restored, everything is in its place, and you stop seeing once more.

There is magic in discovering that the world and everything in it is good and meaningful and whole, in waking up to the fresh and glorious world that is already here, in finding ourselves in the center of it and knowing who we are and what we are, through and through—and in discovering that we like what we see. There is magic also in helping other people. Because we can care for ourselves and our world, we can care for others, including the ant carrying off the crumbs from the countertop.

We can see magic with our hearts. We can find magic by learning to live beautifully, with heart and soul and goodness, with wide-open eyes. We find it by seeing the sacred in a blade of grass, by rediscovering the gods who surround us with their energy and wake us up. We discover magic in the messages of the haunting cry of the loons on the quiet lake, or in the tap-tap of rain on the window pane; we discover it in the energy of the sun and stars, or in the swirling pattern of a wheat field blown by a gust of wind.

Discovering magic is also discovering joy and sadness and love. It is knowing what to accept and what to reject—how to go forward in the light of sanity and how to reject wallowing in the darkness of neurotic mind, the mind that goes to sleep like the setting sun. Discovering magic is feeling the relief of finally relaxing into the world with effortless energy and cheerful good heart. It is not sentimental; it is precise and true.

Basic Goodness Is the Inherent Nature of All Beings

Recognizing and nourishing the sacredness of the world is at the heart of most spiritual and healing traditions throughout the world. Experiencing the world as sacred is common among native peoples in North and South America and in Africa, India, China, Japan, and Australia. But this sense of sacredness has been lost to a great extent in modern technological society. It is nonetheless still possible for those of us captured by the "modern world" to experience the world as sacred and to let this experience profoundly affect our lives.

This possibility, this inherent ability to care for ourselves and the world is an expression of the *basic goodness* of human beings. Our basic goodness lies in our capacity to live fully, passionately, vividly, and wakefully; in our capacity to be fully aware of our lives and to live them wholeheartedly, no matter what twists and turns they may take; and in our capacity to care for others as well as ourselves.

Modern society has, on the whole, rejected the very idea of the basic goodness of human beings. The belief that humans have a fundamental and ineradicable fault—an "original sin"—has become dominant even among those who have rejected traditional religion. The sense of guilt and shame at having committed some unremembered wrong has been transmitted from generation to generation right down to the present. We feel that we did something very wrong, long, long ago, *something that we cannot erase* and that makes us undeserving. Because we have this idea, it is very difficult for us to accept or even understand the idea of basic goodness.

Belief in our fundamental blameworthiness is so deeply rooted in our upbringing that we accept it without question as the final truth about human nature. Yet it is far from being a universal truth. Chogyam Trungpa, the Dorje Dradul, says of this:

> Coming from a tradition that stresses human goodness, it was something of a shock for me to encounter the Western tradition of original sin. . . . It seems that this notion of original sin does not just pervade Western religious ideas. It actually seems to run throughout Western thought as well, especially psychological thought. Among patients, theoreticians and therapists alike there seems to be great concern with the idea of some original mistake, which causes later suffering—a kind of punishment for that mistake. One finds that a sense of guilt or being wounded is quite pervasive. Whether or not people actually believe in the idea of original sin, or in God for that matter, they seem to feel that they have done something wrong in the past and are now being punished for it.

There is some truth to the idea of sin if we understand sin as a pattern of destructive behavior, of self-doubt and self-hate, that has been passed down from parents to children for generations. The idea is helpful when it reminds us of our tendency toward selfishness and egotism—the tendency that the Shambhala teachings refer to as our "cocoon." The idea of *original* sin as a fundamental part of our nature, however, from which we can never be free, only breeds more self-doubt and self-hate. As the Dorje Dradul suggests, the idea of a flaw in human nature, a flaw that never can be healed, has crept unnoticed into many of the institutions that govern our lives: into the sciences, into our educational system, into economic theory, and into many systems of psychotherapy.

We feel that something is profoundly missing from our lives. We express this feeling in many different ways—we say we feel empty, disheartened, emotionally numb, depressed, anxious, or disconnected. Sometimes we feel it physically, as a piercing ache in the center of the chest. This deep inner hunger is felt throughout society, even among those of us who live at the level of relative physical comfort and affluence that would have been inconceivable only a century ago. Our education offers little clue as to how to satisfy this hunger. We grow up with only a narrow and piecemeal vision of how to live our lives. We become driven by empty and pointless goals to which we have no real allegiance. We drift on a sea of anxiety and confusion. We lose touch with our genuine human heart and our basic goodness. Many people today are asking "What do I *really want?*" It is not a shallow question. It is a question that penetrates deeply into the heart.

We want to find meaning in our lives, to find value, genuineness, and depth. We want to find something *real*—to feel and experience intensely and wholly. Yet what we want remains not quite defined. However precisely we try to define what we want, an unspoken longing nonetheless remains. The longing is for something deeper than the dogmas of various spiritual, healing, and religious traditions. It touches a commonality in people's actual experience. The yearning for genuineness is intense enough that we want to *do* something about it, to seek a different way of living. This search is not just for personal development, however; it is a search for community—community with other humans, as well as with all species that share the earth as home. Many of us long to build a good human society that cherishes the earth and all creatures that live on it—a society that acknowledges and nourishes basic human goodness. The assumption of all healing and spiritual traditions is that it is *possible* for all of us to do this.

In place of enduring narrow and distorted lives, we can seek practical experiences of fullness and goodness, a sense of wholeness that does not divide inner and outer, spiritual and material. Uncovering the basic goodness of humans is the foundation of any genuine spiritual path, as well as the focus of the transformative work of some modern psychotherapies. Psychotherapist Thomas Moore, in *Care of the Soul,* says, "This is the 'goal' of the soul path—to *feel existence;* not to overcome life's struggles and anxieties, but to know life firsthand, to exist fully in context." For Moore, soul is "not a thing, but a quality or a dimension of experiencing life and ourselves. It has to do with depth, value, relatedness, heart and personal substance." Many of us have lost touch with soul, and our great longing is to reconnect and to care for this basic goodness of our being.

The belief in the basic goodness of humans is the basis of the Buddhist teachings, as well as the Taoist and Confucian ways of life, all of which influenced the Shambhala teachings. In Buddhist teachings our basic goodness is known as our buddha nature. The word *buddha* literally means "awake." As the great contemporary Tibetan yogi and teacher Ugyen Tulku Rinpoche says,

> Buddha nature is present in ourselves as well as in everyone else, without any exception whatsoever. . . . Our buddha nature . . . is called *empty* and *cognizant self-existing* wakefulness. The empty aspect, the essence, is like space that pervades everywhere. But inseparable from this empty quality is a natural capacity to cognize and perceive, which is basic wakefulness. Buddha nature is called self-existing because it is not made out of anything or created by anyone. This self-existing wakefulness is present in all beings without a single exception.

All humans possess buddha nature, hidden deep within their conditioned, rigid, narrow ways of believing and acting, like a jewel hidden in a heap of garbage. Ugyen Tulku Rinpoche continues,

> The buddha nature is already present as the nature of our own mind, just like the unchanging brilliance of the sun shining in the sky. But due to our dualistic thinking, this sun of the buddha nature is not evident; we don't see it. . . . The conceptual thoughts we have day and night obscure our buddha nature, just like the sun in the sky is momentarily covered by clouds and seems to be obscured. Due to the passing clouds of ignorance we do not recognize buddha nature.

All humans have the potentiality to wake up, to discover their buddha nature and bring it to full flowering. As Buddhists acknowledge, a tremendous exertion and commitment to being genuine is necessary in order for our buddha nature to blossom. They acknowledge the dross, the tendency to dualistic thinking in terms of good and bad, me and you, that covers over our buddha nature. To Buddhists, however, the dross, the garbage, is like manure that can be transformed into food for a beautiful flower bed, rather than something that forever keeps us from our basic goodness.

The Confucian and Taoist traditions, too, saw the basic goodness in humans, as well as the need for training to bring it out. Mencius, who lived from 371 to 289 B.C., was the first Confucian to teach explicitly the basic goodness of human nature:

> If you let people follow their feelings [original nature] they will be able to do good. This is what is meant by saying that human nature is good. If man does evil it is not the fault of his natural endowment. The feeling of commiseration is found in all men and is what we call humanity. Humanity is not drilled into us from outside. We originally have it with us. Only we do not think to find it. Therefore it is said, "Seek and you will find it, neglect and you will lose it."

Almost contemporary with Mencius was another Confucian commentator, Hsun Tzu (298–238 B.C.), who proclaimed that human nature is evil and has to be trained to overcome this evil. Hsun Tzu recognized an almost unlimited capacity of human nature to be trained, however, and for Mencius this capacity is *itself* an aspect of the inherent goodness and shows that the "evil" tendencies are not fundamental. The debate between followers of Mencius and of Hsun Tzu raged over the centuries, but the difference of perspective is not really so fundamental. As the thirteenth-century neo-Confucian Tai Chih pointed out:

> Mencius is talking about the [basic nature,] and what he calls goodness refers to its uprightness and greatness. He wished to encourage it. But Hsun Tzu is talking about [conditioned nature,] and what he calls the badness of human nature refers to its wrongness and roughness. He wished to repair and control it. Thus Mencius's teaching is to strengthen what is already pure, so that defilement tends to disappear of itself. While Hsun Tzu's teaching is to remove the defilement activity.

This debate mirrors a similar debate that can still be heard in the West. Is human nature *fundamentally* sinful, or aggressive in modern terms, or are these qualities simply the obscurations that separate us from our basic goodness? The Great Eastern Sun vision of human nature is summed up succinctly by the sixteenth-century sage Wang Yangmin: "Every person has a sage within his breast. It is just that people do not believe fully in this sage and bury it away." And finally, the eighteenth-century Taoist sage Liu I-Ming said, "At first, human nature is basically good. There is originally no distinction between the sage and the ordinary person. It is because of the energy of accumulated habits that there comes to be a difference between sages and ordinary people."

Basic Goodness Is Unconditioned

Our basic nature of goodness does not exist in contrast with something "bad" in us. Goodness is not something that would dawn if only we finally weeded out all of our undesirable habits, or figured out just how our parents went wrong in raising us, or became thin, beautiful, and rich, or attained our ideal of a spiritual person. The basic goodness of our nature is not the "good" side of a world divided into good and bad. When we divide the world in that way—even in our minds—we automatically put conditions on everything around us, so that we consider a thing good if it fulfills our conditions and bad if it does not. Basic goodness is *unconditioned* because it does not depend on any limitations or boundaries or on conditions of any kind at all. It is like a rock over which a stream is flowing. The rock is there whether the stream is warm or cold, whether it flows quickly or slowly or not at all.

At the most basic level of our being, we have everything we need to celebrate our lives on this planet. Our bodies, through sense perceptions, provide us a connection to reality that *can* wake us up to sacredness. We *can* experience our world as healthy, direct, and real. We only have to be willing to do it. When we stand on the earth, it holds us upright—usually we don't sink in quicksand. When we breathe, we breathe oxygen, which gives us life—usually we don't breathe noxious gases. When we eat, we nourish our bodies with good food grown in the earth—usually we don't eat poison. When we bathe, we clean ourselves with water, fresh and pure—usually we don't bathe in a chemical dump. The earth cares for us. If we care for it, it will continue to care for us. It is trustworthy and good. This is very basic.

But basic goodness is even more basic than *that*. It is the vast open, creative, living space that permeates and illuminates everything. Without this space we couldn't see or hear or move or even exist. It is the most basic of any goodness you can think of. It exists prior to thought or the birth of anything. Everything is created from this space and exists in it. Each one of us is permeated by it. In it we live and move and have our existence. Living space is not an abstract idea; it is as close and intimate to us as water to a fish.

This profound level of basic goodness is hard to think about, but you can feel it. When people are crowded together, you see a crowd. When sounds are crowded together, you hear a noise. When your thoughts are crowded together, you get a headache. Your world closes in on you. You feel claustrophobic, which is basic fear. When you allow the *space* of basic goodness into your mind, however, your thoughts become illuminated—as if you had turned on the light in a dim room.

When you see the physical space around an object, you can see the object clearly and brightly. You can see the details. When there is silence around sound, you can hear each note. That is how the space of basic goodness can change your perception. Mix the creative space of basic goodness with your perceptions, and suddenly, magically, the world *is there* in all its reality, as it is—genuine and good and sacred. You can discover your world of basic goodness both in the space and in the details.

Because we all share the same earth and the same living, creative space of basic goodness, our lives are intertwined and connected at a profound level. The feeling of unselfishness that can guide us at times to acts of generosity great or small stems from this intertwining of our existence. Although we usually take an immediate interest in the "pursuit of happiness" of only a small circle of family and friends, our interest in the well-being of others *can* extend far beyond. Our circle of caring naturally extends to total strangers, for example, when we see reports of wars or disasters on television. People are frequently willing to risk their lives when they see that the life of a complete stranger is in danger. This fundamental caring and intelligence has guided us to cooperate with each other, to build houses and highways, to grow and eat wholesome food, and to create and sustain good human societies. Without the decency and courtesy that springs from our basic goodness, ordinary human community would be impossible. To help to build a good human society, we must start with ourselves, with coming to know ourselves and with rediscovering our basic goodness as real and very personal.

CHAPTER 2

Presence in
the Sacred World

The sacred world is a living world, and its profundity extends vastly beyond the surface of ordinary human perception. It is full of powerful energy that has unlimited potential for new patterns and meanings to arise constantly in a kind of self-created cosmic display. This grand dance is happening everywhere and throughout time, and you can find it at every level from the infinitesimally small to the infinitely large. "The very small is as the very large when boundaries are forgotten; the very large is as the very small when its outline is not seen," said Seng-ts'an. You can see the dance in a swarm of gnats flitting back and forth in the last rays of the evening sun, in the force of a hurricane as it sweeps the coast, or in the majestic but momentary burst of a comet in the night sky. You can see the cosmic dance in the smallest thought flitting repetitively through your mind, in the movement of a herd of animals or migrating birds, or in the compassionate action of a great leader. There are also energy patterns that are not so obvious, but that you can feel when you are willing to open to the unexpected in your world.

When you feel your real, direct connection with the sacred world, you tune in to energy patterns in the cosmos that are like the veins and arteries of the world that carry the world's life-blood. The energy of the world courses through these channels, and since we are part of that world, the energy of the world runs through *our* veins and arteries and nerves as well. These energy patterns are intelligent and responsive to us at the level of feeling. I am not talking about any dramatic revelations here—no sudden flashes of cosmic light or visitors from outer space. I am talking about a responsiveness to subtle energies that we feel in the pattern of the wind, in the pattern of the bark on a one-hundred-year-old pine tree, in the sounds of loons and crows, in the way a rock sits majestically atop a bare hill, in a sudden change in the weather. We can feel the subtle patterns of energy and power in the world; we can see with our hearts the patterns of energy that are ordinarily present but are usually invisible to our gross and cloudy perception. When we can feel those energy patterns, we can communicate with the sacred world through them.

Communicating with the Energy Patterns of the Cosmos

We can feel these energy patterns in the *qualities* of things. When we see only surface appearances, the mere *thing*ness of separate things, we deaden them. The world becomes flat and meaningless. But if we are open to the qualities of things, to the isness or beingness of things—the blue*ness* of the sky, the solid*ness* of the rock, the swirling quality of the wind, the haunting quality of the cry of the loon—and to the connections between things, the meaning of things, then we can feel their energy. We feel it running through us, so that we can respond to it and it can respond to us.

To understand how we can communicate with the energy patterns of the world, we need to remember that there are many ways to communicate other than speech. The musician Jim Nollman is also trained in ethology—the science that studies animal behavior. He has learned to use music to communicate with members of other species. In *Dolphin Dreamtime,* Nollman makes it clear that in order to communicate with other species, we have to change our whole way of being, our way of seeing, thinking, and feeling, and especially our relationship to time. He tells of an experience of entering "buffalo time" when he was working with a film crew in Yellowstone Park. It beautifully illustrates the reality of communication through energy patterns.

The film crew was trying to get a film of Nollman communicating with elk through music. They could find no elk, but they unexpectedly came upon a herd of more than a hundred buffalo. Afraid that the buffalo might charge him,

the crew tried to persuade Nollman not to go near the herd. He went ahead but
heeded the warnings and moved cautiously, taking over an hour to advance
three hundred yards. As he went, he strummed a repetitive drone of four notes
on his guitar:

> Slowly, ever so slowly, I shortened the distance between us. Then some-
> thing strange happened. Suddenly, almost too suddenly, I stood no more
> than a hundred feet from the nearest animal. It was as if, all at once, I had
> been lifted right into place, without any recollection whatsoever of the
> long arduous hour of moving forward at a snail's pace. Perhaps it was
> nothing more than my own sensory reaction to the very hypnotic drone.
> Perhaps it was the shock of staring directly into the big brown eyes of a
> mountain of a buffalo. All my senses were being filtered through the
> lightheaded breeze blowing across the river valley at 8500 feet of elevation.
> All the shapes and colors appeared so sharp and vibrant. The prairie and the
> mountains seemed alive. I was nearly hallucinating—almost, but not ex-
> actly. It was not so much that any particular part of the landscape had
> dramatically altered—rather, that every part seemed more vivid. I had
> entered buffalo time.

He now stood directly in front of the herd. Three bull buffalo stepped to
the edge of the herd.

> The most uncanny thing happened. I beheld a dirty yellow glow pulse out
> from the herd, parallel to the three large bulls. It was like a ring, a
> smokescreen, or a fence expanding outward around the entire herd. It was
> luminous but it wasn't light; rather like individual bubbles or bundles of
> glowing energy. It was dots on fire. It stopped just in front of me, like a
> barrier or signal that defined the group territory: a boundary, a social aura,
> an energy extension of the herd's group body language. Yet it had no real
> substance. I felt it would disappear if I only blinked.
>   That I actually saw what I believed I saw was in no doubt, because when
> I put my left foot directly on the ring, the largest bull, who stood less than a
> hundred feet away, began to paw the ground with his hoof. I pulled my foot
> away. The bull immediately stopped pawing. To be sure that the connec-
> tion was what I thought, once again I dropped my foot onto the glowing
> ring. Once again the big bull pawed the ground.

After Nollman and the buffalo did this dance several more times, the buffalo seemed to recognize that he had come in harmony, not in threat. Suddenly Nollman found that he was surrounded by buffalo, and the ring had disappeared. He waited awhile, and slowly the herd shuffled off down to the river. Nollman had entered buffalo time and communicated with the entire herd of buffalo through a dance of energy and music. The communication was two-way: He had offered his dance of friendship to them, and they had responded. As he says, the almost-hypnotic quality of the four notes affected him as well as the buffalo, but it affected him by opening his perception to the world beyond language.

Usually, we perceive and respond to our world not directly but through the medium of words. Often, when we hear a sound, first we have a feeling toward it—positive or negative—and then we wonder what to name the sound. We recognize the sound, we put a name to it, and only *then* do we respond to it. Sight and the other senses work the same way, so that we perceive our world through a filter of words. This process is usually so fast that we are not conscious of it, but it happens with everything we perceive—we live in a world of words. If you watch your mind in action, you can sometimes catch this whole process happening even with the simplest sounds or sights.

Sometimes, though, we perceive our world directly and we act directly, without the barrier of words. When a child screams, a mother runs to her. She doesn't have to say or think anything—that comes after. People occasionally report moments when they have been particularly relaxed, with nothing on their mind, when they glance at a pet or a child and for a brief moment they clearly see through the eyes of that other being. Although the moment is brief, it changes their relationship to that being.

Through your body and the subtle feelings that it conveys, you can become aware of levels of perception and communication with your world to which you are normally deaf, blind, and numb. We normally have a constant, inner sensation of our body of which we can become aware at any time but that we habitually ignore. Magic happens when your awareness tunes to that inner sense of your body in its wholeness. When you lose that sensation altogether it can be tragic.

Neurologist Oliver Sacks, in *The Man Who Mistook His Wife for a Hat*, reports a case of a woman who lost the inner awareness of her body (a "sixth sense" known to neurologists as proprioception). At first she was totally unable to move—not because she could not use her muscles but because, having no inner sense of her body, she had no feeling for where her limbs were at any moment. Her voice became completely toneless, her face expressionless. After much struggle, she learned again to walk and sit up and live a seemingly normal life by replacing her inner awareness of the body with her sense of sight. As long as she kept her arms and legs within sight, she could use them. Sacks says, "Christina is condemned to live in an indescribable, unimaginable realm—though 'nonrealm,' 'nothingness' might be better words for it. At times she breaks down. . . . 'If only I could feel!' she cries. 'But I've forgotten what it's like.' "

Sacks showed Christina home movies of herself before the illness. " 'Yes, of course that's me!' Christina smiles, and then cries: 'But I can't identify with that graceful girl any more! She's gone, I can't remember her, I can't even imagine her. It's like something's been scooped right out of me, right at the center.' "

When we join mind with body, we become aware of the inner sensation of the body. The body is the dwelling place of the emotions and of the deeper feelings of sadness and joy that lie beneath fear and anxiety and anger.

Right now, gently let your awareness travel into the inside of your right forearm. With your eyes closed, you know exactly where it is just by the feeling of it, by its inner sensation of warmth and aliveness. Although this inner sensation of the body may seem rather unimportant, in fact it is vital. To become aware of this sensation during daily activities and stay with it for a moment is a very powerful practice to connect the mind and body and so to feel the world and communicate with it directly, without the separation caused by language.

Try this exercise: Sit in a café or diner (or bus or train), perhaps one that you have been to many times before. As you sit, instead of losing yourself in your thoughts, feel the presence of your own body. Now take a moment to look around at the details of what people are wearing. Listen to the tones of their voices and to the sounds of traffic outside, and smell the slightly stale coffee and the sweetness of the doughnuts. The place itself suddenly comes alive, as if you had awakened from a dream for a moment. You are actually *here;* the world is actually *here.*

When body and mind are joined, we participate fully in our world and can communicate at a deeper level than speech. By participating physically and emotionally in the world of another being, we communicate with that being. While listening to the troubled story of a friend, you can feel the sorrow he communicates through his body and his environment, perhaps more deeply than through his words. If you stand next to a large sycamore tree with an open heart, you can feel the life in that tree resonating in your own body. Often you can feel a person's presence as she moves close to you even when your back is turned or when you are in a darkened room. Sometimes you can feel aggression in the atmosphere when you enter a room where there has been a bad fight, and you can feel the peace in the atmosphere of a house of healing.

Sitting at the foot of a mountain, a sick person may feel healed. Standing at a particular point on a cliffhead, you may feel disturbed—not because of a strong wind but just because of the lay of the land. Sitting quietly and without anxiety by the bedside of a dying person, you can bring them peace. But you can feel these things only if you are receptive to the sensations of your own body and beyond your body at that very moment. At those times we have no concern about which is my space and which is your space, which are my boundaries and which are your boundaries. When we relax and give up keeping track, there is no limit to how far we can extend our openness, our participation, and our affection for the world.

In *Dolphin Dreamtime,* Jim Nollman relates a funny and illuminating incident in which he participated in the world of a turkey and communicated with its energy. He had been staying in Mexico. Each day he sat out in the yard playing his flute, and "every single time I hit a certain high note on that flute, the tom turkey who lived in the yard next door would let out a single resounding gobble."

Over the next month, Nollman spent an hour a day playing "strange songs and stranger sounds with that turkey." He wondered,

Was I communicating to my friend, the plump tom turkey? To be perfectly honest, part of my mind was quite skeptical about the matter. . . . But there is another level at play here that I cannot so logically explain away. Because, you see, I *did* learn the turkey energy. It is very difficult to say that it is precisely this, or exactly that. . . . It is about my feelings of collaboration with the bird; about the bird finally sitting beside the barbed wire, waiting for me to appear; my own growing sensitivity to the bird's own moods—shared feelings about the weather; a dislike of quick movements, sounds, change. It is about learning to operate on turkey time, the turkey dreamtime. . . . [T]his relationship was not about *observation,* but rather, about *participation*. . . .

Yet what it was that the two of us actually communicated is much more difficult to pinpoint. It was not words. Nor was it emotions either. Not exactly emotions. Rather, it was . . . the exchange of pure energy, the kind we generate so effortlessly when we are young and in love. It is the stuff of talented musicians at play. For me, the experience was immediate and very direct.

When we ourselves have glimpses of such communication, we usually dismiss them as "just imagination" because we are afraid of them. They don't fit into our idea of how the world is. People who experience such phenomena particularly vividly have been so afraid of being thought crazy or "impractical" that they tried to hide their experience and insight even from themselves. Sometimes this refusal to acknowledge their own experience leads to depression or insanity. Why not try thinking that they are *not* fantasy, and see how your world changes?

Intuitive Insight

Probably you are familiar with a sense of intuition or participation in the presence of the world. Maybe you feel it in very small ways: As you walk to your car from the grocery, you may realize the school is trying to call you because your child is sick; or you may know who is calling before you pick up the phone; or you know when someone is thinking of you or that a friend is having a hard time with her lover. Usually we experience such intuitions as slight, fleeting impressions, at moments when we are not involved with something else. Mostly, even when we do manage to glimpse such intuitions, we dismiss them. Only later, when life has become more complicated because we ignored the intuition, do we think back and wish we'd paid attention. A colleague of mine totaled his car when the brakes failed as he went down a mountain road— that morning he had ignored a nagging feeling that he ought to have the brakes checked.

Sometimes these intuitive feelings become much more vivid, especially when intense emotion is involved. But even at these times, although it is harder to dismiss the intuition, we still tend to distrust our own perception. The night before Christina's strange and tragic loss of body sense began, Oliver Sacks tells us, she had a vivid dream that just such a thing was happening to her. A friend of mine experienced, on several occasions, seeing the face of someone she knew in a clear and stark way, just before that person died. Immediately after her mother died, my wife intensely felt her presence in our home.

My father is a civil engineer, a specialist in concrete, a religious agnostic, and as practical a man as I have known. One day he told me this story, about something "that shook my whole world to its foundations." His mother was over ninety and was suffering from senile dementia. She could rarely recognize anyone except my father. But she was very fond of his younger sister, Bettina, who was then dying of cancer. This was the same disease that my grandfather, a doctor, had died from years before.

The day after Bettina died, my father called the nursing home to tell the nurse but asked her not to tell his mother, since he would tell her himself the next day. The nurse said, "Oh, but she already knows. On her bedside table this morning there was a card which she had edged in black. And she had written the name *Bettina* in the middle. When I asked what it was for, she answered, 'Bettina died last night.' " When my father went to visit his mother the next day, he asked her how she knew Bettina had died. She answered, "That night your father came to the window and held up a card that said, 'Bettina died, same sickness.' "

In *The Lost World of the Kalahari*, Laurens van der Post tells how he had been hunting with some Bushmen, and they had killed an eland, which was a cause for great celebration. He said to his companion, Dabe, "I wonder what they'll say at the sip-wells when they learn that we've killed an eland?"

"Excuse me, Master," Dabe said, bolder than I had ever known him, "they already know."

"What on earth do you mean?" I asked.

"They know by wire," he declared, the English word "wire" on his Bushman tongue making me start with its unexpectedness.

"Wire?" I exclaimed.

"Yes. A wire, Master. I have seen my own master go many times to the D.C. [District Commissioner] at Gemsbok Pan and get him to send a wire to them when he is going to trek out to them with his cattle. We Bushmen have a wire here," he said, tapping his chest, "that brings us news."

More than that I couldn't get out of him, but even before we were home it was clear that our skeptical minds were about to be humbled. From afar in the dark, long before our fires were visible from a place where we stopped to adjust our heavy load, the black silence was broken by a glitter of new song from the women.

"Do you hear that, oh, my Master?" Dabe said, whistling between his teeth. "Do you hear? They're singing 'The Eland Song.' "

Whether by "wire" or by what mysterious means, they did know at the sip-wells, and were preparing to give their hunters the greatest of welcomes.

The Sword of No-Sword, a story about sword-master Yamaoka Tesshu, conveys a similar message:

Tesshu developed a kind of sixth sense, frequently surprising his disciples by telling them exactly what they were thinking. When asked about this "magic power," Tesshu told them, "It is nothing out of the ordinary. If your mind is empty, it reflects the 'distortions' and shadows present in others' minds. In swordsmanship no-mind allows us to see the perfect place to strike; in daily life it enables us to see into another's heart."

Stories about people's ability to feel the moods, images, or thoughts of others are so abundant and commonplace that they seem as natural as the splitting of the atom (which has not been as widely observed!). Such phenomena are less "mind-reading" than being in tune with the sensitive receiving and transmitting organ that is our bodymind when it is in harmony with heaven and earth. These experiences are numerous and familiar to all of us. The point is that we should not ignore them.

Even though communication through participation is so common, however, anyone wanting to be taken seriously would hardly have dared to mention it, until recently. This largely is due to our living in a world guided by a philosophy of scientific materialism carried over from the nineteenth century— a view that is deeply ingrained in us. Most people in modern society are simply unable to accept the evidence of their own senses because they are taught by their science teachers, by popular science magazines, and by eminent scientists on TV that "scientists *know* such things are just not possible." By its very nature, science is capable of dealing only with patterns of events that can be repeated. The intimate experiences we are talking about in this chapter are each unique. This makes them no less true than facts validated by science. Candace Pert, herself a highly respected scientist, said in a conversation with Bill Moyers in *Healing and the Mind*, "Too many phenomena can't be explained by thinking of the body in a totally reductionistic fashion. . . . There's another realm that we experience that's not under the purview of science."

For more than fifteen years, at the Engineering Laboratories of Princeton University, a special laboratory has been studying "anomalous" phenomena— that is, phenomena that do not fit into the scientific view of the world. The researchers have found evidence that suggests a pervasive quality of mind throughout space. Robert Jahn, the professor of aeronautical engineering who set up the laboratory, conducted the experiments under the strictest scientific controls. The book *Margins of Reality*, which he wrote with Brenda Dunne, the laboratory manager, demonstrates incontrovertible evidence for the ability of participants, *simply by their intention,* to affect the outcome of a physical event, such as the pattern of Ping-Pong balls falling through a set of pins, or the sequence of numbers shown on the display of a random number generator. Jahn and Dunne found that the most successful participants were those who reported some kind of empathetic feeling of identification with the machines, who in some strange way felt interconnected with the machines.

The laboratory has also demonstrated the validity of precognitive remote viewing, which is perhaps even more startling to minds habituated to a distinctly narrow worldview. Precognitive remote viewing is the ability of an observer accurately to describe a far-distant scene, as much as four thousand miles away, that another person will visit some hours *after* the description has been recorded. Jahn and Dunne's results are highly significant according to all reasonable scientific criteria, and other scientists have reproduced them many times.

We must be extremely careful not to get caught up in wishful thinking. Sometimes we would love to escape to another world to be free from having to deal with this one. What I am talking about here is quite the opposite of such escapism. Communication through participation is being courageous and without self-deception; it is being present now and being intelligently open to what we experience *now and here*. These forms of communication are going on all the time, whether we know it or not and whether we like it or not. When you look and listen with an open heart, you can feel them. Even if you do not recall a personal experience of this kind of communication, the evidence is overwhelming that it happens, and far more frequently than the modern mind admits. When I mention these things at a dinner table of apparently staid professional people, including scientists, I have been astounded to find how many breathe a sigh of relief and then recount their own experiences. It is as if a kind of coming out of hiding were happening, related to a changing view of what is accepted as valid human experience and part of our world. People in all walks of life who have long denied their experience for fear of being considered silly or, worse, being assigned to a mental hospital are now saying, "Yes, we do experience these things."

If we acknowledge that such things happen and let their happening challenge our comforting but narrow beliefs about reality then the world will begin to reveal its vastness to us. We can begin to understand that we participate in a world far richer and more multifaceted and connected than we thought.

A Universal Field of
Unified Energy and Awareness

Most spiritual traditions, including the Shambhala path of warriorship, are based on the realization that we exist within a profundity of inseparable consciousness and energy from which the physical and mental universes arise together and only appear to be separate; and on the possibility of experiencing the presence of this creative mind-energy. Even "energy," "consciousness," and "mind" are merely concepts to describe an essentially unconditioned and unbounded presence. This is the ground of all that can be named and thereby bounded. It is very simple, but it confounds the intellect: there is vastly more to this world than all human philosophies and religions can name or even dream of. By recognizing and naming recurring patterns in this ground, we give them form; by giving them form, we bring them into existence. "Existence" literally means "to stand forth out of the background."

The sixteenth-century Confucian sage Wang Shihuai who, like all Chinese scholar sages, was strongly influenced by Taoism, explains:

> The name "mind" is imposed on the essence of phenomena. The name "phenomena" is imposed on the functioning of mind. In reality there is just one single thing, without any distinctions of inside and outside and this and that. What fills the universe is both all mind and all phenomena.
>
> Students wrongly accept as mind the petty, compartmentalized mind that is vaguely located within them and wrongly accept as phenomena the multiplicity of things and events mixing together outside of their bodies. Therefore they pursue the outer or they concentrate on the inner and do not integrate the two. This will never be sufficient for entering the Path.

The boundless realm or field of mind-energy that is both outside and inside embraces us and in it we live and move and have our being. This field is both mental and physical or, to put it another way, it is neither physical nor mental in the conventional sense. It is mental because we experience it as unconditioned love, uncompromising affection that cuts right to our heart, and warms and nourishes our genuine nature. Yet this field of awareness is not purely subjective—it is *one*, a common realm shared by all of us and we experience its effects as the medium of subtle communication and energy.

This common field *is also* physical, and it is important to understand this if we are to overcome the split between spirituality and the ordinary world we experience with our senses. It is physical because we feel it as energy that enlivens our body and mind. Chinese chi gong and Tai Ch'i masters have demonstrated physical effects of the spiritual energy, qi or ch'i. Masters of chi gong, Tai Ch'i, Zen swordsmanship, and aikido have demonstrated extraordinary feats using the energy of chi. There is a film of Ueshiba, the founder of aikido, being attacked by several of his students simultaneously when he was in his eighties. As the students lunge toward him in a circle he suddenly appears, from one frame to the next (i.e., within one-sixteenth of a second) outside of the circle and the students simply go crashing into one another. I have seen a demonstration by a Japanese master of Zen sword in which he simply held his hand, palm facing down, three or four feet above the head of a volunteer lying on the floor. He asked the volunteer, a big man, to move. The volunteer told me, "I was completely incapable of moving. It was not that I was in any way hypnotized. It was that I felt such a powerful physical force emanating from the man's hand and pressing me down that I simply could not get up."

In a scene from *Ring of Fire,* a documentary video by two British brothers, Lawrence and Lorne Blair, who spent ten years traveling and filming in the volcanic island chain of Indonesia, one of the brothers went for treatment to an acupuncturist in Jakarta, the capital of Java. After successfully treating him, the acupuncturist demonstrated his chi. First he touched the hand of one of the brothers and, after a brief pause, the brother pulled his hand away quickly after feeling a sudden burst of intense heat. The doctor repeated the effect with one of the camerawomen who was especially sceptical. She too pulled her hand away after a pause with a look of shock and delight on her face. The doctor explains that anyone can generate this energy if they practice "meditation every day." He ended by crumpling a newspaper supplied by the film crew and causing it to burst into flames through the energy of the chi projected from his hand which he held several inches from the newspaper. The astonished look on the faces of the Blair brothers and the film crew, quite apart from the humbleness and obvious ingenuousness of the doctor, leaves little doubt about the authenticity of this scene. The doctor emphasized that it is important in working with this energy not to have negative emotions and aggression because this energy is neutral and could be harmful to others rather than beneficial if it is misused.

So chi is the source of both spiritual awakening and remarkable physical power, and forward-looking scientists are now beginning to accept that such a field must exist. For example, physicist Hal Puthoff, director of the Institute for

Advanced Studies at Austin, Texas, has shown theoretically that what we normally think of as vacuum—completely empty space—is in actuality *not* an empty passive container, but is full and dynamic and interacting with all that is within it. He is in the process of conducting experiments that demonstrate the reality of this energy. Puthoff suggests that chi is a manifestation of the vacuum energy, and is also conducting experiments to test this. As Wang Shihuai says, "The great ultimate [the Tao] is our true nature; it is the primordial. When it moves it gives birth to the creative force [chi], which from then on belongs to material energy, to the temporal. True nature can give birth to material energy: true nature is not outside of material energy."

We must keep in mind that this all-pervading mind-energy field is not external to our own mind and body. We must also be careful not to turn it into a "something" outside of us. Here, the Buddhist view is always a helpful reminder. Suzuki Roshi puts very clearly the sense that there is nothing, which nevertheless is full.

I discovered that it is necessary, absolutely necessary, to believe in nothing. That is, we have to believe in something which has no form and no color— something which exists before all forms and colors appear. This is a very important point. . . . It is absolutely necessary to believe in nothing. But I do not mean voidness. There is something, but that something is something which is always prepared for taking some particular form, and it has some rules, or theory, or truth in its activity. . . . This is not just theory. This is not just the teaching of Buddhism. This is the absolutely necessary understanding of our life.

The Cosmic Mirror

This originating mind-energy from which time, space, consciousness, and all mental and physical forms arise is profound and ungraspable by thought. In the Shambhala tradition, it is called the *cosmic mirror.* It is called *cosmic* because of its vastness and its primordialness. Primordial means that it is before space and time and is not caused by anything, not created or formed by anything outside itself. It is, in itself, empty of all forms, but full of all possibilities and potentials. Buddhists tend to emphasize the formless or empty aspect of the cosmic mirror to avoid creating the idea that it is a substantial *thing* external to us and giving rise to the natural tendency to turn it into an external creator god. However, the teachings at the highest level of Tibetan Buddhism do recognize the energetic and luminous aspect of the mirror.

The cosmic mirror is called a *mirror* because everything we perceive as having form and existing as a "separate" entity arises within it like a reflection in a mirror. And it has no bias toward whatever arises in it, just as a mirror has no bias toward what is reflected in it. Nowadays we have the analogy of a hologram, which is perhaps more helpful because through the hologram we can begin to get the feel of how things can appear in three-dimensional space and full living color apparently from nowhere. From *Zen Dust:* "The entire world is your eyes; the entire universe is your complete body; the entire universe is your luminance; the entire universe is within your own luminance."

The Dorje Dradul speaks of it in this way:

The realm of perception is limitless, so limitless that perception itself is primordial, unthinkable, beyond thought. There are so many perceptions that they are beyond imagination. There are a vast number of sounds. There are sounds that you have never heard. There are sights and colors that you have never seen. There are feelings that you have never experienced before. There are endless fields of perception.

By perception the Dorje Dradul is referring not just to what you perceive, but to the whole act of perceiving—the interactions between consciousness, your sense organs, and the object of perception. He goes on to say,

Because of the extraordinary vastness of perception, you have the possibilities of communicating with the depth of the world—the world of sight, the world of sound—the greater world.

In other words, your sense faculties give you access to possibilities of deeper perception. Beyond ordinary perception, there is super-sound, super-smell and super-feeling existing in your state of being. These can be experienced only by training yourself in the depth of meditation [mindfulness] practice, which clarifies any confusion or cloudiness and brings out the precision, sharpness, and wisdom of perception—the nowness of your world.

All that we perceive, feel, and experience in our world arises within the cosmic mirror. The cosmic mirror is the wisdom that gives rise to all images, living symbols, archetypes—all those profound meanings that organize and energize our life, yet it is felt in the simplest perception: smoke curling up from a chimney, rain washing over the hood of a red car, a child calling in the park. The cosmic mirror is beyond the discriminating intellectual aspect of mind that distinguishes between opposites, one and many, good and evil, black and white, friend and enemy, our side and their side, existence and nonexistence. The conceptualizing mind is always dichotomizing, dividing everything into opposites, and most modern people do not know that a state of mind beyond dichotomizing exists or could exist. It is presumed in our educational and political systems that the intellectual mind that creates opposite views, which then have to battle for the truth, is the highest function of the human mind. Is it any wonder we have wars! However, the fact is that all of us *are* capable of recognizing opposites and not being caught up in taking one side or the other, thereby harmonizing them. That awareness that recognizes dichotomies is itself beyond creating and dwelling in opposites, beyond conceptualization. And by developing this awareness, through the practices that we will describe in Part Two, and paying attention to the depth of our ordinary perception we can learn to let our mind become one with the wisdom of the cosmic mirror.

CHAPTER 3
Patterns of Living Energy

In the Shambhala teachings, the patterns of living energy that we can feel and with which we can communicate are called dralas. *Drala* is a Tibetan word that means "transcending enemies." The dralas are our links with the reality beyond us. They are the liaison between that loud, colorful, smelly world that we sense and think we "know" and the vast and fathomless world of formless energy and limitless potential that supports our little world and nourishes it. The world that we perceive and know with all its boundaries and distinctions is just the surface of reality; it is an elaborate play, like a holographic sound-and-light show. Our bodies and minds, our feelings and perceptions, and the "things" that make up our world are part of that show. By calling on the dralas, we can draw down the energy that drives the show, that unseen fullness behind the surface world. As the Dorje Dradul says,

> When we draw down the power and depth of vastness into a single perception, then we are discovering and invoking magic. By magic we do not mean unnatural power over the phenomenal world, but rather the discovery of innate or primordial wisdom in the world as it is. The wisdom we are discovering is wisdom without beginning, something naturally wise, the wisdom of the cosmic mirror.

Patterns of Living Energy

How real are the dralas? They are as real as we are, as real as the trees, as weather patterns, galaxies, supernovas, and nuclear forces. But how real is that? The dralas are not masks or deceptions, and they are neither "otherworldly" nor "supernatural." It is a mistake to think of them as separate entities existing outside of us, just as it is a mistake to think of ourselves as fundamentally separate from one another and the world. According to the Dorje Dradul:

One of the key points in discovering drala principle is realizing that your own wisdom as a human being is not separate from the power of things as they are. They are both reflections of the unconditioned wisdom of the cosmic mirror. Therefore there is no fundamental separation or duality between you and your world. When you can experience those two things together, as one, so to speak, then you have access to tremendous vision and power in the world—you find they are inherently connected to your own vision, your own being.

We can relate to the dralas as if they were other than ourselves, however, just as we relate to each other. We can call on them and invoke their response and help. They will not save us from ourselves—that is up to us—but they can help us and are willing to help. The dralas come into existence in our world and make themselves known to us, so long as we call on them with heartfelt longing, motivated by genuine caring for ourselves and others.

The dralas are not merely "subjective" structures of the human mind, as some modern psychologists would have us believe. This attitude is human-ego-centered, as it interprets everything according to human perceptions and beliefs. A snake perceives no "tree" in its world, a fish perceives no "air," nor an ant "clouds." For us, knowing the dralas may be a little like a prairie dog perceiving a herd of buffalo—a cloud of dust, a thundering noise, vibrations felt through the ground. These might be about the extent of the prairie dog's experience. Perhaps it communicates with the buffalo through the circle of yellow light, just as Jim Nollman did. Ed McGaa, Eagle Man, an Oglala Sioux, puts the dilemma this way: "What are the spirits? Who are they? In a way that question could be analogous to wondering what a grasshopper knows about a locomotive that goes whizzing by. No doubt the grasshopper might ask if it had the means or intellect to speak. No doubt the locomotive would be discovered to go quite beyond the grasp and comprehension of the crawling one who has but one summer's life span."

We cannot feel dralas, least of all dance with them, if we are trapped in small-minded logic, in fixed ideas that we all got from books, teachers, and schools that themselves inherited them from the past. Thus we perpetuate a certain view of the world, a modern myth, *without realizing* that it is one particular creation myth among many. Some of our beliefs tell a small patch of the story of the cosmos, but it is arrogance to believe it is the *only* myth, the final solution to the limitless wonder of the cosmos.

We do not have to be great shamans or special people to invite the dralas into our world. We are all ordinary people and special people at the same time. We can call on the dralas, but we need to have the proper attitude and intention. We cannot invoke dralas from an attitude of grasping and ambition. We cannot think and reason our way into that connection. We can connect with the dralas only from a mind and heart that is gentle and profoundly relaxed. We need to let go of our fixed ideas about ourselves and our history, about how the world is. We can let go and relax body and mind together, let go and relax, relax, relax . . . until we have nothing on our mind. With that open and gentle mind we can invoke the dralas.

We cannot feel the dralas unless we let go of our certainty and feel, feel, *feel the world*. We cannot feel the dralas unless we let our minds swim in a whirlpool of uncertainty, a fog of confusion. How delightful! At last you can give in. You probably always knew that you didn't really know, now you can just let go into that. Now you can feel the multitude of questions buzzing in your brain and heart. Did you not feel these questions as a child? Where have they gone? How did they die?

Let your questions come alive again. Feel your small mind dissolving in a glorious intoxication of questions. Let yourself feel awful and awe-full: the world is magnificent, wonderful, hot and cold, pissy and shitty, vibrant, boring, extraordinary, powerful, frightening, exhilarating. *Now* can you feel the energy of the dralas?

We have to be in drala time and space, which is now and here, to communicate with reality. The dralas are like bubbles that expand and pop. They snap, crackle, and pop, and we can pop with them. When we pop with them, we are part of the same energy. We just have to pop *on the spot,* we have to pop *now.* We have to be willing to let our minds explode on the spot, *now.*

When we let go and pop, we can hear the dralas in the cry of the loon, the sound of wind and rain. We can feel the dralas as the leaves shift and twinkle in the sunshine, as the spring stream comes rushing down the hillside splashing little sprays of cool water on our hands, as thunderclouds gather and hail comes pouring down on our heads in the middle of a warm summer afternoon. We can feel the dralas gathering on objects that we care for, in sacred places, in power spots on the land, in meaningful coincidences, at times of creative inspiration, and throughout our world when we give it attention and care.

That the world can respond to us in this way may be shocking to our mundane minds. Most modern men and women arrogantly believe that humans and other animals are the only beings that feel and communicate, even though intelligent and sensitive peoples all over the world have sung and danced with greater and smaller patterns of energy for tens of thousands of years.

The Drala Principle Is Found in Most Human Societies

The drala principle is found in every human group as far back as we know. It is found in the ancestors, helpers, and spirits of the Native American tradition; in the pagan gods of the Greek, Roman, Germanic, and Nordic peoples; among African tribes and Australian Aboriginals. It is found in the Japanese kami, which are the basis of the naturalistic, shamanistic Shinto tradition. Persons of great authentic presence often have a relationship with heaven and earth so direct that they seem able to dance with the dralas of the natural world.

The Dorje Dradul says,

There are many ... examples of invoking external drala [dralas in the environment]. I have read, for instance, that some American Indians in Southwest grow vegetables in the desert sands. The soil, from an objective standpoint, is completely infertile. If you just threw a handful of seeds into that earth, nothing would grow. But the Indians have been cultivating that soil for generations; they have a deep connection to that earth and they care for it. To them it is sacred ground, and because of that their plants grow. That is real magic. That attitude of sacredness towards your environment will bring drala. You may live in a dirt hut with no floor and only one window, but if you regard that space as sacred, if you care for it with your heart and mind, then it will be a palace.

He goes on to point out that the so-called pagan traditions of Europe also had a connection with the dralas.

The Greeks and Romans laid out their cities with some understanding of external drala. You might say that putting a fountain in the center of a square or at a crossroads is a random choice. But when you come upon that fountain, it does not feel random at all. It is in its own proper place and it seems to enhance the space around it. In modern times, we don't think very highly of the Romans, with all of their debauchery and corrupt rulers. We tend to downplay the wisdom of their culture. Certainly, corruption dispels drala. But there was some power and wisdom in the Roman civilization, which we should not overlook.

Understanding of the drala principle has been renewed in modern times. People today do not quite know what to call them and have begun to call them *angels,* which is a quite limited term, influenced by traditional Christian dogma. Certainly some very silly stories are circulating about "angels" appearing to help people out—for example, when a tow truck seems to appear out of nowhere in the middle of a snowstorm. Dralas do not appear miraculously as truck drivers, although the auspicious coincidence of a *human* driving a tow truck and appearing just when needed is worth paying attention to. There we might find a pattern of energy beyond our usual experience.

The extraordinary experiences at the Findhorn garden in northern Scotland may be one example in our time and culture of communication with dralas, very similar to the Dorje Dradul's description of the Native American connection with the dralas of their land. Dorothy Maclean tells of her experience at Findhorn:

Yes, I talk with angels, great Beings whose lives infuse and create all of Nature. In another time and culture I might have been cloistered in a convent or a temple, or, less pleasantly, burnt at the stake as a witch. . . . Being a practical, down-to-earth person, I never set out to learn to talk with angels, nor had I ever imagined that such contact would be possible or useful. Yet, when this communication began to occur, it did so in a way that I could not dispute.

Concrete proof developed in the Findhorn garden. . . . This garden was planted on sand in conditions that offered scant hospitality and encouragement for the growth of anything other than hardy Scottish bushes and grasses requiring little moisture or nourishment. However, through my . . . contact with angelic Beings, . . . specific instructions and spiritual assistance were given. The resulting garden, which came to include even tropical varieties of plants, was so astonishing in its growth and vitality that visiting soil experts and horticulturists were unable to find any explanation for it within known methods of organic husbandry, and eventually had to accept the unorthodox interpretation of angelic help.

Maclean goes on to speak of the crux of how and why renewed connection with dralas is vital:

To learn to talk with angels is really learning to talk with ourselves and with each other in new and profoundly deeper ways. It is learning how to communicate with our universe more openly and how to be more in tune with our role as co-creators and participate in its evolution. Modern communication has developed marvelously and very quickly in the physical, technological mode, but deeper and more subtle forms of communication remain untapped. For the future of our world and ourselves, we must now begin to use those deeper forms. . . . It requires a joyful enlargement of our view of reality, a readiness to be open to ourselves and our environment, and a conscious movement to embrace our own wholeness.

In every culture we find human collaboration with dralalike energies. Like electricity, however, these energies are neutral. Whether the outcome of collaboration is beneficial or harmful depends on the training and intention of the people involved.

The English author D. H. Lawrence, who had an extraordinary understanding of the old spirituality of the native peoples of Mexico, writes:

The Indian does not consider himself as created and therefore external to God, or the creature of God. To the Indian there is no defined God. Creation is a great flood, for ever flowing, in lovely and terrible waves. In everything the shimmer of creation, and never the finality of the created. Never the distinction between God and God's creation, or between Spirit and Matter. Everything, everything is the wonderful shimmer of creation, it may be a deadly shimmer like lightning or the anger in the little eyes of the bear, it may be the beautiful shimmer of the moving deer, or the pine boughs softly swaying under snow. . . .

There is, in our sense of the word, no God. But all is godly. There is no Great Mind directing the universe. Yet the mystery of creation, the wonder and fascination of creation shimmers in every leaf and stone, in every thorn and bud, in the fangs of the rattlesnake, and in the soft eyes of a fawn. Things utterly opposite are still pure. . . .

It is a vast, old religion, greater than anything we know, more starkly and nakedly religious. . . . In the oldest religion everything was alive, not supernaturally but naturally alive. There were only deeper and deeper streams of life, vibrations of life, more and more vast. So rocks were alive, but a mountain had a deeper vaster life than a rock, and it was much harder for a man to bring his spirit, or his energy, into contact with the life of the mountain, and so draw strength from the mountain, as from a great standing well of life, than it was to come in contact with the rock. And he had to put forth great religious effort. For the whole life effort of man was to get his life into direct contact with the elemental life of the cosmos, mountain-life, cloud-life, thunder-life, air-life, earth-life, sun-life. To come into immediate felt contact and so derive energy, power, and a dark sort of joy.

A modern spokesman for one of the Native American traditions, Wallace Black Elk, a Lakota, describes his communication with spirits this way:

I learned from the spirit how to find those rocks that contain the sacred powdered paints. . . . We go [to the Badlands] and pray . . . and you can see those special rocks glow in the dark. They look like little colored lights in the dark. You can see the colors that are on the inside. So we go there and take the colors we need. . . . I learned their songs, but there are many songs out there. There are countless songs. Like the fire, it has a song. That fire shapes and forms all life, and each shape has a song. And the rocks, the rocks have songs. Like this rock I wear around my neck, it has a song. All the stones that are around here, each one has a language of its own. Even the Earth has a song. We call it Mother Earth. We call her Grandmother, and she has a song. Then the water, it has a song. The water makes beautiful sounds. The water carries the universal sounds. Now the green. This tree, every green has a song. They have a language of their own. There's life there. . . .

If you see a tree, it doesn't move. It doesn't talk or walk. You just see it. You just see a tree. That's all. But the trees talk. They have a language of their own. So all this green that you see, they communicate. . . .

So each one of the winged-people [birds] has a song. It is the same with the four-legged and creeping-crawler creatures. So that's how come we have an eagle song, a buffalo song, and even a serpent song, a serpent language. . . . So I want to tell you that you have a lot to learn. What you know today, it's just a little bit—like the blink of an eye. So that power is immense.

Douchan Gersi spent many years studying with shamans of the Haitian voodoo tradition, and he recorded his experiences in *Faces in the Smoke*. In voodoo, the dralas are known as loas. Voodoo was long banned by the Catholic Church and so was given the bad name that it has for most of us. But as Gersi says, "Theologians have begun to consider Voodoo as more sacred and solemn than they had previously thought. More than a religion, Voodoo is a mysticism, a culture, a philosophy, a way of life. And because it is a living and dynamic religion, which, instead of being dogmatic and moral—as most western religions are—is based on initiatory and metaphysical principles, it is impossible to describe Voodoo in everyday language. One can only experience it."

According to Gersi,

The invisible world is all around us, among us, behind the cosmic mirror. This world is like a reflection of our visible world. The inhabitants have the same needs and passions as we do. It is populated by the souls of the deceased and by an infinite number of *loas,* who are the original inhabitants of this world. Sometimes called spirits or angels, loas are energies or entities that have been made divine. They are divided into different families, groups and sub-groups. Some have great power.

The loas are available to humans to act as guides in the visible world and intermediaries with the invisible world. Loas generally are neither good nor evil in themselves and can be used for either good or evil. But, as Gersi emphasizes, "Voodoo is a religion in search of the sacred: it uses the cosmic force only in a positive way, and loas are never used for evil purposes."

The loas with greatest power came from African traditions, notably the Yoruba, whose culture was as sophisticated and equal in power and beauty to the "great civilizations" with which Westerners are familiar. These loas are connected with the elements of nature. One is the father-protector of main entries, thresholds, and doorways; another is the energy of fecundity, symbolized by a snake; another, the ruler of crossroads; another, the energy of war, symbolized by a piece of iron. Other loas are the energy of thunder and lightning, the energy of passion and sex, the energy of the sea (symbolized by a boat), and the guardians of the deceased, chief of whom is the Brave, symbolized by a cross or grave.

In the Shinto tradition of Japan, the dralas are called kamis. The creative function of the world is realized not by one creator god but by the kamis harmoniously cooperating as they carry out their responsibilities. According to Seigow Matsuoka:

> *Kami* has no physical body; its body and essence exist as a vacuum, a place entirely void of matter. But "void" does not mean nothing is there. . . . In the beginning the *kami* was thought to visit, to dwell temporarily in the mountains and the sea. The line of the mountains and hills against the sky, the horizon over the water, these were the *kami's* proscenium arches. Here the *kami* were accustomed to enter and exist. . . . *Kami* does not abide; its nature is to arrive and to depart. The Japanese word *otozureru,* meaning to visit, is a compound of *oto* (sound) and *tsure* (bring). The ancient Japanese may truly have perceived the sounds of utmost mystery and elegance that accompany the visitations of *kami*. No doubt this was what today is perceived as *ch'i* by those involved in martial arts and meditation. . . . This concept of *kami* as the atmosphere of *ch'i* which fills a void has given the entire Japanese culture its striking quality. [In contrast,] European culture adopted the Aristotelean principle of "Abhorrence of the Vacuum."

According to Sokyo Ono, "Kamis are the guardian spirits of the land, occupations, and skills; the spirits of national heroes, men of outstanding deeds or virtues, and those who have contributed to civilization, culture and human welfare." There are kamis associated with natural objects such as the sun, mountains, rivers, trees, and rocks; natural phenomena, such as wind and thunder; the qualities of growth, fertility, and production; some animals; and ancestral spirits.

Each kami has its particular characteristics and mission and is considered the protector of some definite object or phenomenon. For example, one is concerned with the distribution of water, another with the manufacture of medicine, and still another with the healing process. They are protectors in the sense that the real heart and authenticity of something cannot be found unless the kami are respected properly. As Ono tells us:

> The Japanese people themselves do not have a clear idea regarding kamis. They are aware of kamis intuitively at the depth of their consciousness and communicate with the kamis directly without having formed the kami-

idea conceptually or theologically. Therefore it is impossible to make explicit and clear that which fundamentally by its very nature is vague.

Joseph Campbell tells the story of being in Japan for a conference on religion when he overheard another American delegate, a social philosopher from New York, say to a Shinto priest, "We've been now to a good many ceremonies and seen quite a few of your shrines, but I don't get your ideology, I don't get your theology." The Japanese paused as though in deep thought and then slowly shook his head saying, "I think we don't have ideology, we don't have theology . . . we dance."

Most older Japanese, whether their actual religious worship is Buddhist or Christian or Shinto or none at all, respect the kami. They feel their presence and understand the need to communicate with them in order to maintain the proper flow of energy in their world. Even a businessman building a bank at a particular location will perform the appropriate ceremonies to pay respects to the kami of that place before beginning construction. More ceremonies will be performed throughout the building process to gather the energy and power of the kami. The Emperor himself spends much of his time in ceremonies honoring the kami.

This very brief survey is merely a hint of how the drala principle appears in so many cultures around the world, whether they are small, tribal groups or large, national, city-based cultures. The drala principle appears in many different forms, but there is a common heart to all of these: they are ways that humans have found to connect with the energy, profundity, and power of the real world. Some of these cultures may seem quite strange to your way of thinking and living and you may wonder whether there is any way for *you* to connect with the dralas. It *is* possible for all of us, even in our modern culture, to reconnect with the dralas and bring that energy into our world to heal it and enliven it and to re-sanctify our lives. This is one of the principal messages of the teachings of Shambhala. Furthermore, the Shambhala teachings do not just vaguely suggest that it is possible to connect with the dralas, they provide *methods* to connect that are practical and workable in the context of modern life.

The Dralas of Shambhala

Like the kami, the dralas of Shambhala are natural phenomena, not connected with a particular religious doctrine but available to everyone who is open to them. The Shambhala understanding of dralas derives from the indigenous Bon tradition that existed in Tibet before the arrival of Buddhism in the tenth century. The Buddhist philosophy and psychology do not exclude the existence of dralas. As Tulku Thondup Rinpoche says, "In Tibetan tantric (esoteric) Buddhism there are methods of training, particularly ritual ceremonies such as [invoking] gods or spirits which originated from or were influenced by Bon. . . . In Buddhism we believe that there are numerous systems of living beings besides the ones that we see. What prevents us from seeing them is our lack of common karma and the limited power of our physical eyes." Each time Buddhism entered a new country, it accepted and acknowledged the local deities, making no attempt to suppress them, while providing a larger spiritual and psychological context for understanding these deities as neither purely man-made nor truly separate and external. For example, ever since its introduction to Japan, Buddhism has existed side by side with the indigenous Shinto tradition.

The Dorje Dradul was recognized and trained in Tibet as a *terton,* a person who has the ability to discover *mind-terma,* or the teachings that great teachers of the past left in the safekeeping of protector dralas. *Terma* are discovered or revealed (rather than authored), somewhat like taking dictation, by great teachers like the Dorje Dradul, who have been thoroughly trained to do so. Tulku Thondup Rinpoche describes the *terma* tradition in *Hidden Teachings of Tibet:*

> The tradition has two aspects. First, appropriate teachings can be discovered by realized beings, or they will appear for them from the sky, mountains, lakes, trees and beings spontaneously according to their wishes and mental abilities. Second, they can conceal teachings in books and other forms and entrust them to gods . . . to protect and hand over to the right person at the proper time.

The *terton* process is a form of shamanism that probably derived from the ancient Bon tradition. Shortly before his year-long retreat in 1977, the Dorje Dradul had discovered the first Shambhala texts as *terma,* and it was based on these Shambhala *terma* that the Dorje Dradul founded the Shambhala Training Program after his retreat. His Holiness Dilgo Khyentse Rinpoche, one of the Dorje Dradul's first teachers and himself recognized as one of the great *tertons* of Tibet, later confirmed the Shambhala texts as genuine *terma.*

In his ability as a *terton* to join the mundane world with the power and wisdom of the dralas and the cosmic mirror, the Dorje Dradul showed the characteristics of a shaman as well as a great teacher and leader in the Buddhist tradition. However, there are some important differences between the Dorje Dradul's shamanism and the shamanism of older, more local cultures. Generally in the past, shamans arose within a particular tribal culture and provided teachings and healing within that tribal family. The Dorje Dradul, on the other hand, opened up the teachings and powerful warrior practices and ceremonies of Shambhala for anyone who cared to journey on that path.

The Dorje Dradul did not call himself a shaman or himself claim to be one, but he was proud of the fact that his family name was Mukpo, the same tribe in Tibet from which the great warrior Gesar came. He would often say to Shambhala students, "You are all the Mukpo family." By this he did not mean to be exclusive, nor that students should reject their own family heritage. Rather, he meant that the Shambhala teachings that he had revealed are open to the whole world, regardless of racial background or family creed. Whoever wanted to practice these teachings was welcomed into the Mukpo world family.

Ruth-Inge Heinze, at the University of California–Berkeley, has been researching living shamans and shamanistic rituals for thirty years. Her research, reported in her book *Shamans of the Twentieth Century,* shows that the shamanistic community is beginning to open up even in traditional shamanistic societies in Indonesia, Thailand, and China as well as North America.

Shamans continue to play a vital role and fulfill special needs of their community which otherwise are not met. I have to add here that, in the twentieth century, "community" does not necessarily mean people living together in the same geographical area. . . .

Becoming more closely involved with one shaman, however, does not necessarily lead to the formation of a new cult. Such open-ended relationships escape the effects of rigidifying codification world religions are suffering from.

After her lifetime of study and personal experience of shamanism, one of the main reasons Heinze says she wrote the book was "to show that the services of shamans are needed when the relationship between man and the universe has weakened or has been interrupted. Shamans stay close to the 'source.' They are called to be the mediators between the sacred and the secular."

Shamans are always in touch with changing time and place, according to Heinze.

In the twentieth century, we cannot revive the heritage of the paleolithic. Nobody can bring back the past. Our environment, the society we live in, even the climate, kept changing and so have forms of shamanism. Like a snake shedding its skin, shamanism has kept renewing itself, from the inside out. Imitators of ancient traditions, therefore, deceive themselves when they "religiously" repeat old patterns. Not familiar with the belief system on which "old" rituals have been built, their "blind" imitation obstructs the process of ritual development. In other words, different times give birth to different rituals.

Kenchen Thrangu Rinpoche spoke of the dralas in a talk to students at Gampo Abbey, the Tibetan Buddhist monastery in Nova Scotia founded by the Dorje Dradul. Thrangu Rinpoche was one of the closest colleagues and friends of the Dorje Dradul and accepted the role of abbot or spiritual guide of the abbey at his invitation. Thrangu Rinpoche says,

Trungpa Rinpoche once said to me that, although there was great develop-ment and appearance of wealth in the Western world, through a lot of the manufacturing, mining of the earth, and so forth that had gone on, much of the vitality of the land had been harmed, had deteriorated, and because of that the drala had departed. As a method for restoring the vitality, for healing a wounded situation, he had given the practice of drala and so forth, so that people could bring brilliance and dignity to their physical world and body; potency to their speech; and courage, or strength of heart, to their minds, so that both from the point of view of dharmic [spiritual] activity and from the point of view of worldly activity, people could experience brilliance and dignity. The oral instructions he gave regarding this are extremely important. Please don't forget them.

The dralas are expressions of the interdependent co-creation in which everything takes part. Dralas, humans, rocks—all exist only within the inter-connected, ever-changing, mutually co-creating web of existence.

The most all-encompassing and in that sense the ultimate or "highest" dralas are called by the Tibetan name *Rigden*. The Rigdens are the presence, wisdom, and unwavering compassion within the cosmic mirror. They are the dralas that embody cosmic basic goodness. Some people might like to compare the notion of Rigden with the idea of "God," but this is not appropriate. *No* dralas—not even the ultimate drala of basic goodness—exist as objective entities, outside agents of salvation or grace, like the popular Western conception of God. There is no one "creator" drala.

The Native American traditions have many different terms that are closer than *God* to the idea of the Rigdens. This is very well explained in the editors' note to the beautiful book *Wisdom Keepers: Meetings with Native American Spiritual Elders* by Steve Wall and Harvey Arden. They write:

> Terms now commonly used, such as *God, Creator, Great Spirit,* are not adequate names for *Sakoiatisan, Wakan Tanka, Taiowa* and *Kitche Manitou.* That is the failure of the English language, not of the idea. *God* is a term that connotes an anthropomorphic being who dwells outside of humans and nature. *Creator* is a term that also assigns a male gender to the First Cause. . . . These supernatural beings—who could create worlds and other forms of life—could be male or female. *Taiowa* and *Wakan Tanka* are not male deities. These names represent the sum total of all things. . . . Even *spirit* has its limitations in English. The English term *Great Spirit* attempts to define what is incomprehensible. . . . We must understand that these terms—*God, Creator, Great Spirit*—have been used [by the Wisdom Keepers] to convey the concept that all things are interrelated and an equal part of the whole: that we are like drops of rain which will one day return to the ocean, that we are like candles lit by the fire of the sun, forever part of it.

Dralas dwell at the level of energy, feeling, and the inherent luminosity of things. It would be as well to call this the "space" or "realm" of the dralas as the "level." Whether we think of them as levels, spaces, or realms, these ways of connecting with dralas are not outside of the ordinary world—they are not "outer space" or "other realms" but are right here. The living space of the dralas interpenetrates the ordinary world, just as physical space interpenetrates all material things, although material things *seem* to be solid and to take up space so that the material and spatial realms *seem* different. The dralas embody qualities such as gentleness, bravery, and sharpness of intellect. They are connected with the body and the environment; with natural objects, such as trees and rocks, lakes and mountains; with natural phenomena, such as rain and hurricanes; and with human activities, such as cooking, weaving, woodcarving, and building.

Connecting with dralas through ritual and through paying attention to the sacredness of the world brings harmony to our individual and group being. Harmony begins within oneself, within the harmony of body and mind, and extends to create harmony with others, within the community, between communities, and with the cosmos. All of these harmonies are necessary for wholeness and health.

Harmony should not be confused with total bliss or quiescent peace. The word tends to be taken this way nowadays because we are so used to discord and war that we can understand harmony only in opposition to them. Harmony is the correct functioning of everything according to its nature. There is tremendous harmony in a hurricane and in the eruption of a volcano and in the exploding of a star. There is harmony in the thunder and in rainstorms that nourish crops. There is harmony in an angry roar, if that is what is called for. Harmony is awake, passionate, powerful, and spotless. It is to preserve and cultivate harmony in this sense that the dralas are invoked.

Being in harmony *is* health. When the harmony is broken, disease (disease, dis-harmony) arises, and healing is needed. Connecting with the dralas can help us in healing, but this is really a secondary outcome of invoking dralas. We need to be healed only when we feel diseased. The important point is *not* to become diseased in the first place, and this is where the connection with dralas is vital. Traditional peoples relate with their dralas through dance and song and ritual in order to *maintain* health.

The Japanese portray the interaction and collaboration between their dralas and humans in their shadow theater, the wayang. Wayang plays are performed, usually at night, primarily for the local "gods," ancestors, and all manner of spirits and demons—the human audience is just passing through. A wayang play portrays the Japanese view of reality. Within it, as in reality, many worlds and times—of the dralas of raw nature, of the ancestral heroes, of the ancient gods, and of human clowns—simultaneously coincide and interweave.

The performance of the play is itself considered a meeting, a meaningful coincidence of dralas and humans. It is in these coincidences that the subtlety of the wayang lies. According to anthropologist Alton Becker, the wayang places the present in the context of the past and the small human world in the context of the energies and power of nature and the cosmos.

> Wayang teaches men about their widest, most complete context, and it is itself the most effective way to learn about context. . . . Shadow theatre, like any live art, presents a vision of the world and one's place in it which is whole and hale, where meaning is possible. The integration of communication (art) is, hence, as essential to a sane community as clean air, good food and medicine to cure errors. In all its multiplicity of meaning a well-performed wayang is a vision of sanity.

Harmony in human activity is seeing how things are and acting according to that vision. When we wake up and are fully present, here and now, we can catch a glimpse of the patterns of drala energy; we can see how things are—their true nature. But the order can be reversed as well: We can work with our mind and body, our emotional and physical reality, actually to cultivate this energy of drala and invite it into our life. Then the dralas can *help* wake us up to the reality of how things are. We can invoke them and even provoke them to come along.

The dralas are presenting themselves to us now. They are offering their help to heal us and cheer us up; to uplift the earth and its inhabitants and make us whole. But if we want to run away, they cannot chase us, they cannot investigate our plight further. They cannot do anything for us until we connect with them and communicate with them. All they can do is plant the seed in our hearts and wait for us to open to them. As Ed McGaa, an Oglala Sioux, says, "Spirit people from the spirit world are called on in the *Yuwipi,* spirit-calling ceremony. They have a higher realm much freer from the constraints of time and space than that in which we dwell. Therefore they can be of help to us if properly beseeched."

One of the most powerful sessions that I experienced with the Dorje Dradul came when he began to teach about dralas. He asked the question, What went wrong in modern society? How did we lose touch with basic goodness and the sacredness of the world? He then started to talk about dralas, and about how relationships with the dralas have been cut in the destruction of paganism. The whole room seemed electrified and shimmering. I looked across at my wife, who was pregnant with our daughter, and saw her as if through a heat haze. It was as if some primordial power, so long repressed in the Western world, were being restored.

The Dorje Dradul insisted that he was not the only one who could meet the dralas directly—we also could meet them face to face. He made it clear that although he had introduced us to them, it was now up to us to call on them. "I have introduced you to these ladies and gentlemen. Now they are waiting to meet you," he said. Indeed, during his life and since his death, some of his students have had powerful experiences of meeting drala energy.

The dralas have the power to bring peace and harmony because they transcend the very idea of enmity and therefore are completely free from aggression. When we touch that energy, we feel the world to be alive, authentic, and precious. Feeling drala energy provokes us to care for our world. If the world is *alive* and you are a part of that living world, you would no more wish to violate it than you would wish to violate another human or other living being. The dralas support and protect the natural order and the dynamic harmony of the cosmos. When you connect with them, you can feel this greater harmony. You can find your own place in that natural order and put your own energy into supporting that greater harmony.

We need to appreciate the world we have. It doesn't help to reject it and try to find something better—to become deaf and dumb and to try to ward off the energy coming to us. It doesn't help to blame everything and everyone else for our own lack of connection. But it also doesn't help to want always to see or hear only beautiful or fantastic things. Either way, we ward off the dralas. Sometimes reality is painful, boring, and ugly, but it is always workable—we can still appreciate its raw and difficult qualities.

When we appreciate the world, we *experience* it as sacred and want to take care of it. There is no separation between sacred and "profane"—everything is sacred in the world of the dralas. Appreciating sacredness begins by taking an interest in all the details of life. Even the seemingly mundane aspects of your life—where you live, what you wear, what bowls or plates you eat from—can contribute to this overall sense of sacredness and the feeling of the presence of dralas. We need to be inquisitive and look into things more: to listen to people, to frogs, to the sounds of rain; to see deeply rather than glance at things casually. We need to let our heart be touched, to stop thinking about things as problems to be solved and start appreciating the magic and mystery of our lives. If we live with these attitudes and intentions, we will attract the dralas so that they can help us wake up to the harmony, beauty, and power of the sacred world.

Windhorse banner

PART TWO

The Practice
of Warriorship

CHAPTER 4
The Cocoon

In Part Two, we will learn how to open to and connect with the sacred world. We will go through the education of the warrior. To begin, however, we must ask ourselves why we don't feel our basic goodness and the sacredness of our world and live from that. If sacredness is universal and yet intimate, close, and genuine, why don't we experience sacredness all the time and base our activity on it? If we did base our activities and relationships, our political structures and cultural norms, on basic goodness and sacredness, then the world would clearly be a quite different place. What keeps us from doing that?

However intense our first discovery of basic goodness may be, it is inevitably brief. No matter whether we try to hold on to it or let it go, it passes as we return to the monotonous drone of our same old habits of thought, emotion, and physical posture. The fresh and clear quality of our minds and the warmth of our hearts seem to get covered over so quickly by the more familiar cloudy mind. Sometimes, these clouds are pink-tinged—we become lost in romantic fantasies of falling in love. At other times, the clouds are dark and threatening, accompanying fantasies of murder. Frequently, the clouds reflect the same memory of hurt or happiness over and over again. Later in our journey, we will come to understand that not even the clouds—pink or green, blue or black— are really separate from basic goodness. For the time being, however, it certainly feels as if they cover a precious discovery, leaving us with our same old, thoroughly familiar selves.

As sixteenth-century Confucian-Taoist sage Liu Wenmin said, "If you do not recognize the root source of the myriad transformations, then you submerge yourself in clever artifice and defiled habits. You see everything under Heaven as a welter of countless different appearances. Thus your spirit is blinded and confused, and your whole life is toil and suffering."

Yet there is a paradox here. Even though the clouds seem to be covering a freshness and openness of heart that we would dearly love to hold on to, at the same time they feel cozy and comforting. They are what we know. No matter that they feel neurotic, no matter that we have seen the same clouds over and over again, their very familiarity makes them seem precious. They are a safe place for us to hide. This is where we feel "real."

Why We Do Not See the Sacredness of the World

Most of us fail to connect in a simple, genuine way with ourselves and with the world around us. We avoid who we are and the world we live in. Some of us feel inadequate and become depressed, while others try to be superhuman and feel stressed out. In both cases we are trying to be somebody other than ourselves. We are not paying attention to our own experience but are measuring ourselves against some imaginary standard. We invent ourselves and our experience. We can sometimes see quite clearly the ways others are constantly inventing themselves, but it's hard to believe that we ourselves do it. The fact is that most of us do it all the time: We substitute for our genuine human person and our genuine human experiences another person whose experience exists only in our own minds. For some reason, pretending to be someone else feels better than being ourselves, *and we believe our own pretense to be truly who we are.* When we begin to pay attention to our lives and minds, it is these habitual patterns of pretense that we see first.

In the Shambhala teachings, this stale, familiar place patched together with habitual thoughts and emotions is called the *cocoon.* Its staleness is the key to seeing the cocoon—the thoughts we have heard, the mental movies we have seen, the emotions we have felt before. Whenever anything fresh or sharp or unfamiliar threatens our usual way of being, we race back to the cocoon.

The Cocoon

The Dorje Dradul describes the cocoon as the state of mind of the coward:

When we are constantly recreating our basic patterns of behavior we never have to leap into fresh air or onto fresh ground. Instead, we wrap ourselves in our own dank environment where our only companion is the smell of our own sweat. We regard this dank cocoon as a family heirloom or inheritance, and we don't want to give that bad-good, good-bad memory away. . . . It is comfortable and sleepy.

Most of us have a place like this in our minds and hearts where we go when we feel hurt and fearful. We spend a great deal of time in that place. It is cozy, closed in, "safe," and protected. It is cozy because it has our own intimate taste—the taste of "me." Hearing about the cocoon, I was reminded of my experience as a small boy in England during the Second World War. The only thing left standing in bombed-out houses would often be the staircase. When the air-raid sirens went off during the daytime, my sister and cousin and I would be put in a storage closet under the stairs, just big enough for two or three children and an adult. We used to take candles, snacks, and games under the stairs with us, and we felt cozy and secure there. Although we did not really understand what was going on, we picked up on the adults' fear when the sirens shrieked, but under the stairs we felt safe. The phrase "under the stairs" came to symbolize for me a warm cozy place to escape from fear—a cocoon.

Nowadays, physical "cocooning" has become a fashionable concept in big cities. It has even been the subject of magazine articles. Those who can afford it create a cocoon in their apartment so that they don't have to go out at all to face the danger and ugliness of the city. They buy lots of electronic gadgets, CDs, and videos, order in pizza and gourmet foods, and stay home.

Whole cocoon towns have been built, like those in Green Valley, Nevada. Green Valley is planned and managed by a development corporation. Subdivisions are growing up in Green Valley that are entirely surrounded by walls. Each house is also surrounded by a wall, and homeowners pledge not to make any changes in them. One of the developers explained, "It's safe here, and clean. And nice. The schools are good and the crime rate is low. It's what buyers are looking for."

Children who live outside a subdivision are allowed to visit their friends who live inside only after a phone call to the security guards, who are on duty twenty-four hours a day. David Guterson, who wrote about Green Valley for *Harper's* magazine, found a nine-year-old, with dirty fingernails and sun-bleached hair, playing alone in a small piece of desert within Green Valley that had eluded the developers because it was unbuildable. The little boy was on his knees poking in a hole for lizards. He said, "Most of the time I'm bored out of my guts . . . the desert's all covered up with houses—that sucks."

Signs on corners read, WE IMMEDIATELY REPORT ALL SUSPICIOUS PERSONS AND ACTIVITIES TO OUR POLICE DEPARTMENT. On garages there are signs that read, YOUR NEIGHBORS ARE WATCHING. In spite of all the regulations, a rash of burglaries broke out, and the neighbors discovered that the burglars were living in houses within the walls of the subdivision. For all their efforts, they hadn't managed to keep reality out of their lives.

The real cocoon, though, is in our own being. All of us have walls around our hearts to ward off anything that disturbs us or doesn't agree with us. Naturally, we don't want to be hurt, so we try to keep out anything that threatens to attack us or seduce us away from our familiar and pleasantly lukewarm states of mind—sometimes we are successful and sometimes not. We have been building these walls since before we can remember, and they are firmly in place by the time we become aware of them. The cocoon is not just a facade that we wear for others. It is a way that we hide from ourselves as well. We tell ourselves our life stories over and over again, improving on them each time. We get so caught up in our fantasies about how we are and who we are that we don't really feel our uncertainties and fears and longings for a more fulfilling life.

Buddhist teacher and psychologist Jack Kornfield calls the cocoon a "body of fear." He says, "Our fear creates a contracted and false sense of self. This false or 'small' self grasps our limited body, feelings, and thoughts, and tries to hold and protect them. From this limited sense of self arises a deficiency and need, defensive anger, and the barriers we build for our protection. We are afraid to open, to change, to live fully, to feel the whole of life; a contracted identification with this 'body of fear' becomes our habit."

We see ourselves as the main character in a book or movie or television sitcom, and we try to beat our bodies into conforming to that image. At the same time, we habitually deny what our bodies are actually feeling—hunger, exhaustion, and the need to be touched—dragging them along with us as if they were unruly children, drugging them into speed or sleep. We are plagued by a stream of chatter in our heads, and at the same time we experience a vague—or perhaps full-blown—feeling of frustration, unhappiness, and un-fulfillment. To others, we may appear to be efficient, successful, and happy. Yet inside we are afraid that we are missing out on our very lives.

Vernon Cooper, Native American elder and healer, says,

I just wasn't cut out for the age we're living in. Everybody's hurrying but nobody's going anywhere. People aren't living, they're only existing. They're growing away from spiritual realities. These days people seek knowledge, not wisdom. Knowledge is of the past; wisdom is of the future. We're in an age now when people are slumbering. They think they're awake, yet they're really sleeping. But this is a dangerous age, the most dangerous in human history. People need to wake up.

The cocoon severs the connection between head and heart, so that we do not have to feel the rawness, subtlety, or unpredictability of our ever-changing world. We dwell in the lifeless masks that our minds have created for us and that cut ourselves off from feeling the response of our hearts to living energy. Ironically, by maintaining the cocoon we are deadening ourselves to our creative energy. By avoiding life, we are starving ourselves to death.

The Masks We Wear: Our Many ''Me's''

When we look at the cocoon more closely, we see that we have not just one idea of "me" but many. We have different "me's" for different occasions. Spiritual traditions have long known of this fragmentation, and now many psychologists and therapists, too, are recognizing this strangely well-kept secret. Psychologist Roberto Assagioli, the founder of psychosynthesis and one of the first to join spiritual understanding with psychotherapy, called these different "me's" *subpersonalities*. "The organization of the sub-personalities is very revealing," he says, "and sometimes surprising, baffling or even frightening—different and often quite antagonistic traits are displayed in the different roles. . . . Ordinary people shift from one to the other without clear awareness and only a thin thread of memory connects them; but for all practical purposes they are different beings."

The subpersonalities are like roles that we play—a different one for each situation—or like masks we put on to cover how we are really feeling. One Shambhala warrior, Adam, describes this phenomenon quite clearly:

When I am with my boss, a meek, trying-to-please role comes out. When colleagues are there, I get into the one-upmanship role, trying to be smart and witty; but sometimes a kind of feeling-put-down role suddenly comes up, and I want to run away. When I'm with an old buddy, an altogether different role appears that plays itself in the old familiar way. And when I'm alone, I play either the planner/daydreamer or the depressed role. These seem to grip me just as uncontrollably as the roles I take on when I'm with people.

We slip into our roles automatically, without even realizing it. Each role has different thoughts, different feelings, different moods, and even different muscular tensions and bodily postures. The change of role is so smooth and the roles themselves are so familiar that we don't really even notice the change happening. We think each role is the same "me" feeling a different way. We don't notice the automatic nature of the whole process. If we were asked to describe ourselves, we would probably describe one or another of our various roles.

Alex, another student warrior, reports:

I had had a wonderful weekend and arrived at work a little late on Monday morning. One moment I was in the car saying good-bye to my lover. I felt a bit puffed up and very romantic. But I felt generally pleased with my life. I walked into the office and caught one glimpse of my supervisor and started to shrink physically and mentally. I felt a little nervous and quickly began to think whether I had left anything undone. The lover role was gone for the rest of the day. My subordinate role was able to take a break when I went out for lunch with a friend, and we spent the whole hour gossiping about the boss and feeling irritated about him. But we felt very smug with each other. Thinking about it afterward, I realized that these three roles—the lover, the subordinate, and the conspirator-buddy—are as familiar as my old T-shirt.

Particular emotions are part of our self-image in each role, and when we leave one role and enter another, we often disown the former role's emotions and hardly believe that we could have felt them at all. Frequently men who abuse their wives and children in one role become bitterly remorseful and disown the abuser in another role. But then the abuser reappears later. All of these emotions are part of our conscious self-image of the moment—"I am angry," "I am in love," and so on—the patches that make the cocoon.

Some roles are actually very appropriate, while others make an awful mess of things. Some people have developed very appropriate roles for their professional lives and feel successful and satisfied with them. Meanwhile their family lives are in chaos. As one successful lawyer said during a Shambhala training discussion group, "The role I often wear at home seems to act like a spoiled brat that still wants something it didn't get when it was four years old." Other people have smooth and joyful family lives, but in their roles at work they cannot manage and feel depressed and incompetent. Many people have developed roles that function beautifully when they are with other people, but they have depressed and confused roles when alone.

The point of seeing the cocoon is not to judge which roles are good and which are bad; or to try to get rid of the "bad" ones and foster the "good" ones. The point is simply to see that so much of our psychic energy is taken up by these completely habitual and automatic modes of thinking, feeling, and acting. Most important of all is to see that the cocoon is not a solid, permanent, unified thing but is rather a constantly changing flux of masks and roles. It was patched together higgledy-piggledy as we grew up, and now this hodgepodge is what we believe we are.

Understanding the multiple roles we play and the multiple "me's" that we are is very helpful on the path of warriorship. So many of us believe that we are a single and unified if maybe somewhat neurotic person. Somehow, we think, to grow as a warrior means to change this single but not very sane person into a sane person. When we understand the patched-together nature of the cocoon, however, and the multiple personalities that make it up, we can see a different approach. We can discover that person who we genuinely are and who already is sane. We can nourish our genuineness so that we become able fearlessly to step out of the cocoon, taking along the roles that are helpful and leaving the rest behind. We can step out when we feel the warmth of basic goodness, and we can extend that warmth and gentleness to the cocoon itself.

Whatever can help us to see the cocoon clearly, as in a mirror, without getting caught in it further, can be helpful on the path of warriorship. The focus of a path of warriorship is on discovering our basic goodness and on opening to the sacred world beyond the cocoon. This is the reason for looking at the cocoon—so that we can step out of it, again and again, rather than withdraw further into it. Sometimes when we first see our cocoon, we become fascinated and absorbed by its depth, history, and structure. This fascination can become a problem, for we could spend all our lives exploring the cocoon and never realize that there is anything beyond. Rather than constantly going over and over our pain and delving into its history, we can cultivate glimpses of our basic goodness, no matter how insignificant they feel in comparison to our wounds. No matter how much pain we are in, such moments of discovery and opening do occur. When they do, however, it is important that we avoid turning the new sense of self, the warriorship that we discover, into another layer of the cocoon. We can easily make a cocoon out of the "me" who treads the path of warriorship if we become arrogant about it and stuck in it.

Getting Out of the Cocoon

As warriors, we do not try to get rid of the cocoon or to destroy it, even if we could. The cocoon is a necessary phase in growing into human society, and in that sense it is itself a manifestation of basic goodness. It is the armor and arsenal of weapons with which we have managed to survive. At some point in life, the habits that make up our cocoon were helpful to us and protected us. Later, these same habits came to prevent us from living responsively, from opening to new possibilities. One young woman grew up in a household filled with a great deal of bitterness and unspoken wounds. Her father was usually silent, and whenever she spoke to him with any real feeling, he snapped back at her with a sneering, angry tone. She learned to protect her heart from him. Now, whenever she is with especially quiet men, she feels suspicious and threatened, imagining them to be brooding and quietly putting her down. She realizes that not all quiet men are like her father, but she has great difficulty seeing another side to them.

There is no problem at all with the cocoon in itself. It is a natural phenomenon, just like the cocoon in which a butterfly begins its life. The butterfly's cocoon is a living part of the caterpillar, kept alive by its constant patching. But when the butterfly is about to be born, the cocoon dries up and becomes a dead shell. Just like the butterfly, we begin life in a cocoon, but if we can see and feel its layers in the light and warmth of basic goodness, it will fall away of itself and we can step out. This falling away is unforced and unmanipulated. It is a natural process, just as bark peels from a birch or sycamore or hickory tree as it grows from within.

The cocoon falls away when we see it in contrast to the freshness of a moment of basic goodness, much as we may realize the air in a room is stale only when someone opens the window to let in a fresh breeze; or as we may realize that it's getting dark only when someone comes in and turns on the light. As the Dorje Dradul says,

The Cocoon

In the cocoon there is no idea of light at all, until we experience some longing for openness, some longing for something other than the smell of our own sweat. When we begin to examine that comfortable darkness— look at it, smell it, feel it—we find it is claustrophobic. So the first impulse that draws us away from the darkness of the cocoon towards the light of the Great Eastern Sun is a longing for ventilation. . . . With that longing for fresh air, for a breeze of delight, we open our eyes, and we begin to look for an alternative environment to our cocoon. And to our surprise, we begin to see light, even though it may be hazy at first. The tearing of the cocoon takes place at that point.

When we connect ourselves to a larger world, our harsh feeling of separation is diminished. Our inner chatter is dulled, and we feel it is possible to open to a fresh world without our stale cocoon and to realize our inherent connection to it. Albert Einstein said,

A human being is part of the whole, called by us the Universe, a part limited in time and space. He experiences himself, his thoughts and feelings as something separate from the rest—a kind of optical illusion of consciousness. This delusion is a kind of prison for us, restricting us to our personal desires and to affection for a few persons nearest to us. Our task must be to free ourselves from this prison by widening our circle of compassion to embrace all living creatures and the whole of nature in its beauty. Nobody is able to achieve this completely, but the striving for such achievement is in itself a part of the liberation and a foundation for inner security.

So the point is for you to discover how to make connections with the real world—the real world beyond your static conceptualizations. The only way really to do this is to *pay attention to the details of your most ordinary experience.* For it is there that you will find basic goodness. You will never find it just by believing in it because someone else says it is so, nor by striving for some alternate reality, some other world. You can experience basic goodness only here, for yourself.

Basic goodness is to be found in your ordinary experience of just being alive: in the warmth of your body, in smells and sights and sounds, in the taste of a delicious meal. It is so simple, yet we rarely experience it directly. Most of the time we are in too much of a hurry or are too preoccupied to feel that joy. We take so much for granted and get so lost in the tedium and anxiety of trying to survive and to compete, or trying to find out what is *really* wrong with us, that we rarely appreciate living.

For example, whatever experience you may be having at this moment, the fact is that you are *experiencing*. You can feel the beating of your heart, the in and out of your breath, the weight of this book in your hands. Perhaps you hear the sound of the wind whistling past the chimney, the hum of the refrigerator, or the traffic down in the street. If you look around, you may see people's faces, or automobiles, or the pictures on the wall of your room, or the little flowering plant that needs watering.

You have reactions to all these things. You consider them good, or you consider them bad. You feel excited, or you feel blue. You may be so caught up in your judgment or your mood that the fact that you are experiencing at all seems unimportant. But think back to a time when you had just recovered from a fever—how fresh and pleasing simply eating a meal or taking a walk was. Those who have been desperately ill and have come back from the brink of death almost always describe the extraordinary joy that they feel at their mere ability to experience their world again. Those who have been temporarily blinded or deafened express tremendous gratitude for their sight or hearing when it is restored. We take these things for granted, yet they are in themselves quite magical.

All of us *can* learn to be aware of our lives as we live them. Rediscovering and coming to know our basic goodness is a natural process that is available to anyone. The beliefs of a particular culture and the way children are brought up may facilitate this process or may serve to thwart it, but the experience is available to any human being—it is the experience of being truly human. To find basic goodness, we need to stop running and look at who we are. Although basic goodness is the very basis of all our experience, it cannot be found—at least, not at first—by searching outside of yourself. Basic goodness is not an external object. Discovering basic goodness begins with appreciating who you are, as you are. To do that, you need to stop for a while and pay attention to yourself, to your body, to your thoughts, and to your emotions and feelings.

The Epidemic of Mindlessness

When we do decide to be with ourselves for a while, we often just follow our thoughts and feelings along wherever they take us. When we do that, we very quickly find that we are no longer present. We have lost our sense of being in this room, sitting in this chair. We have lost the sights and sounds and smells of our immediate surroundings.

Instead, we think about what happened a moment ago, or a few hours ago, or yesterday, or years ago. We recall memories to make ourselves feel better. We replay over and over a deal we lost to make it a deal won; a challenge we avoided becomes a victory. Or we plan for what we expect or want to happen later. We are not present with our immediate experience, nor are we aware that we are thinking—our thoughts are just dragging us along. In this sense we are mindless.

In a recent popular comic strip, a young nurse who is always busy at work or with some project or other finally has a moment to herself. She says, with a sigh and a bright smile, "No TV. No radio." Then: "At last I am alone with my thoughts." In the closing panel, grimacing and holding her head, she ends, "Boy! It's noisy in here." This is the problem. When our environment is not distracting us, our own thoughts drag our attention hither and thither so that we still cannot be wholly in the present moment. It is not that thoughts themselves are the enemy—we *can* think and be aware of our environment and our own living presence together, but we don't.

Being mindless, absent from our bodies, our feelings, and even our thoughts in the present moment—being on automatic pilot—is the activity of the cocoon, and it is our condition in daily life almost one hundred percent of the time. Some people think it is very clever to be mindless: to be planning a future deal while they are walking down the street, watching TV, or talking to a colleague. Some deliberately cultivate mindlessness to distract themselves from the tedium of their jobs. Muzak is played everywhere to relax and entertain us. We sometimes have to hear its mind-dulling drone even while we wait to speak on the phone. Entertainment has become largely the social cultivation of mindlessness—leading us into a fantasy world so that we need not be present to our daily drudgery.

Ellen Langer, a psychology professor at Harvard, has spent many years researching the roots of mindlessness and its costs in daily life. In her book *Mindfulness,* she summarizes these researches and says, "Unlike the exotic 'altered states of consciousness' that we read so much about, mindfulness and mindlessness are so common that few of us appreciate their importance or make use of their power to change our lives." Her book is about "the psychological and physical costs we pay because of pervasive mindlessness and, more important, about the benefits of greater control, richer options, and transcended limits that mindfulness can make possible."

Many people near the end of their lives ask, with a tinge of regret and nostalgia, "I have done many things, but did I really live?" Or they lament, "Life seems to have slipped by without my really noticing it. It went by so fast." Warriorship is really living your life, not letting it slip by unnoticed. The basis of warriorship is paying attention to your life in all its nitty-gritty, slimy, mucky, joyful, and occasionally brilliant detail. The foundation of warriorship is mindfulness.

Paula, a Shambhala training participant, recently described her experience of realizing the wildness of her untrained mind. She was first brought face to face with her life in the Kimberley region of Northwest Australia, the most remote and rugged area of the country, on an Aboriginal reserve. She had received a grant to tour the area's schools to present workshops on a communication technique using drama. She had done this work for several years but had only once before been on an Aboriginal reserve.

As she describes it:

There was much in the Aboriginal way of life that completely turned my American cultural pride inside out. I thought I had thoroughly divested myself of that vulnerability by being a left-wing, New-Agey, anti-American whatever. The society I was dealing with was so in contrast to my conceptual world that "I" became totally undermined. It was by no means an ideal social order, and if I were to go back now years later, I am sure that I would see this even more. The important point is that gradually my mind became apparent to me. It was swirling, distraught, contradictory, a cacophony of ideas, statements, worries, ambitions, fears, hopes, delusions, and so on. And it was constant—no gaps at all. I started to feel desperate and inwardly crazy. I am grateful now.

The Aboriginals told me they thought whiteys were sick. They were always trying to smoke me in a purifying fire or dump me in some sacred pool. They were very kind. Then they started asking me why I wasn't in my own country with my own people. It made no sense to them, and pretty soon it made no sense to me.

One day, in a state of extremely heightened confusion, I walked a little from this bizarre desert settlement. I sat on the edge of an enormous cliff overlooking hundreds of miles of flat red desert dotted with mounds resembling large-nippled breasts. There was a tremendous amount of sky, horizon, and air. Great expanses. And I heard my mind—it felt small, cramped, and painfully claustrophobic. The space felt real. My mind felt sick. The thought arose that if I could let my mind go into all that space, mix it with that space, there would be relief. Let it go with the breath. Just that. Mix my mind with vast space. Maybe I even did it for a moment, but it was fleeting. I knew I could not do it on my own and that I needed someone to teach me how to do this.

Three years later I returned to the United States. I went to Shambhala Training at the suggestion of my therapist, who said he thought in the long run it would be more effective and a lot cheaper than treatment. I had seen enough spiritual silliness to be extremely wary. I was not convinced by the talks; words were cheap in a mind like mine. During one of the mindfulness practice sessions, the leader nodded off to sleep and awoke with a snort. The *genuineness* of mindfulness practice got me.

Like Paula, when we first sit down quietly with ourselves, our thoughts and feelings seem to run wild. *They* seem to drag *us* along with them. Paula could not just be there on the cliff, letting her mind go out to that vast space, resting in that present moment. Yet she had no other plans. She had walked away from the community for a moment, and there was nothing that she was expected to do. She recognized that the landscape was gorgeous, and she was moved by it. She wanted to let her mind dwell there for a moment, but she could not. Her attention simply refused to be there with her body and her experience. She realized that she needed to *train* her mind.

Try this exercise now: Put this book down, and for five minutes, while sitting in a comfortable but firm chair, try to be aware of the sensation of your backside pressing on the chair. As well, try to be aware of your thoughts. Do your thoughts keep trying to pull you away from the simple task of being mindful of your backside? Do you keep forgetting the exercise and have to start over?

You most likely found that within a few seconds your mind was caught up in a thought or an emotion. You were no longer mindful of the sensation of your body, and you had even forgotten your intention. Each time you remembered and brought your attention back, it was probably only a few seconds before you were lost in thought again. This may not have been exactly your experience, but it is close to the experience most of us have the first time. Many people are quite shocked to discover how little influence they really have over what is going on in their own minds—the part of themselves that they believe most certainly to *be* themselves.

How much more difficult it is to remain mindful in the middle of an office meeting! Being mindful in daily life, with all the demands that our environment and our habits of thought place on our attention, is asking too much of ourselves at first. It is like giving a rank beginner a pair of skis and putting him at the top of an Olympic downhill race course: A curve or a bump would send him flying. This same kind of careening out of control would happen if we were to say to ourselves, "Gee, that's a good idea, I'll be mindful from now on." Within a few moments we will be lost in the next thought and bouncing back and forth helplessly, having altogether forgotten our intention to be mindful.

If you tried the exercise, you probably discovered the untamed quality of your mind. It was probably constantly running from one thing to the next or was stuck in a groove from which you could not budge it. The mind does not seem to want to be with immediate experience at all. So we need to train our mindfulness, to *practice* mindfulness. This is a very important beginning step. If we don't initially tame the wildness of our mind—at least partially—we have no way to continue our journey.

 Suggestions

1. Meeting Yourself
Each day for a week, have a fifteen-minute meeting with yourself sometime during the day or evening. Choose a different time each day, but make a specific appointment, and write it down on your calendar. Maybe Monday it will be 10:00 A.M., Tuesday 9:15 P.M., and so on. The purpose of this meeting is to stop what you are doing for a while and pay attention to yourself—your body, your thoughts, and your emotions. Pay attention to the details. Start with your body: How are you sitting? Is your posture straight or slumped? Where are you holding tension—in your shoulders, your jaw? Now move on to your thoughts: What were you thinking just before the appointment? Are you concerned with something you just can't "get off your mind"? Are your thoughts moving quickly from subject to subject, or are they quite sluggish? Are you thinking about what else you should be doing? Do you feel you are avoiding something you don't want to relate to? Notice how you're feeling in general: Are you tired, anxious, restless, slow? Now pay attention to your emotional state: Do you feel irritated, angry, resentful, passionate, excited, happy? Do you see any patterns or habits in the way you are now that repeat in the way you usually experience

yourself? Do you often sit in this posture, think and feel this way? The point is to be with yourself fully and honestly, but not to be solemn about it. You don't have to try to change anything, although if changes do occur as you pay attention to your present state, notice them. You can do this exercise of "meeting yourself" spontaneously at any time you remember it, but do it at least once a day for a week.

2. Getting Acquainted with Your Masks

Write down some of the main roles you play in your daily life. For example, you may play the roles of doctor, mother, wife, intimate friend, acquaintance, and professional colleague. Think about what circumstances these roles occur in and what masks you wear for each of them. Keep it simple. In your role as doctor you may wear a mask of efficiency and knowledge (even at times when you may not know what you're doing), or a mask of compassion (even when you may be tired and don't really care). In your role as wife, you may wear a mask of love (even when you feel angry) or one of anger or resentment (even when you feel loving). You may have a mask of love even when you actually do feel loving— the mask may be covering your soft, vulnerable heart. Look at your posture in each of these masks. How do you feel as you wear it? What are your usual thoughts? Recall what you do when you feel disturbed in your masks. Just look. Don't judge whether the mask is good or bad, and don't try to figure out how to change anything.

3. Seeing the Wild Mind

Find some time to be at home alone. Now turn on the TV, the CD player, the cassette player, and the radio—all at once—everything you have. Vacuum the floor, make a to-do list, eat, and keep as busy as possible for half an hour. Then turn everything off and sit down in a comfortable place in your favorite room or outside and listen to the silence; listen to your thoughts.

4. Getting a Feeling for the Cocoon
as a Whole

This is an exercise to imagine, visualize, and let yourself feel the extreme of cocoon claustrophobia. It may feel highly artificial at first, but when you actually do look through your mask, you may discover the reality of feelings that you don't want to face. This is not an exercise to make you feel comfortable or good, but it might give you a new insight. In addition to feeling the tension and staleness of the cocoon, the other important aspect of this exercise is to realize that you are creating it. This will seem obvious in the context of the exercise, but if you look closely at the details of your cocoon world, you can see how you are creating that world continually.

Take your time with the instructions, and try to feel the details of each step of the exercise. For example, when the instructions say, "Imagine your body wrapped tight with coils," feel your entire body constrict. Imagine what the coils are like. Are they thick, heavy, black, and ropelike, or are they thin, blue, wire? Feel the coils start from your toes and wrap around your body, up your legs, step by step, until they are crushing your head entirely. Let your imagination lead you in detail through each section. At the end, be sure to come back gradually, and let yourself sit quietly for a while. Here is the exercise.

Go to a quiet room where you can be alone. Lie on the bed, or sit in a comfortable chair. Close your eyes, and let your mouth droop. Feel the tension in your body, in your stomach, in your arms and shoulders—feel it getting tighter and tighter. Imagine your body wrapped tight with coils. Feel what it would be like to be actually inside a cocoon, with no light or fresh air. Feel black, stale, airless space suffocating you. Think: "I am creating this now. My body is tight and crushed. I am creating this." Let yourself feel a longing to go out to the world to communicate with others. Feel the way you protect yourself. Feel the walls you create to keep yourself safe and separate. Think: "I am creating this." Let yourself feel the hurt of being isolated and alone. Know you are creating this. You make your own cocoon. Put each of your favorite masks on inside your cocoon—one by one. Laugh in the mask; grimace in the mask. Feel the drama. Think: "I am creating this." Gradually let yourself come back. Open your eyes, look around, be quiet.

5. *Appreciating Who You Are*
How you think about yourself affects deeply how you feel about yourself and your life. Having looked at your cocoon world, spend a little time contemplating your personal feeling of basic goodness. Do you feel that you are basically good in a deep way, beyond the conventional concepts of "good" and "bad"? What are your doubts about the basic goodness of yourself *and* others? Having acknowledged your doubts, put them aside for a moment and think that you *are* basically good. Contemplate how you feel caring, gentleness, and affection toward other people, animals, or places in your own life; how you feel affection from others; how it affects your life. How does basic goodness show in your life? Have you had moments when you experienced the world in a simple and genuine way? Forget about ideas, concepts, *shoulds,* and obliga-

The Cocoon

tions: What makes you laugh and cry? What touches your emotions? Where is your heart?

Have the intention, for a whole day, to acknowledge moments of freshness and genuineness when they occur in your daily life. These occur all the time, but usually we don't notice unless the moment is dramatic. Having the intention to recognize these moments is the first step to seeing the sacredness of the world.

CHAPTER 5

Practicing Mindfulness

In Shambhala training we use a technique to help us be with ourselves thoroughly and deeply. This is the practice of sitting, or mindfulness practice, a form of eyes-wide-open meditation. It allows ourselves the time and space to discover who we are, to discover and face our wild untamed mind and our fears, and to discover the basic goodness of ourselves and our world.

Practice always involves simplification. Practicing the guitar means doing lots of scales, and training to be a football player means doing a lot of practice sprints, blocks, and tackles. Just as you cannot pick up a guitar and instantly play beautifully, there is no instant mindfulness. Practice takes effort, but with the right vision and intention the effort can be joyful because it feels wholesome and good. Practice *is* only practice. The point of playing scales is to be able to play the guitar; the point of the sitting practice of mindfulness is to be mindful in daily life.

Mindfulness, the antidote to the mindless activity of the cocoon, is part of the American tradition of psychology and therapy, going back at least to William James, who said, "The faculty of voluntarily bringing back a wandering attention, over and over again, is the very root of judgment, character and will. An education which should improve this faculty would be education *par excellence*. But it is easier to define this ideal than to give practical direction for bringing it about."

More recently, therapists such as Joan Borysenko and Jon Kabat-Zinn have shown how mindfulness is a key element in working with chronic physical pain and psychological suffering. Kabat-Zinn, who was featured on Bill Moyers's television special *Healing and the Mind,* is director of the Stress Reduction Unit at the University of Massachusetts Medical Center. In his book describing this program, *Full Catastrophe Living,* he says, "Knowing what you are doing while you are doing it is the essence of mindfulness practice. . . . This leads directly to new ways of seeing and being in your life because the present moment, whenever it is recognized and honored, reveals a very special, indeed magical power: *it is the only time that any of us ever has.*"

Only at the moment when we are attentive to our lives, mindful of our lives, are we really living at all. Nadia Boulanger, a French music composition teacher whose many famous students included Aaron Copland and Leonard Bernstein, once commented, "Life is denied by lack of attention, whether it be to cleaning windows or trying to write a masterpiece."

Mindfulness and insight-awareness practices also lie at the heart of Buddhist and Taoist training. Recently, Christian teachers and scholars have begun to reclaim mindfulness meditation as the root of Christian prayer. According to Father Laurence Freeman, spiritual director of the World Community for Christian Meditation, "What all religions share is a deep tradition of meditation that stems from the original teachings of their founders. In the experience of meditation we all face the human struggle with ego and distraction."

Father George Timko, a Greek Orthodox parish priest, says, "Christianity became trapped at some point by thinking that prayer is verbalization and asking. That's a wrong understanding of prayer. The Greek word *prosevkomai* [translated as 'prayer'] . . . simply means to be in a mindful state of awareness. *Theoria* [usually translated as 'contemplation'] is watching, observing, simply looking. It is an interior looking of the mind, of paying attention without expectations."

The ability to guide our attention to be present to our experience is our human birthright. Doug Boyd, author of *Rolling Thunder,* spent many years living with native medicine peoples in a number of cultures. His story of the year he spent with Native American healer and shaman Rolling Thunder is both down-to-earth and evocative. Boyd emphasizes the key role of mindfulness in shamanistic rituals of all kinds. Spotted Fawn, Rolling Thunder's wife, spoke to Boyd about the drums that she heard incessantly throughout the night during peyote rituals. "The drums speak," she said. "They talk to you and they help you. They keep you there. I remember times I would start to drift away, 'space out' as they say, and the drums would say, 'Pay attention, pay attention, pay attention.'"

Boyd observes, "This reminded me of the night of the purification ritual at the hot springs in Carlin when Rolling Thunder had conveyed those words to me without speaking. Rolling Thunder, like . . . perhaps all 'medicine people,' gives first priority to the capacity to control attention, to maintain 'one-pointedness of mind.' There can be no healing, no meditation, no meaningful spiritual experience without that highest of disciplines."

Mindfulness practice is not just a tool for therapy, a spiritual exercise, or an educational technique. It is a natural function. *It is, more than anything else, what makes us human.* We all have the capability to be mindful of our body, feelings, perceptions, and thoughts as they happen, unless we are diseased or brain damaged. But most of us use this ability only partially and intermittently, hardly realizing that we are doing it. There is no training for mindfulness in our upbringing, and we therefore do not realize the fullness of living and the creative potential that its practice can unfold.

In modern society conventional religious doctrine and conventional science alike teach that our minds and bodies are not one but forever separate. Actually, mind and body have never really been separated—except by fear and by the walls that the cocoon has built to separate mind from heart and from bodily feeling. Awareness and feeling are in our bodies, which include our brain but are obviously more than our brain. Our society's belief that mind is somehow localized in the brain—or in the most extreme cases, that mind *is* the brain—is very deep rooted. Most people have no idea that their mind fills their body and radiates out beyond its surface.

In *Healing and the Mind,* TV host Bill Moyers interviewed neuroscientist Candace Pert. One exchange went like this:

> MOYERS: You're saying that our emotions are stored in our body?
>
> PERT: Absolutely. Didn't you realize that?
>
> MOYERS: No, I didn't realize that. I'm not even sure what I mean by that. What's *down* there?
>
> PERT: You're still thinking it's your brain, but it's the wisdom of the body. Intelligence is in every cell of your body. The mind is not confined to the space above the neck. The mind is throughout the brain and body.

Like many modern men and women, Moyers so identified his mind as being in his head that he thought his body was "down there." He seemed to have no idea that the body could be the location of anything having to do with mind or that it could be a source of feeling and joy—so long as we *can* feel it. On the path of warriorship we practice mindfulness to rejoin our mind, body, and emotions so that they function together as one harmonious whole. We do not practice mindfulness to attain a state of being described by any particular spiritual tradition or an altered state of consciousness; nor do we practice it to free ourselves from pain or anxiety, nor even to discover basic goodness. We practice mindfulness—"bringing back the wandering attention over and over again"—simply so that we can be present in our lives as they happen. When we are fully present in our lives, then we enjoy them and truly live.

The fact is that we can all train our mindfulness if we want to. This is a lasting contribution that Eastern spiritual traditions have made to world culture: to remind us of our human birthright of mindfulness and, as William James sought, to "give practical direction for bringing it about."

The Sitting Practice of Mindfulness

The practice of mindfulness begins with sitting, alone or in a group, for a certain period of time each day. You might try this alone, but it is always good to get personal instruction from a qualified teacher, especially if you want to continue it. Sitting practice is often easier to do at first with the support of a group. To get you started, here is a detailed description of the practice.

Schedule a specific time during the day when you will be uninterrupted, then use the time to practice. It may feel a bit awkward at first, but if you persist, it will start to feel more natural. Make a commitment to practice sitting mindfulness for a specific period of time, perhaps twenty or thirty minutes—less than this, and you really will not have time to let your mind settle. There is nothing magic about twenty minutes, however. As Sogyal Rinpoche comments, "I have not found that it says twenty minutes anywhere in the scriptures; I think it is a notion that has been contrived in the West, and I call it 'Meditation Western Standard Time.' " You might practice three days a week or every day—whatever is manageable for you. Often people manage to find as much as an hour a day to sit during some periods of their lives.

It is important to make a commitment to a definite time of the day and for a definite length of time; otherwise, habitual distractions can keep you procrastinating endlessly. Try to practice even when you do not really feel like doing it. Making an effort at those times can be especially fruitful. If on a particular day you find a great deal of resistance even to starting sitting practice, ask yourself:

What is the cause of my resistance? What am I afraid of? If you understand the value of practice and you want to do it, making the commitment to yourself and scheduling it is the way to leap into it.

Decide on a quiet place to practice. Find a suitable firm cushion—one that has some height is best—and turn on your answering machine so that you will not be interrupted. Sit cross-legged on your cushion on the floor, back straight and upright, shoulders relaxed, hands palm-down on thighs. If this posture is difficult for you, you can sit in a dining-room-type chair with your feet flat on the floor and your back unsupported. Keep your eyes open, glancing slightly downward with your gaze unfocused. Your mouth is slightly open as if you were about to say "ah."

Notice the firm pressure of the ground on your buttocks, the strength of your upright spine, the soft openness of your chest. Let your body relax into this posture. Sitting in this way itself expresses and embodies the basic dignity of being human. You have found your spot on the ground and settled onto it, and you can just remain quietly there—you do not have to do anything else to express your humanness. The firm strong back with your head resting upright on your shoulders and your gaze forward embody the fearlessness of not bending or giving in to your burdens but always looking forward. The open, soft, vulnerable chest embodies gentleness: You can be open to experience, whatever that may be. You can be not armored and protected from your life but willing to be affected by it.

Now notice your breathing. As your breath goes out, let your awareness go out with it. Try to feel that you actually *are* your outgoing breath. Acknowledge the gap between the end of the out-breath and the beginning of the in-breath, and simply let go. Don't try to continue to be mindful—don't try to check yourself at all. Just let go, and let your attention return to your body and posture.

Touching the outgoing breath—feeling yourself go out with it—and then letting go, simply and without fuss, is an expression of how to be mindful throughout your life. *Touching* means fully experiencing each thought, emotion, perception, or sensation and entering fully into life, however difficult it may be at that moment. *Letting go* means not holding on to your experience as it continually changes. In sitting practice we let go of even pleasant thoughts and feelings rather than prolong them; and we let go of painful emotions rather than analyze them or get rid of them.

As you follow your out-breath, inevitably and probably very quickly a thought will come along. That thought will be followed by another, and another, until a whole stream of thoughts has started up. These thoughts will bring images, emotions, and moods. What do you do with them? First, understand that *you are not trying to stop thoughts.* You are trying to know your mind as it is, to be with it as it changes moment by moment. You are not trying to be something other than what you are or to change your mind into something "better." Whatever comes to mind—whether it is a verbalized thought or a visual image, a mood of elation or glumness, a heavy emotion of passion or anger—regard it as simply part of the stream of mental process. All of it is the same as thinking. We often consider emotions and moods as somehow different, more intense, more real than thoughts. But the end product of an emotion, the moment we notice it, is always a thought: "I am so depressed," "I am angry," "I am so much in love." Each time you notice yourself distracted by a thought or emotion, label it "thinking," then return your attention to the breath.

The practice of labeling "thinking" is especially helpful when you try to return your attention to the breath from a heavy fantasy or a strong emotion that grips your attention and will not let go. Perhaps you are thinking of a business deal that you are about to make. You fantasize how the deal will go and get so completely caught up in a grand fantasy of conquering your competitors that you altogether forget where you are. When you try to break out of this fantasy, it still pulls you. Struggling to bring your attention back to your breath at that point feels quite harsh. Labeling that fantasy "thinking" enables you to touch it gently and loosen its grip on your attention, so that it can pass through naturally. But whether your thoughts are heavy-duty or light and fleeting, your reaction to them is the same: Look at the thought, with its emotional quality, directly; feel its quality; label it "thinking," and return to the breath. There is no special significance to the label "thinking." It simply marks the moment when you realize you are distracted and return to the breath.

Each time you do return your attention to the breath, you can regard it as a fresh start. Do not strive to attain a particular, predetermined state of mind. Students sometimes try to grasp the positive aspects of the sitting experience and hold on to them and try to make them recur, which inevitably leads to disappointment. After the first moment of sitting down on the cushion, which is very open and mindful, thoughts may come swarming along and the sitter wages a subtle struggle to regain mindfulness. When people deliberately strive to get into a peaceful state of mind and hold on to it, they usually end up asleep. We are not trying to create a special state of mind. These strivings about the outcome of sitting practice are just more thoughts. Let go of them just like all the others, by taking the attitude of making a fresh start each time you take a new breath.

Take a break at any time during your practice period—as many breaks as you like. Just pause for a few seconds, relax, stop practicing mindfulness of breathing, and just be there. When you resume your practice, again make a fresh start. Those moments of "just being there" can sometimes be as mindful as the practice itself. However, thoughts and emotions will most likely distract your attention quite soon, and you will need to return it to your breathing to provide a reference point for mindfulness.

No matter what insights occur, continue to sit until the end of the time period you have set aside. If the telephone rings, you don't need to jump up to answer it. If you remember a missed appointment, you don't need to apologize at that moment. You can do that later. If a brilliant thought occurs, you don't need to run and find a pencil and paper. Whatever occurs in your mind, just continue to sit. Quite often, as the more superficial memories and fantasies become boring and wear out their welcome, deeper hurts come to the surface. Memories that have been blocked by constant inner chatter or constant busyness finally have a chance to claim your attention. In the privacy and safety of sitting practice, nothing is pushed away as bad or invited in as especially good. Whatever occurs, treat it exactly the same—touch it, thoroughly acknowledge its presence, feel how it feels and what mood it brings with it, and let it go gently when it is ready to go.

This evenness toward all thoughts, hidden desires, and deep wounds is a fundamental expression of gentleness and fearlessness. In sitting practice we are gentle and kind to ourselves: We reject nothing, we push nothing away as childish or silly or wild. We are fearless: We do not hide from anything but instead look directly at our experience, just as we face forward with open eyes in our physical posture. This is the beginning of warriorship. For if we can be gentle and fearless toward ourselves, we can then be gentle and fearless toward others and toward the world. There is tremendous human dignity in just sitting upright and facing our inner lives directly, without manipulation or judgment.

Sitting practice is a way to be kind to yourself and to have the courage to find out who you are and to be who you are. It is a way to stop running: running from anxiety, running to catch up or keep up with your neighbors, running to fulfill your own and others' expectations of you, running away from knowledge of your own mind and heart, running toward your death and rarely ever tasting the richness of your life.

The most crucial aspect of sitting is your attitude toward the practice. You are not trying to manipulate yourself or to be something other than you are. Nor are you trying to sort out what is good in you and what is bad, what you like about yourself and what you don't like, so that you can change from the bad to the good. In this sense, sitting practice is not the same as therapy—at least, not those kinds of therapy that aim to remold you into a particular model of a "healthy" person. You are sitting simply to express your genuineness and humanness. Treat each thought as it comes along precisely the same way: Look at the thought straightforwardly, touch it, and let it pass on of its own accord. Your attitude is expressed in your posture; you fearlessly look at whatever comes up in your mind and heart, then gently and softly touch it and let it go. At that very moment you are being fundamentally kind to yourself. You are expressing basic goodness.

The much-loved Zen teacher Shunryu Suzuki Roshi used to call this state of mind "beginner's mind" or "original mind." He said,

Our "original mind" includes everything within itself. It is always rich and sufficient within itself. You should not lose your self-sufficient state of mind. This does not mean a closed mind, but actually an empty mind and a ready mind. If your mind is empty, it is always ready for anything; it is open to everything. In the beginner's mind there are many possibilities; in the expert's mind there are few.

In the beginner's mind there is no thought, "I have attained something." All self-centered thoughts limit our vast mind. When we have no thought of achievement, no thought of self, we are true beginners. Then we can really learn something. The beginner's mind is the mind of compassion.

I will summarize the basic instructions here so that you can easily refer to them when the time comes for you to practice:

1. Sit cross-legged on a firm cushion on the floor, back straight and upright, shoulders relaxed, hands palm-down on your thighs, mouth slightly open, eyes open, gaze down.

2. Let your body relax while keeping good posture—not too tight and not too loose.

3. Notice your out-breath, let your awareness go out with it—actually try to go out with the breath. At the end of the breath, notice the gap before the breath starts to come in. Let your attention return to your body and posture. Notice the next out-breath, and so on.

4. Whatever comes to mind, take the attitude of "touch and let go" with a sense of humor.

5. If you notice your attention has been carried away by a thought or emotion and you are forgetting to be present with your breath, label the thought "thinking" and return your attention to your breath. Don't try to control or manipulate your thoughts.

6. From time to time, take a break from the technique. For a few seconds to a minute, just relax and think that you are not practicing mindfulness. Then start again with a fresh start.

7. Continue practicing until the end of the time period you have set aside—unless your house is on fire.

During the training process, going away from home for a few days or a week or maybe even longer can help to deepen your experience of sitting. You can hold a retreat in an isolated country home, a meditation center, or even in an apartment in a city (although that is more difficult). Regardless of what location you choose, you can go there and practice sitting, to be with yourself fully.

You may even look forward to this trip as a vacation. But you may soon discover that there is no holiday from your own mind. Sometimes the very thought of being alone with the mind is so sad and lonely and frightening that we can't imagine doing such a thing. Being alone, really alone, maybe for the first time—with not even a telephone to call a friend if you freak out—can be shocking or even terrifying. But if you manage to survive the first few days and face your fear, something surprising and magical might happen (although there are no guarantees).

Perhaps you will discover a little sore spot on your heart, a little feeling of tenderness for yourself and your plight—your sorry state. You may feel so sad that you fall in love with yourself. It's lonely. You can't share yourself with anyone yet. But that sadness slows you down and makes you sensitive to your world. You start to feel the space, which *is* basic goodness, and you start to come alive. You start to appreciate yourself—being alone with yourself is so rich. You start to appreciate the whole world of colors and sounds—the trees, the greenery, the chipmunks and birds, even taxicab horns for that matter. These sensations can attach themselves to your senses and wake you up out of your deep sleep. The world becomes alive and bright, and the more you can open to it, the more you can see. So when your sad and lonely and joyful and tender retreat is finished, you may venture back to your world a little tentatively, but you may see with new eyes—the eyes of basic goodness.

Early Experiences of Mindfulness by Student Warriors

Practicing together in a group is another powerful way to be with yourself. The presence of others, practicing in the same space with you, can strengthen your own practice. Nonetheless, you face your own experience alone. A few accounts of group sitting practice, told by student warriors in the Shambhala Training Program, illustrate this vividly. Anne, Kathy, and June went through a lot—a whole journey in one weekend—each in her own way. Sometimes the practice was painful and difficult, sometimes joyful and delightful. But these student warriors all accepted the challenge of warriorship, the challenge of their lives. They didn't give up and so were able to make a fresh discovery of themselves and their world.

Anne spoke about her change in perception:

I guess what I remember about the first day is the total surprise of having all these thoughts go on and on in my mind while I was focusing on my breath; and realizing that I wasn't creating these thoughts—they were happening on their own. I didn't sit down to think, I sat down to focus on my breath and go out with my breath. So that was a revelation just to realize that thoughts arise and move with their own energy.

On the second day I had my first experience of the gap between thoughts—going out with my breath and staying out there for a moment. There was an absence of any barriers or sense of separateness between me and the point on the floor where my eyes rested. I felt a sharp shock that this was so. It was the first time that I experienced the fact that I am not just this cubic unit named Anne.

It is difficult to communicate the intensity of that experience. The best I can do is to use an analogy. Imagine that you live your entire life with a pair of binoculars attached to your eyes backward so that everything seems out of your reach and you always feel slightly off balance. Every time you try to capture the beauty in your life, it is just beyond your grasp. As you are sitting one day you see things clearly for the first time. What a shock! That momentary glimpse of how life could be and that it is possible to truly experience this world purely as it is, I shall never forget.

Kathy's experience was initially quite painful.

I knew my core was basically good. But I felt my core was conditionally starved. I was so unloving and angry that I felt soul-murdered. I worked constantly at falsifying myself by doing what was "right." Then I found myself here [practicing sitting meditation], and I can never turn back.

That weekend I was to sit on a cushion and be with myself. While I sat, I thought I would never make it through. I was in excruciating pain physically and mentally. It was absolute awfulness, but I placed it on myself and I was going to stay with it. This ordinary human felt like I was losing it, because all my life I just did. I was someone with no power within. I was what I did, so I was always busy. Now there was nothing to do but just sit and be with myself. I was so frightened, it was so painful to be with me, not doing.

By the time I left on Sunday evening, I realized that everything I would ever need—everything good, every awareness, every fear, all sacredness, all beauty—existed right inside me. All my "doing" was to keep me from going inside myself, because I thought I was an empty shell. After considerable pain of just sitting, I realized the opposite was true. Once you become aware of that, you can never go back.

Toward the end of a weekend of sitting practice, participants often notice a softness and gentleness in the atmosphere and in themselves. Many feel present in their bodies for the first time in years; their perception of colors and sounds becomes a little brighter. Although they may still be pushing and being hard on themselves as they have during the week, they also find that they are starting to relax and be kinder to themselves. These subtle sensations may be quite enough to suggest to them the profound sense in which all their experience is a manifestation of their basic goodness.

For many students, the first glimpse of their basic goodness is a tremendous relief, like letting go of a huge burden that they have carried for many years. Some participants weep at their momentary freedom from anxiety. Others associate the experience with childhood memories of joyful times when they were truly themselves. Some feel an intense, almost physical warmth in the heart, as if they were actually connecting with their hearts for the first time. For others, it is like coming home to a warm hearth after a long hard journey.

June had been in a very difficult marriage for two years. "Especially the last year was distressing," she says, "and a lot of energy was focused on whether to get divorced. There was a lot of pain involved, and I noticed that I was dealing with the pain in a way that I really did not like. I would have temper tantrums and panic attacks, and they were exhausting, and I lost a sense of basic trust and respect for myself."

June found the first weekend of sitting practice difficult, but she continued to sit daily when she returned home.

The reason I didn't stop sitting practice was probably because the separation from my husband was so upsetting me. The sadness and misery I was feeling so strongly since I began meditating felt real. I was grieving, and it would simply take time. So as I sat with my depression, the idea of "basic goodness" started to make sense to me. I began to appreciate the sad, slow, heavy feelings and my lack of interest in the outside world. The process seemed natural and necessary to me, and basically okay. The sitting meditation itself seemed like that to me, too. It did not make me feel good, but it felt good in its basicness.

In spite of continuing to feel depressed when she sat, June took part in a second weekend of group sitting in Nova Scotia.

On Saturday morning I had my normal experience of feeling that sitting was bringing me down. I left for the lunch break feeling as though I were a piece of gum stuck to my shoe.

After lunch we continued to sit, and I had my interview with the director. I told him that it troubled me that sitting meditation always either depressed me or frustrated me. And he said it sounded like I was being very hard on myself. And, *ping!* I got it. He said maybe I could try to be more gentle with myself. And, *ping!* the word *gentle* entered my vocabulary at age thirty-six. He said that maybe the depression I was feeling was the true sadness of my heart. And again, *ping!* the feeling became more real, and I could feel my dignity return, in the way that color returns to frozen cheeks when you go sit near the fire and sip a warm drink.

The talk Saturday night was about the cocoon of habitual patterns from which the warrior emerges, moving into fear and through it into fearlessness. I was confused by this, and the next day in my discussion group I said that I thought a cocoon is a wonderful and necessary place to be periodically and that I'm sure that every warrior returns again and again to his or her cocoon. The director said something to the effect that once you are out, you want to stay out. Now this really shocked me.

The shock I felt when I heard that the birth of the warrior is for real was perhaps like the shock of remembering something valuable that had been cast aside due to shame and convenience and conformity, the shock that something cherished and then sacrificed could spontaneously and unexpectedly return. Driving back through Nova Scotia and then crossing the water in the ferry and continuing south, I felt that something had happened that had tried to happen many times before in my life and had not succeeded. Then, it just happened.

Again and again you may find yourself back in the cocoon, depressed or overexcited in a habitual way. The challenge of warriorship is to *see* that cocoon of tired habits of mind and heart. When you see it, you can let it go and step out of it. Each time you step out, you are taking a step on the path of warriorship. You can see the cocoon especially clearly in sitting practice because it is a safe situation in which you have deliberately chosen not to do anything. The cocoon is constantly active, constantly reacting to your situation. It tries to manipulate your world to fit your expectations or manipulate your thoughts and feelings to fit the world. In sitting practice, there is no threat and nothing to which the cocoon can react. It begins to relax and lose its energy. Gaps can occur in it, allowing you a feeling of freshness and freedom from anxiety.

Of course, during a first weekend of sitting practice (and sometimes for long after that), practitioners struggle with all kinds of negativity, which all comes from their own minds. Doubt frequently attacks them. After the initial joy and relief of finding that you can be with yourself, you may begin to wonder why you are doing it. Kathy and June both felt this during their first weekend. Your speedy or depressed mind will come back in full force and accuse you of wasting time, of being naive, of losing contact with reality. Doubt is a universal experience for everyone on a path of warriorship.

Such twists and turns are to be expected. Because these negative feelings come from an aspiration to be genuine, they are themselves an expression of basic goodness. The fact is that many people just feel deeply relieved to sit. No matter what turmoil they find in their thoughts and feelings, noticing it for the first time is profoundly healing. This realization is itself the discovery of basic goodness. Once you have glimpsed basic goodness or even just vaguely felt its reality, you can begin to gain a sense of direction for your life. You can aspire toward that vision of basic goodness.

CHAPTER 6

Fear: The Gateway to Fearlessness

After you begin to practice mindfulness, sooner or later you are bound to encounter fear. Very often, fear becomes a reason to give up the practice. The Shambhala teaching regards fear as the blessing of the dralas, however, because without experiencing fear, we could never discover fearlessness. Fear is the energy and motivating force that drives our habitual ways of pretending to be alive. Fearlessness, discovered through being willing to experience fear gently and honestly, makes us fully human, makes us warriors. In this chapter we will look at fear and see that it can become a gateway to fearlessness and experiencing the sacred world. The reason to face our fear is to discover who we are. Fearlessness is daring to be genuine.

Through our habitual patterns of body, emotions, thoughts, and behavior, our cocoon manipulates the world we live in to fit our fantasy of ourselves. To a large extent we perceive the world according to our *expectations* of it. We do not see and hear the external world as it actually is. Our eyes and brains do not function like perfect video cameras, taking accurate movies of things that exist in the "objective world." What we consciously perceive is patched together by the mind, the senses, and the outer world in a constant drama of interaction and feedback. As far as it can, our cocoon creates the world that best fits it. We don't live in just any old world, then, but in one tailor-made to keep us as secure and comfortable as possible.

Fear: The Gateway to Fearlessness

Once the cocoon adapts us to the world, the world fulfills our expectation of it, as is illustrated by an old folk parable. An old man is standing at the entrance to a village when a sour-looking young man comes along. He says, "Old man, what are the people like in your village? I am wondering whether to settle here." The old man asks, "What were they like in the village you left?" To this, the young man replies, "Horrible! They were mean-spirited, lazy, and humorless." The old man replies, "Son, you will find the people of this village exactly the same." Later another young man comes along and asks the same question. When the old man asks about the people in his previous village, he replies, "They were wonderful! They were full of humor and joy, and so generous." The old man replies, "Son, you will find them just the same here."

You may not feel that you are manipulating your world, but if you look closely, you can see that the world actually conforms to your beliefs in very simple ways. If you are feeling down on yourself, everyone seems to be belittling or not appreciating you. If you think of people as friends, they appear to like you. If you believe that the world is out to get you, it appears to be full of sharks. If you are in love, the world constantly reminds you of your lover.

Of course, we can't manipulate the world as we want it to be *all* the time. When we cannot remake the world to fit our expectations, when something happens that simply does not fit our idea of how the world should be, then we experience fear. Biologically, fear exists as a warning system to alert the organism to the presence of something foreign or unrecognizable, something strange. Psychologically, we twist this basic and valuable biological function into a warning system for our cocoon. Whenever a sudden event occurs that does not immediately find a place in our cocoon world, we feel fear. It may be just a twinge of anxiety or outright terror, but it is the certain response to unpredictable change. When anything unexpected or unrecognizable comes along, we feel threatened, and we doubt our ability to go toward the new. We fall back quickly into our habitual roles. While we are in these habitual roles, we hardly feel the underlying fear that maintains them. If something or someone forces us to change or simply to experience something out of the ordinary, fear can manifest itself as laziness—an unwillingness to change due to inertia—or as irritation, sometimes amounting to outright aggression.

That we fear anything even slightly out of the ordinary or strange is beautifully illustrated by a story reported recently in my local newspaper. Ms. Mars, who taught a performance art class, gave her students their final assignment: to walk very slowly through a mall to the shop where they could buy bottled water. During the walk, security guards approached the group and informed them that they were making customers feel uncomfortable. After the group explained that they intended to buy something, they were not asked to leave after all. "As soon as you move outside of the normal tempo or rhythm of what people expect, it's looked upon as a paranoid and suspicious way rather than as a curiosity," Ms. Mars said. "Whenever we do something that is unexpected, even if it's not aggressive, it's perceived as aggressive." In other words, we regard anything unexpected with fear.

Everything we do and don't do in our habitual world comes from fear. We are afraid to die, yet we are afraid to live fully. Too many of us, when we see an injustice happening at work or at school right there in front of our eyes, shrug our shoulders and walk away. Often we suppress our outrage because it feels like "anger," then tell ourselves that we should not interfere, that it is some-one else's problem. When we feel mistreated, too often we explode in an-ger without pausing to look at what is behind the anger. Often, when a friend tells us of her affection, we shrink back and become polite and distant, or, alter-natively, make it into an opportunity for an affair. We do not open ourselves to the affection and let it flow through us, then respond to it from our own hearts.

There are so many ways that we avoid our own energy because we are afraid of it and because we have no idea what the result will be if we follow it. So we avoid living genuinely. We make excuses for ourselves and feel righteous. We want to be "together" as people—upright, integrated, and sane. If we feel "together"—whether good and kind and soft-hearted, or tough and "streetwise"—when fear arises we don't know where it comes from or whose it is. We don't identify with it as our own.

Our ultimate fear is that we will die and be obliterated from the earth, losing all our connections with family and friends. Tibetan Buddhist Sogyal Rinpoche writes:

Why do we live in such terror of death? Because our instinctive desire is to live and go on living, and death is a savage end to everything we hold familiar. We feel that when it comes we will be plunged into something quite unknown, or become totally different. We imagine we will find ourselves lost and bewildered, in surroundings that are terrifyingly unfa-miliar. We imagine it will be like waking up alone, in a torment of anxiety, in a foreign country; with no knowledge of the land or language, no money, no contacts, no passport, no friends.

Fear: The Gateway to Fearlessness

Death is very frightening, but the reason we feel so afraid of it is that we already feel separated from others. Our fear has already closed us off and separated us from everything we love and care for. Our fear covers the sadness and tenderness of our heart, which feels affection for those whom we love and connection with the reality beyond our cocoon. When we open our eyes and hearts, we can feel that the world itself is full of sadness and suffering. We can see the way we pass on our own habits of fear and denial to our children, and the way habits of hatred and brutality are passed on from generation to generation. Everything changes, yet we all try to hold on to people and things as if they would last forever. All of this is so sad that we turn away from it in fear. As the Dorje Dradul says, "If we look into our fear, if we look beneath its veneer, the first thing we find is sadness."

When I was in college in England in the early sixties, I had a very dear friend who was Greek and very passionate. He loved women in a very earthy way. One day as I sat on a couch with him, he put his arm around my shoulder in simple warmth. I immediately stiffened and leaned forward—a response that came from my fear of physical closeness, especially with men. To this day, thirty years later, I remember the mixed feeling of uptightness and intense sadness at having rejected his simple gesture of friendship.

Fear Underlies Habitual Patterns

Fear is covered over by the habitual patterns of the cocoon. The slightest interference of these habitual patterns brings an immediate response of fear. If we experiment with changing one of our habitual patterns, or if the circumstances of our life forces us to change without warning, we will quickly encounter the fear that lies below the surface. Our effort to go beyond fear begins with becoming mindful of all the ways that create a familiar, habitual, and safe world to close off fear. We can start by looking closely at our habits of body and speech, emotional habits of reaction, and habitual thoughts and beliefs. By applying mindfulness practice to them we can see how each of these patterns recur in our life, and we can become familiar with them and acknowledge them.

Habits of the body include how we walk, how we enter a room, how we sit down, and so on. Some people stride forcefully forward, chest puffed out, nose leading the way, as if they were determined to save the world. Some people, men and women, walk with their shoulders swaggering and stiff hips, as if they imagined themselves to be football players. Some people slouch, their chests caved in, their stomachs loose, as if they would like to melt into the ground. Everyone has a characteristic way of tensing their body against the threat of the world.

We also have habits of speech. Some people speak loud and fast, like a machine gun—to attack before they are attacked. Others speak softly, slurring their words a little, perhaps hoping no one will hear them. Others speak with an excited, speedy optimism that would like to turn the whole world into a party. Still others speak with a soft, musical tone that would seduce the world onto their side. Each way of speaking is appropriate in some circumstances, but when it is our habitual way, it sorely limits our flexibility in relating to the world. Our speech habits are part of the armor that keeps the world away from us and keeps us from feeling our fear.

Emotions can also become rigid and stereotypical—we may be habitually angry, or resentful, or enthusiastic, or fawning. We learn to regard certain situations or types of people as threatening and others as friendly, and we react accordingly. Many psychologists suggest that our ways of reacting to others were firmly established in our early years as ways of surviving in our family—ways of being "good" and pleasing the adults in our world. For particularly strong and rigid patterns, it can sometimes be helpful to look back into the past and seek their origin. The path of warriorship, however, emphasizes becoming mindful of these patterns and the underlying fear in *present* experience. During sitting practice, try simply to become mindful of your habitual emotions as they arise, directly and honestly, and see how they limit the scope of your response to the world.

Finally, we have habitual ways of thinking about ourselves and the world. We carry around an image of ourselves and a story of who and how we are. We have a visual image of our face, a sense of our bodily shape, an idea of the sound of our voice, a view of how we are coming across to other people. These images are so strong and definite that we are often surprised and shocked when we look at ourselves in the mirror or hear our voice on tape. Sometimes when we hear other people's views of what we were like at a meeting or a social gathering, we simply do not recognize the person they are describing.

Most people find it very difficult to hear, let alone accept, ideas that don't fit into their belief systems. Some people instinctively feel that the ways of foreigners or of people of a different race are somehow inferior to their own. Even if they try to be kind to foreigners, they may not quite regard them as equal. Fundamentally, most of us are afraid of strangers, just *because* they are strange to us. The mere *difference* of others has been the cause of many wars.

Likewise, different religious beliefs stimulate anger and fear in some people. Many people actually are more frightened by an open mind than by differing religious beliefs. Someone who strongly believes in the existence of an external creator God is often more disturbed by someone who, when asked if they too believe, replies, "Well, yes and no," than by someone who simply says no. Likewise, someone who vehemently denies the existence of such a creator can be more angered by an agnostic than by someone who affirms belief in that external God. A contrary belief is something to fight against, by which people can test and strengthen their own views. Openness and uncertainty in others arouses uncertainty in ourselves, and it is this uncertainty that we all most truly fear.

The rigid belief that science is the *only* way we can know the truth about the real, vast universe can cover a profound fear of that uncontrollable vastness. *Unexamined* scientific beliefs are as rigid and restrictive as any other culturally transmitted and automatically accepted beliefs, and they profoundly affect the way we perceive and act in the world. Many people are frightened by the idea that they could have a direct intuitive understanding of the world and their profound connection to it. They dismiss intuitive insight as a way of knowing the world because it goes too much against the modern, scientific, rational, information-based view of knowledge. They turn away in anger—beneath which is fear—from insights of their own that could show them the fullness and interdependence of their world.

Doubt as a
Primary Expression of Fear

On the Shambhala path of warriorship, one of the most powerful expressions of fear is doubt. Doubt is the root of many of the obstacles students encounter. It can cause us to lose faith in the power of warriorship to transform our lives and we collapse back into the cocoon. Each time we fall back, we seem to fall in more deeply than we were when we started. Such doubt occurs at any stage and on any path of warriorship. At any point on your journey, doubt can prevent you from going further, especially when you feel ready to stretch out and take part in the world as a warrior. Just when you feel ready to connect genuinely

with your world—to look afresh at your relationships, job, and domestic life—
you may be hit with a powerful attack of doubt.

There are healthy and intelligent forms of doubt that do not pull us back
into the cocoon and that are important in developing warriorship. Healthy
doubt, for instance, is the wholesome skepticism of a sharp mind that does not
accept anything on authority alone. The Shambhala path of warriorship does
not demand that we blindly follow instructions. It encourages us to intelligently
question and test what we are told against our own experience. Through
mindfulness practice, we sharpen our awareness and perceptions and can to
some extent see through the fog of self-deception and confusion that generates
masks and false ambitions, as well as the confusion that others propagate. We are
no longer so gullible.

But other forms of doubt drag us down and steal away our awareness and
cheerfulness. In this negative pattern of thinking, we doubt our own experience
of the practice itself and of the path of warriorship. We may doubt that basic
goodness exists within us or that we are able to nourish it and base our lives on
it. The sham world of masks and false ambitions can at times seem so vivid that
our experience of basic goodness and the dignity of mindfulness seems more
like an escape from reality than a genuine experience of it. The world is full of
people who have no inkling of spirituality (often only because they have not
heard of it). Amid so much mindless confidence that the "real world" is harsh
and aggressive and that humans are fundamentally selfish, we doubt our own
insight and experience.

Since I was trained as a physicist, I had a very long journey to see through
the harsh doubt that I brought to the world of feeling and direct perception.
Even now, I occasionally find my scientist mind jumping in and doubting my
own insight. I am not talking about the truly open, inquiring mind of science,
but about the heavy conceptual doubt that repeats again and again, "But we
know this cannot be true." This doubting mind brings with it a change in
perception, a sort of narrow and cold tone. In the doubting mode, the world
seems to become flat and empty and lose its living quality. At those times, I
feel as if I have been dragged deeper into my cocoon, and I feel the old
familiar tension in my chest, neck, and throat as I put on another layer of
armor.

The word for "doubt" in Tibetan literally means "having two minds," and
this is precisely the problem with doubt. When we doubt, we have two
minds—one that is actually living the experience, and one that watches anx-

iously, holding back from living, constantly checking that we are doing the "right thing." When we are in a happy mood, for example, as long as we are watching ourselves be happy, doubt and fear still underlie our happiness. We do not want simply to be happy, we want to be *sure* that we are happy. So we are in two minds—one that experiences happiness and one that makes sure we are happy, and we keep flipping back and forth between these. We keep checking to make sure we really are happy and to watch out for something that might interfere with that happiness. The nagging fear that happiness is temporary means something will always come along to break our contented mood—even if it is just hunger pangs.

The only way to go beyond doubt is to face it directly, to question it and listen to it until we recognize the basic goodness of doubt itself. By doubting, by protecting our cocoon, we actually *believe* that we are protecting our sanity and comfort. To release ourselves from this trap, it is important to reflect on the genuineness of our mindfulness practice. Our own experience of its effectiveness develops in us faith that is intelligent and not blind. This kind of faith is quite different from the common understanding of faith, as the belief in something we are told without any verification of it for ourselves. The word *faith* is related to the word *confidence,* both containing the Latin root *fides.* *Confidence* literally means "with faith." So it is because we are confident—"with faith"—in our mindfulness practice and in our experience of basic goodness that we can overcome doubt.

Doubt is often a kind of *laziness.* We have heard about basic goodness and the benefits of sitting practice, and to some extent we have experienced them. But when a challenge comes, the effort to connect with basic goodness and confidence sometimes may not seem worthwhile. We are so used to making an effort only when we are threatened by external punishment or promised a reward. Besides, we may think, "My life is not *that* bad. Feeling my basic goodness makes me raw and less certain of everything than I usually feel. Why lay another burden on myself?" We go along with our laziness and accept its negative instructions. This further strengthens our doubt, and we begin to generate more reasons for doubting.

Laziness and the doubt that it conceals are ever-present dangers of any personal work. Once we have overcome the original pain that originally made us seek a spiritual or therapeutic path, we feel better. We feel cozy again, we see the world more clearly, and we have a new point of view. But we don't want to go beyond that point. We relax too much. If we merely dwell in our newfound self-respect, however, we can easily become smug and self-satisfied. The new belief system becomes too comfortable, and we don't work at seeing our fear anymore. We have merely created a new patch on our cocoon rather than a liberating force. This is yet another expression of the underlying fear of being genuine.

To experience our fear, we need to look beneath the habitual patterns and masks that make up the cocoon like patchwork on a quilt. As soon as we look directly at these patterns, we discover gaps between one mask and the next. We see fear most clearly in the gaps between our masks. There is always a moment of hesitation and vulnerability before we put on a mask. That is the moment to catch fear.

Waking up in the morning can be a good time to catch the masks changing. Occasionally you may wake up from such a deep refreshing sleep that you wonder at first, "Where am I?" or even "Who am I?" Perhaps you look across at your spouse or lover and wonder at the strangeness and newness of that familiar face. You feel the freshness, and you feel you *could* respond in a new way. Then you might become slightly anxious, and you very quickly remember who you are and all you have to do that day. You begin to dress in your mask. As your partner wakes up and says good morning, you respond with your habitual greeting. You are already trapped in your habitual role.

Gaps in the cocoon are usually filled in quickly by the constant stream of images and chatter that runs through our heads all the time. This stream is not random. It carefully covers over the underlying fear that motivates us, so that we don't have to really face ourselves. Catching a glimpse of the gap is frightening at first. It means that we are not who we think we are. In fact, *I* am not one solid person at all—*I* am full of holes. I keep patching the cocoon for fear that it will fall apart. Deep in my heart, I know that it *will* fall apart. Once I have seen it, I simply cannot keep it together any longer.

The Dorje Dradul says,

Basically, we are uncertain of who we are, so there is a huge, gigantic fear in the back of our minds, which is hidden very neatly behind the veil of ignorance, of ignoring. But even though it is hidden, we are still uncertain—as though there were a huge, cosmic conspiracy happening. Whether the bomb is going to explode from the inside or from the outside is uncertain. But we don't talk about the inside bombs. On that side, we pretend that nothing has gone wrong at all. At least we have to have some place to sit, to live, to dwell.

Fearlessness Is the Willingness to Face Fear

There is an alternative to turning away from fear. We can *stay with fear* and go into it rather than run away from it. *The only way to practice with fear is to stay with it and go through it, no matter how intense it may be.*

Joan, a Shambhala student, tells of going through fear while she was attending a weekend outdoor workshop for abused women who were trying to overcome the fear and sense of abandonment with which they had grown up.

The group was gentle and supportive, and all the exercises were physically safe. There were several group exercises to develop trust in ourselves and in other people. In one of these the group stood in a circle, and we were asked one by one to fall back and allow ourselves to be caught by our neighbor. I was afraid—I simply could not trust enough. At a deep level, I did not believe there was anyone in the world at all upon whom I could rely for support. I had no sense of trusting *others* in my life. I left the circle in tears. Next, we moved on to some physical challenges. First we had to climb a thirty-foot-high pole and then cross to another pole walking on one wire while holding on to another wire at chest height—wearing a safety harness, of course. As I watched the others go across one by one, I was paralyzed with fear, and again I refused to take my turn. I felt even more alone, now that I had cut myself off from the very group that could support me.

Finally, we were to climb another thirty-foot pole, attach ourself by a harness to a long wire sloping down through the trees to another pole about one hundred feet away, and slide. I climbed the pole and stood on the small platform at the top and I just *froze*. It felt as if we were being asked to leap into space without any way to get back to the ground. I attached my harness to the wire and just stood there, unable to move. I thought I could not go back (although afterward I realized I probably could have climbed back down the pole). There seemed to be nothing but space. I lost all sense that I was being held by a safety harness and that there was someone behind me, as well as on the ground, to watch out for my safety. I seemed to have no way forward and no way back. I thought, No way am I going to jump.

For a moment I did check out my harness and the people on the ground below watching me. That reality check seemed important. Then I just leaped. It seems now as if the courage to leap actually came from the energy of the fear. I just leaped into the fear and used the energy. It was a feeling of riding the fear. As I was sliding down the wire, I spread out my arms in a gesture of relief and joy and shouted to my friends, "Here I am." I felt alive and *with* everyone again. Some weeks after, the main thing that stays with me is that sense of taking a leap and *riding* the energy of the fear. At the moment you leap, you just *go,* and the energy carries you with it.

This beautiful story captures everything I am saying in this chapter. Fear itself is not the problem. It is our *avoidance* of fear, our fear of fear, that closes us off from the world. Recognizing fear is an extremely positive step. Fear is a message that something unknown is beckoning us. It is simply the boundary that we have to cross to open to a larger world of energy and joy. *Fear* is related to the word *fare*—fear is the dues we have to pay to get across to fearlessness. Far from being a problem, fear is a blessing. Without fear, we would be forever stuck in our cocoon.

When we face fear—or situations and thoughts that we are afraid of—and acknowledge it with kindness, the fear does not necessarily go away. It may even seem to become deeper and stronger, but nonetheless it changes its quality. As we stay with the fear, no longer covering it over but gently touching it and coming to know it, a new strength develops in us. We find we really are capable of facing fear, without running from it. This *willingness to face fear is itself fearlessness.* Fearlessness is not merely the numb absence of fear. It is the strength and dignity that are nourished each time we face fear directly.

When we stay with our fear, we will begin to be able to feel the reality beyond it. We will begin to feel our hearts, to feel our sadness, and to experience the way the world is actually working. This is the boundary at which we find ourselves, again and again: feeling fear, and feeling the possibility of going into it directly without deception, connecting with basic goodness and opening to the sacred world beyond. This is the razor's edge, the constant hurdle, the cliff from which we have to leap, the sweet and sour blood of our life. No matter how long we have practiced and journeyed on the path of warriorship, fear is the stepping-stone between the cocoon and the sacred world. Gently opening to fear, experiencing each of our fears one by one, and going through them *is* the path of the warrior.

Just as seeing the cocoon begins in sitting practice, when we're not distracted by daily life, so too does recognizing fear. This is especially true of the deeper fears that we avoid so cleverly in everyday life. You may not think that you experience fear in sitting practice, but it is there in each thought or emotion that you turn away from and quickly push back. That turning away expresses the fear of fear. As you acknowledge unpleasant thoughts and painful emotions that you have long rejected, you can feel the fear behind them and begin to face that fear.

In daily life fear hides itself in those things that we need to do or would like to do but "don't want to do," or "don't have time to do." It hides in that person we know we have to see but feel uncomfortable with; in that meeting we have to arrange and keep putting off; and so on. Fear lies just below the surface of these hesitations and doubts. They conceal the fear of stepping into an unfamiliar and strange world. Each time we step across our fear into that world, the cocoon dies a small death. To discover our own fears, we can practice facing the small hesitations and discomforts that occur daily. It is not necessary to cultivate fear deliberately by putting ourselves in dangerous situations. Since fear is near the surface all the time, we need only make the decision to face it and go through it, however painful it may be. Trying to be genuine is enough to show us our fear.

Unlike most adults, teenagers still possess the natural wish to face fear and enjoy the fearlessness that comes from going through fear. This is one reason for the seemingly harsh rites of passage through which many traditional societies put their young men and sometimes women before they become adults. In modern Western society we have few ways to guide teenagers through the process of developing fearlessness. In fact, we often condemn teenagers for their longing to face fear. Not surprisingly, many teens go through a short period of shoplifting and "borrowing" cars and going for joyrides. Instead of understanding this as a way to experience fear and fearlessness, adults turn it into yet another source of fear and see in it signs of a "criminal mentality." I am not suggesting that teenagers should be encouraged to break the law, but society should provide them with real challenges and encourage them to encounter genuine fear within the bounds of legality. Social programs that bring "delinquent" inner-city adolescents into contact with the elements—the raw earth, rain, wind, and sun—and present them with genuine challenges have an extraordinary success rate. Teenagers who have never seen a tree, who don't know that milk comes from cows, flourish in natural situations in which they can confront their fear and act through it. Indeed, many adults are afraid of teenagers just because they feel the openness in them to strangeness and to fear.

To face fear, you can start anywhere. If you tend to avoid being alone, try to take some time to be alone. You might start with an hour or two. Notice how you feel, what thoughts tend to repeat, what you do with your body. Then try extending the time to a day or two. If you do not like to be out in the countryside, spend an evening alone in the woods. Every sound will seem strange to you; every sound will touch off fear. Just experience the fear—you don't need to do anything about it. Some people have the opposite fear—they feel nervous in a group of people. If this is your fear, then next time you are with a group notice how you feel and what thoughts keep flickering up that you try to push away. Do you think, "They don't really want me here," or, "No one likes me that much"? Perhaps you are walking down the street and see someone on the other side with whom you always feel slightly nervous. Instead of walking by, hoping that she will not notice you, try crossing over and greeting her. As you speak to her, simply pay attention to your thoughts, your feelings, the sound of your voice, and the way you stand. You need not try to change anything—just be mindful of how you are with her. Perhaps you are at a meeting and you feel something is not right. Wanting to speak out can arouse fear. Stay with the fear for a moment, feel it, listen to what it is saying to you. Then speak out if you want to, again paying attention to your feelings and fleeting thoughts as you do so.

On one occasion, when the Shambhala Training Program was still quite new, I was teaching a program attended by several hundred people, most of whom had been studying with the Dorje Dradul for some years and many of whom were my friends. I was very nervous and uptight, and my talk on Friday night was quite doctrinal and rigid. Afterward, my colleagues were merciless in their criticism of it. On Saturday evening, while I was waiting to give the second talk, the Dorje Dradul's private secretary called to tell me that he had thought of "something else that was wrong with the talk last night—it had too much of a 'true believer' quality." I was furious and began the lecture even more uptight than I had been the previous night. A little way into the talk, I was overwhelmed by panic. I felt numb and speechless. I simply waited, saying nothing, feeling the fear. Then I remembered what the secretary had said. I put down my notes and started to speak from my heart, energized by the fear. The words seemed to flow freely, without calculation, and I *felt* what I was saying rather than merely mouthing the words. Rather than keep to what I was supposed to say, I shared my life with people. The same colleagues who had been so upset the night before were happy that night. That evening permanently changed my understanding of the teachings and how to communicate them.

Do you tend to sleep late because you fear that you will be tired if you don't get enough sleep? Try getting up an hour earlier for a few days. Do you always buy the same vegetables at the supermarket? Try a different kind, even if you are afraid you will ruin dinner. Do you tend to doodle during meetings or in class? Try not doodling for once, and notice the feelings and thoughts that come to you. The possibilities for examining fear and the habits that cover it are endless.

Discovering who you are does not have to be solemn. You can play with your fear, as long as you do not endanger yourself or others. Once I traveled with my family to the Black Canyon in Colorado. The Black Canyon is many hundreds of feet deep, and its narrowness exaggerates the feeling of depth. Knowing that my body has an intense fear reaction to heights, I climbed onto a narrow ledge. As I stood there looking down, waves of fear went through my body and mind—fears that I would fall, that I would lose control of my mind and jump, and so on. I simply stayed there for a while and felt fear as well as exhilaration. I could feel the powerful living energy of space radiating up from the canyon. It was not really a dangerous thing to do—though I would not recommend it to anyone—but it taught me a great deal about fear. Some years later I went with my daughter to a fairground. There was the roller coaster. Merely looking at it aroused fear in me, but I went on it with her. When we had finished, we enjoyed it so much that we went around twice more.

The metaphor of life as a roller coaster is very appropriate—but are we willing to ride it? For example, many people find their jobs depressing and unfulfilling but are unwilling to quit them. They fear the loss of their steady income and the roller coaster of not knowing how they will make the next rent payment—even though that steady income may be maintaining life in a dead world. A woman physicist recently told me that she had headed a team of engineers in a major engineering company. She was the only woman on the team, and she perceived subtle and not-so-subtle sexual bias. It was painful, and she felt it stifled her creativity and her enjoyment of the work. After much discussion, she and her husband moved to another city, not knowing what awaited them. After they moved, Anne discovered that the town they moved to was near to a mountain that was sacred to the Native Americans who had lived in that region and she began to experience the healing presence of the mountain. Anne found a teaching job at a liberal arts college nearby, her life began to open, and her interests extended into leading-edge consciousness research.

The fear of running out of money, and thus of energy and life, holds many people in bondage to the shadow world of the setting sun. If you are brave enough, look at your relationship with money, feel it, and imagine other possible ways of handling it. Feel the fear of losing money and the hope of having more, and feel how this hope and fear sustains the cocoon.

As you practice discovering and going beyond your little fears, you may begin to see how to go forward into fear, and you may discover something quite remarkable: that honestly going through fear is enjoyable. It is actually a relief to be able to face fear. You may find that it is all right to be afraid and begin to feel gentle and tender toward your fearful mind and heart. Fear wakes us up. We may be shaking in our boots, but we know that we can go on, and so we are kind to ourselves and we *can* go on—into the fear and beyond it, without losing our minds. At the same time, you should always know how far you can go. Do not push yourself further than that. Don't create a state of panic in yourself that can only be harmful or that can really lead you into danger.

Fear is the gateway to fearlessness. When you don't run away from fear, a new pattern, one different from the habitual patterns that make up the cocoon, can begin to take root. This new pattern is not simply one more patch on the cocoon. It is the start of a new pattern of fearlessness. Bravery doesn't come from obliterating fear—it comes from knowing that fears are the stepping-stones of the journey. It comes from opening to the tenderness and vulnerability that underlie all fear. As the Dorje Dradul says, "Nervousness is cranking up, vibrating, all the time. When we slow down, when we relax with our fear, we find sadness, which is calm and gentle. Sadness hits you in your heart, and your body produces a tear. . . . That is the first tip of fearlessness."

Having discovered the strength that comes from stepping directly into fear, you will know that you need never give up, whatever twists and turns your path may take. The path circles and spirals back on itself. It is not a linear path that is neatly laid out, and it does not exist as something outside of you. You will not be following a path that is already completely prescribed so that all you have to do is fit yourself into a mold. The path is unique to each of us because our fears, our stepping-stones to bravery, are unique. Maps for the path, such as this book, can only provide signposts—ways to help you unfold your own unique way of being.

Once a farmhouse near where I lived in Vermont burned to the ground—only the basement was left. The family had nowhere to go and had no insurance. So they built a roof on top of the basement and lived there until they were able to build walls. The foundation of the entire path of warriorship is the willingness to see, explore, and let go of our cocoon gently by crossing through fear. It is like the foundation of a house, the solid base on which the rest of the house is built, whether it is a country cottage or a huge mansion. Even if we renovate the house inside and out, we do not change the foundation. The foundation of the warrior's path, too, is always there for you to go back to. Whenever you lose your way, you always know how to begin again.

Sometimes the path will seem dark and obscure. You may feel stuck, or you may not know where you are going or if you are really going anywhere at all. Yet you move forward even when you seem stalled. This is very important to remember. Again and again you will find yourself at the beginning, yet it will feel like a fresh start from a beginning that you have never known before. You will go through this process over and over again. Each time you go through the gateway of fear, you touch a more profound level of fearlessness and genuine confidence.

At other times your way will seem bright and clear, and you will see far ahead. No matter how short a time you have traveled the path of warriorship or how strong your resistance to it, you can have a glimpse of all the stages of the path *at any time*. In a sudden moment you may feel profound confidence and joy and realize who you genuinely are. Such glimpses of unconditioned genuineness may themselves evoke fear, because they can be so different from your habitual image of yourself. But they do give you the bravery and inspiration to go forward. They provide you with a vision for your life and with guidance on your journey.

 ## Suggestions

1. Uncovering Your Fear

To uncover your underlying fear, you need to discover its hiding places. Look closely at your habits of body, speech, emotions, and beliefs. For one week, pay particular attention to when you feel uncomfortable, nervous, irritable, or lazy. What is it that you don't want to do? How do you feel around strangers? How do you feel if you have to do something unfamiliar—give a public talk or a report to a class, go for a job interview, or get up two hours early or stay up two hours beyond your usual bedtime? How does your body feel when you enter a room with everyone watching? How do you feel when someone presents ideas you find unacceptable, stupid, naive, or foolish? Do you usually feel that you are right and get angry when people disagree with you? Notice when you feel a resistance to change or when you feel pushed.

These are simply suggestions as to where you might look for situations that make you uncomfortable—the sharp points of your life. You can best find your own sharp points. It is easy to know when you are uncomfortable or irritated if you are willing to look and be a little bit honest with yourself.

2. Working with Fear

Choose one of the situations that you discovered in the previous exercise. Notice how you try to avoid uncomfortable feelings and the situation that provokes them. Maybe you've been aware of these habitual patterns for a long time but you try to ignore them or run away from them. Notice the ways you usually turn away from them. Keep looking at the discomfort in your life. Find the fear in each situation as it arises.

When you do notice the fear underlying your habitual thoughts, emotions, and actions, try to let it be there without pushing it away or reacting to it. When you feel your fear, really feel it. Go toward the situation instead of running away from it (as long as the situation itself is not dangerous or overwhelming), and go toward the fear in your own mind instead of ignoring it. Give in when you feel the fear. Don't struggle or try to build yourself up. Let it make you meek—shy, almost. Feel your soft heart and vulnerable body. See what happens. Remember, it's all right to be afraid. This is just an exercise—if you begin to panic or the exercise interferes with something practical that you need to do, stop and try again another time.

3. Playing with Fear

Play with your fear—as long as it's not life-threatening or hurtful to yourself or others. Begin to see how to go through fear and that there is something delightful about going through it. You may want to go to extremes, such as bungee-jumping or parachuting, but that is not necessary. There are plenty of ordinary daily-life fears to play with. Talk directly to someone you usually feel nervous around; see if you notice any humor in your nervousness. Take a freezing shower, if the thought of it makes you afraid you'll get pneumonia on the spot. Watch a horror movie, listen to ghost stories, ride a roller coaster, or sit in a dark room. What frightens you? Is there a slight thrill in that? Where is the fun in the fear? Take a playful leap into fear and see what happens.

CHAPTER 7
The Joy of
Being Fully Present

Stepping through the gateway of fear begins in sitting practice. The next challenge is to extend your mindfulness practice from its foundation in sitting practice to action in the world. Indeed, we practice mindfulness first in sitting practice precisely so that we can later carry it into daily life. The whole point of mindfulness practice is to be present without losing mindfulness in the middle of daily-life activities. Even those who go on retreat for three years, three months, and three days—as some do in the Tibetan Buddhist training—have to come out and find their place in the world again and take part in daily life. Sogyal Rinpoche says, "I cannot say it strongly enough: to integrate meditation in action is the whole ground and point and purpose of meditation. The violence and stress, the challenges and distractions of modern life make this integration even more urgently necessary."

Mindfulness in Daily Life

Mindfulness in daily life is not the same as self-consciousness. When you are self-conscious you are split into someone who is acting and someone else who is watching. You are in two minds—and are filled with doubt. Self-consciousness can become a problem for practitioners of mindfulness, especially if they take a heavy-handed, "religious" attitude to it. In that case "mindfulness" becomes another reason to beat themselves over the head, to doubt their basic goodness. Mindfulness actually means being one hundred percent *one* with what you are doing, so that your mind is paying attention to what your body is doing and vice versa. Your mind and body are joined, synchronized, and in harmony—they are one. Your attention is fully in the present. Your mind is no longer constantly racing ahead of your body, planning and scheming. It no longer drags you behind as it tries to dwell in yesterday. Instead, your body and mind experience the world together. You are mindful of sense perceptions at the very moment you have those perceptions. As you reach for a coffee cup, your mind is actually paying attention to the color of the cup, the smell of the coffee, the feel of the solid curving handle between your fingers, its weight as you pick it up.

If you practice in this way, mindfulness becomes a source of joy rather than worry. It brings joy because when you let go of the doubting watcher and can just be with your life as it is, much more energy and vitality are available to you. Practicing mindfulness in the midst of activity, however, takes some effort and discipline. When you're not used to it, mindfulness does not come as naturally as your heartbeat, although it *is* a natural function. First you have to form a deliberate intention to be mindful, although the effort you make doesn't have to be heavy and dutiful. Mindfulness in action can have both humor and a light touch.

You can begin to bring mindfulness into your daily life by retaining your mindfulness as you rise from your practice cushion and leave the space. At this point, do not use your breath as the focus of mindfulness. Rather, pay attention to the soles of your feet as they press on the floor and the way your legs feel as they walk. Next, you can practice mindfulness in the midst of simple physical tasks such as pouring milk into a bowl of cereal, carrying wood in for the stove, or typing a letter. Pay attention to each detail of your movement while remaining present, so that your mind and body are doing the same things. As you pour the cereal into the bowl, notice how the bowl feels and looks—the colors, the light reflected on it—how the cereal sounds hitting the bowl, what happens when the milk touches the cereal, and so forth. There are innumerable details for you to notice.

When you try to practice mindfulness in this way, another distraction will likely come along pretty quickly. Don't worry about it. Simply remember mindfulness again—it might be two minutes, two hours, or two days later— and then again pay attention, mindfully, to whatever you are doing. When you are not deliberately practicing, mindfulness will come to you from time to time, suddenly. This *is* a result of your previous practice, and such moments will accumulate as you practice more. Acknowledge your moments of mindfulness when they occur, and remain mindful for as long as you can without struggling. The more you do this, the more often mindfulness will return.

When mindfulness comes to you, practice for a while and let it go. The key to bringing mindfulness into your daily life is relaxation in your efforts. Forcing mindfulness will not work. If you try too hard to hold on to mindfulness, you will turn it into a struggle. You'll be thinking about mindfulness rather than actually doing it. Your thought will again be divided from your action—this time, in the name of mindfulness. When mindfulness arises in the middle of activity, simply acknowledge it and let it go, just as you would any other thought. If you try to grasp it, you will lose it; if you let it go, it will come back. Just as you once learned to walk as a child and then trusted that you could walk, you can trust that mindfulness will return. Just like walking, mindfulness is a natural function—once you have learned to be mindful, you don't have to keep checking that you are doing it.

In a Shambhala discussion group, John told of a moment of mindfulness that occurred to him while he was driving down the street. "I was in a sort of sullen, gray, mildly depressed, mildly anxious mood," he says. "Just closed in my little world. No big deal, just stuck. Out of the blue I remembered a photography class, where we practiced looking at color. Out of a corner of my eye I noticed something—I think it was the green leaves on the trees. Suddenly, wow! There was a world out there! It was as if a curtain had been pulled back. Suddenly a huge colorful world was just *there*. My dull mood simply evaporated. It wasn't exactly *dramatic;* it felt very simple and ordinary. But it made a powerful difference to me. For several minutes afterward, I was able to practice mindfulness with real delight."

As you continue practicing mindfulness, you will become familiar with the sense of being present. When you are mindful, you are *here,* actually living your life, and your mind and body function harmoniously together. Practice itself develops trust in the effectiveness of practice. Gradually a "residue of mindfulness" develops naturally in you, a general atmosphere of mindfulness in which you need not struggle. Your mind can appreciate resting in mindfulness, almost naively. Whenever your mind relaxes to touch that naive natural mindfulness and harmony of body and mind, you can touch a profound source of energy and joy.

Mindfulness of Speech

Mindfulness in daily life includes mindfulness of speech, which is a very important practice. Speech is the link between body and mind. If body and mind are not joined, they communicate different messages. Since we cannot manipulate our body as we can our words, our body will give us away. Bodies communicate in many ways. Posture, gestures, facial tension, the way you walk or enter a room—these visible communications may say something quite different from the words you speak. If this is the case, your speech will inevitably be deceptive to yourself and to others.

In *The Man Who Mistook His Wife for a Hat,* neurologist Oliver Sacks tells a story that illustrates how our bodies can tell a different story from our words. The story concerns patients with very severe cases of aphasia, a disease that makes the patient unable to understand the literal meaning of words. Yet Sacks's aphasia patients could usually understand what was said to them because they were able to pick up on nonverbal clues—tone of voice, emphasis, gestures, and so on. Sacks demonstrated that these patients were aphasic only when he artificially removed all these nonverbal cues from his speech. Sometimes, to reduce the speech to pure words he had to go so far as to totally depersonalize his speech by using a computer synthesizer.

Sacks writes that he heard

a roar of laughter from the aphasia ward, just as the President's [Reagan's] speech was coming on, and they had all been so eager to hear the President speaking. . . .

There he was, the old Charmer, the Actor, with his practised rhetoric, his histrionisms, his emotional appeal—and all the patients were convulsed with laughter. . . .

In this, then, lies the power of understanding—understanding without words, what is authentic or unauthentic. Thus it was the grimaces, the histrionisms, the false gestures and above all, the false tones and cadences of voice, which rang false for these wordless but immensely sensitive patients. It was to these (for them) most glaring, even grotesque, incongruities and improprieties that my aphasic patients responded, undeceived and undeceivable by words.

This is why they laughed at the President's speech.

Being fully present in the moment, with mind and body joined, is the basis of genuine speech. Speech, at its most superficial level, involves only the literal meanings of words. But when someone is speaking, vastly more is happening than the literal meaning of the words. We choose particular words, but the sound and tone of our voice as we speak also has meaning. The rhythm, pace, and precision with which we speak and the quality of the silence between words also communicate meaning.

When your body and mind are working together, you speak differently from the way you speak in your cocoon. You actually hear and feel the words as they come out of your mouth. You feel the place in your body where they originate. They may come from the heart center in your chest, or off the top of your head, or from a tight little knot in your throat. You may speak with feeling for what you are saying, or you may speak as if you were reading a press release. You may be speaking too fast, so that they come tumbling out before you know what you are going to say. Do the words come out sharply like bullets, or do they have a gentler quality? Do they stroke the listener or strike him? You can be aware of all these aspects of your speech when you speak mindfully.

As a warrior, remind yourself of the importance of your words. Ask yourself if you are saying what you mean to say. Are you being fundamentally honest and direct in your communication? Or is there some deception in your words or attitude, either toward yourself or others? The purpose of speech is to communicate, but even in a request as simple as "Please pass the salt," there is almost always something besides words. There can be communication of hatred or love, of cold indifference or appreciation.

Words have power—they are not merely bearers of dictionary meanings. They carry the wisdom of generations. When you say, "I love you so much," or, "The sky is very black," or, "Just thinking about it made my mouth water," your words carry a whole world of subtle meanings. When you speak with synchronized mind and body and open heart, listening to and feeling your words, you tune in to that flow of power, and you become a conduit for it. With body and mind together, you say neither more nor less than you mean, and the words you speak have clarity and the power to affect your world. When you speak automatically, by contrast, you have only the power of a mechanical doll or a broken faucet.

Sometimes in Shambhala Training Programs, we practice mindfulness of speech, or elocution. Participants are invited to read exercises or poems, clearly enunciating and differentiating each vowel and consonant. When people take part in elocution practice, they hear how they are speaking and feel how they are forming the words in their mouths, throats, and bodies. Often it is the first time they ever realize how they speak. So much of people's habitual identity is embodied in their speech, however, that when they are asked to change the way they speak, they become arrogant. Even though they have volunteered to do the exercise, they often feel tremendous irritation and resistance at first.

However, some remarkable changes take place in participants, even in the course of just one ten-minute exercise. Those who began by slouching to the microphone in their familiar posture, with shoulders bent over and head down, slurring their words so that they were barely audible, have ended standing straight, head up, speaking forcefully and clearly and in a forthright manner. Others who come to the microphone jauntily with a smirk of confidence and a loud aggressive voice have become softened and able to listen.

Kathy, whose early experience of sitting practice and discovery of basic goodness we discussed in Chapter 5, continued to feel tremendous inner resentment and shame as she journeyed along the path of warriorship, although the opening in her cocoon that she had sensed right at the beginning gradually penetrated through the anger. Her experience of speaking practice may be extreme but it is not atypical:

> The night of elocution practice I was irritated beyond belief. I hated Shambhala, thought the elocution was long and painful. I stormed to my room, thinking this practice is not for me, it's absurd. I hated everything that I was doing here. I was going to talk to someone tomorrow and leave. I don't remember ever having felt so irritated, or ever having so little faith in the Shambhala path. The next morning, though, I woke up and said aloud, "The rain in Spain stays mainly in the plain." [This was not one of the exercises!] I burst out laughing. I couldn't believe how good and cheerful I felt. It was not like me to wake up like this. I didn't know how I got to this flip side of the coin of my emotions. I left the room and took pictures of trees and plants and mushrooms as I walked along the path to breakfast. Everything at breakfast was delicious. What the hell happened! At the talk that night the director said how irritability opens things up. It was a magical connection. I had never before felt that flip in that kind of way. Never. Thank you.

When we speak mindfully, from our whole being and not just from our head, mind and body are joined and we are fully present. When we are fully present with open heart, we communicate genuinely. The cloudy mind that comes from so much inner talking clears for a moment, and we feel connected to the earth and to the sky. When mind and body are joined and the inner chatter clears, we can cheer up in a very magical way and take a joyful leap out of the cocoon, as Kathy did.

> The breeze at dawn has secrets to tell you
> > Don't go back to sleep.
> You must ask for what you really want.
> > Don't go back to sleep.
> People are going back and forth across the doorsill
> > where the two worlds touch.
> The door is round and open.
> > Don't go back to sleep.

> RUMI

Awareness

As you continue to practice, mindfulness expands to include awareness of the outer environment as well as the inner environment of your thoughts and emotions. The distinction between *mindfulness* and *awareness* comes from the Buddhist tradition of practice. The Sanskrit word for mindfulness is *shamatha,* which literally means "development of peace" but is sometimes used to mean "taming the mind." The Sanskrit word for awareness is *vipashyana,* which is also translated as "insight." *Mindfulness* is the attention to detail and settling of the mind that you need in order to begin practice. *Awareness* is the more global sense of space, openness, and clarity that develops out of mindfulness as your practice strengthens. Awareness is almost like having antennae radiating all around you and above and below. Mindfulness, with its precision, and awareness, with its openness and clear insight, are both necessary aspects of practice in action, like the two wings of a bird.

After you have had some experience with practicing mindfulness in your sitting practice, your mind naturally starts to slow down and your body starts to relax. At that point, while still paying attention to the out-breath, allow your attention to expand to include more of your environment. Allow your sense perceptions to open so that you can literally be aware of more of the space around you and notice more sounds. This is a relaxed, natural process that should not be strained or focused. Your awareness expands of its own accord, and you should let it happen. A simple instruction in Shambhala training is to put twenty-five percent of your attention on your breath, and seventy-five percent on your environment. These numbers are simply a guideline—there is no way you can take them literally. But they do suggest that at a certain point you can begin to include a larger space in your awareness while still being mindful of your breath.

As awareness increases, you will find that you are naturally paying attention to your environment and the space around you. When practitioners let go of their struggle to control the world and their own energy, a sudden feeling of freshness often dawns. This freshness is bright and aware. With it comes a sense of humor and perspective. Just for a moment, you might feel refreshed and awakened, as if you had plunged into a deep, cool lake on an oppressively hot and humid day. These sudden glimpses of freshness and openness come from outside the normal stream of inner dialogue, emotional upheaval, habitual worry, and anxious hope—that is, from outside the cocoon. They come from a larger sense of being—from basic goodness. Basic goodness is not a personal possession. We can feel it not only in ourselves but in the world all around us and in others as well.

We are immersed in a world larger than our ordinary, narrow, and fearful state of mind knows. It does not necessarily take a long period of warriorship practice for this insight to occur. Your life may be in a terrible mess, and you may be in a lot of pain. Still, if you are willing to be true to yourself, sometimes for a moment you are able to let go, and your awareness can expand to include the environment and the feeling of energetic space and larger perspective that comes with it.

When we look with awareness, we literally include the space around us in our attention. We notice peripheral sights and sounds—and they no longer feel like distractions to our mindfulness. When we are talking to someone, we notice the space within, between, and around the two of us and the subtleties of our exchange. We slow down and hear the silence between our words. When we slow down, we don't need to react defensively or with speed.

Shortly after I first met the Dorje Dradul, I was doing garbage-collection duty at the contemplative center that I was staffing. The Dorje Dradul, who was teaching there all summer, was staying in a cottage in a nearby village. I went over to his house to pick up his garbage. The door to the living room was open. The Dorje Dradul invited me in and offered me tea. As I sat at the table with him, I became very self-conscious and nervous. The space around me seemed to get smaller and smaller, and my attention narrowed down to the table in front of me and to the Dorje Dradul, sitting opposite and smiling. Embarrassed and struggling to find something to say, I began to complain about the sloppiness of other staff and the dirtiness of the center.

After a few minutes, the Dorje Dradul cocked his head to one side as if he were listening and then interrupted me, saying, "Is that a lawn mower?" I stopped and listened, and indeed there was a lawn mower way off in the distance. At first I felt a surge of irritation that he seemed not to have been listening to me, but then suddenly my awareness expanded. I felt the whole room around me, and I became aware of the evening sun shining outside and the fields around the house. My body relaxed, I sat back in my chair, and I was able to continue to talk with him about the general situation at the center and its possibilities, while dropping my nervous complaining.

When awareness develops, you are able to relax and see the larger patterns of your own and others' behavior. You can see more of the whole context, the bigger picture. It is like being able to see all around you—360 degrees rather than just straight ahead. You begin to see with your whole being rather than with your eyes alone. Through the practice of awareness, you begin to connect mind with body. You can pay attention in this way and *still* talk to a friend. When the Dorje Dradul drew my attention to the sound of the lawn mower, he actually increased my awareness of the room around me and of my body sitting at the table, instead of diminishing my awareness, as one might suppose. Even as I now sit typing at a computer monitor, I am aware of the room around me, the sounds coming from the street, the larger space above me, and the solid chair, supported by the earth beneath me.

Awareness also brings attention to the inner environment that the emotions carry with them. If you pay attention with awareness, you will notice that each emotion brings along with it a trail of other thoughts, emotions, and moods— feelings of expansiveness or contraction, of sadness or joy. We do not have merely an angry thought about a friend—our anger has something behind it. It brings all kinds of assumptions about the friend's attitude and behavior, for example; it may bring jealousy and even passion along with it. Strong emotions always bring fear and grasping. When you look directly at your emotion, with clear insight, you will see that it is fleeting and insubstantial, having no permanence other than your attempt to hold on to it. Seeing this, you can begin to let go of the fear and feel the energy of the emotion as it is.

When we are more aware of the inner environment of our emotions, we no longer get them so mixed up with the outer world. We don't mistake our own emotional reactions about people for the final truth about them, and we don't confuse our past associations with people with their present situations. We remain open to what other people have to say and show right now, regardless of our past interactions with them. Too often we jump to conclusions about people without slowing down enough to look at them, feel how they are feeling, see what *they* are going through. Awareness enables us to discriminate between authentic and inauthentic words because with awareness we not only hear the words that are being spoken but sense the meaning and feeling behind those words.

A colleague, for example, might make a comment to you that on the face of it seems insulting, and you might impulsively react with a corresponding insult. When you are aware of the demeanor of the colleague, however, the tone of voice, and so on, you can see that the felt insult is actually an expression of his own insecurity and that you have the possibility of reacting with compassion. With the freshness and openness that awareness brings, you can let go of your own self-righteousness. Without deception, you can feel the energy of your own and your colleagues' emotions, and genuine communication can take place.

A natural sense of humor develops when we are willing to acknowledge the sudden, unpredictable flashes of awareness and insight. One participant at a Shambhala training weekend, Lorin, told us:

Early in our marriage, my wife and I sometimes got into some pretty ferocious fights. Somehow we seemed to be talking on completely different levels. We just locked into something that neither of us could seem to stop, once it got going. One day we were in a frenzy of shouting and insulting each other. I picked up one of my wife's favorite vases and threatened to hurl it at the wall. I looked across the room, and there was our black cat sitting on the back of the sofa, staring at us. At that very moment he yawned.

Seeing that cat's open, blank stare was like hearing a crack in my mind. Suddenly I realized how emotionally indifferent that cat was to all that was going on between us, even though he seemed to be watching us with intense curiosity. I felt an urge to laugh that was so strong, not even my anger could suppress it. I suppose I realized how comical the whole fight was. My wife stared at me for a moment, then she started laughing as well.

A sense of humor is a very helpful, necessary ingredient in the practice of warriorship. As the Dorje Dradul says,

When we begin to realize the potential goodness in ourselves, we often take our discovery much too seriously. We might kill for goodness, or die for goodness; we want it so badly. What is lacking is a sense of humor. Humor here does not mean telling jokes or being comical or criticizing others and laughing at them. A genuine sense of humor is having a light touch: not beating reality into the ground but appreciating reality with a light touch. The basis of Shambhala vision is rediscovering that perfect and real sense of humor, that light touch of appreciation.

The warrior's development of awareness fundamentally means a greater and greater recognition of space. Warriors recognize psychological space in their own being, the open space of egolessness, as if their mind and heart were full of holes constantly letting in the fresh air of unfamiliar and perhaps strange ideas and feelings. They recognize the living, dynamic, responsive quality of the physical space of the world. They feel the space around and within other people. They feel the living space that surrounds trees and rocks and encircles the earth. Gradually, they recognize that the space "inside" is no different from the space "outside." As Suzuki Roshi says, "The inner world is limitless, and the outer world is also limitless. We say 'inner world' or 'outer world' but actually there is just one whole world."

The Dorje Dradul comments,

In the ordinary sense, we think of space as something vacant or dead. But in this case, space is a vast world that has capabilities of absorbing, acknowledging, and accommodating. You can put cosmetics on it, drink tea with it, eat cookies with it, polish your shoes in it. Something is there. But ironically, if you look into it, you can't find anything. If you try to put a finger on it, you find you don't even have a finger to put on it! That is the primordial nature of basic goodness, and it is that nature which allows a human being to become a warrior. . . . The warrior, fundamentally, is someone who is not afraid of space. The coward lives in constant terror of space.

Four Qualities of a Warrior

The Shambhala teachings describe four qualities or "dignities" that develop in the being of accomplished warriors as they develop their awareness, let go of ego-centered concern, and allow the power and joy of space, of unconditioned goodness, to enter their being and their lives. The qualities are *meekness, perkiness, outrageousness,* and *inscrutability.*

These qualities may seem strange to those of us used to the most up-to-date slang use of words. However, the Dorje Dradul, who chose the names in collaboration with his group of student-translators, often used words in ways that seemed strange to his students' ears but that were in fact more accurate based on the words' etymology. For example, the word *perky* is nowadays used in a slightly silly and derogatory way, sometimes even chauvinistically to stereotype women. However, *Webster's Collegiate Dictionary* defines one meaning of the verb *to perk* as "to gain in vigor or cheerfulness, especially after a period of weakness or depression." This definition brings us very close to the sense of the word *perky* as a quality of warriorship, although in this usage it has more profound connotations.

The first quality, *meekness,* is the ground of a warrior's being. Whatever their accomplishments, warriors remain genuine, modest, and without pretense. They are self-contained and alert. Because they do not have an inflated image of themselves, they are inquisitive and interested in the world around them.

The second quality, *perkiness,* is the playfulness that treats everything with a light touch of humor. The playfulness is not casual, however, but is thoroughly trained in mindfulness and continually exerts itself joyfully. It is a fresh and uplifted state of being in which body and mind are completely in harmony. Its youthful zest overcomes all doubt and laziness, as well as the feeling that it is not worthwhile to keep going forward into new challenges.

The third quality, *outrageousness,* enables warriors to enter completely into any situation without trying to measure their own ability to respond to it adequately or to guess the outcome. Warriors at this stage are not caught up in fear or in hoping for any particular result. To accomplish what is needed, they are not afraid to go beyond conventional responses or the limits set by their habitual patterns of thinking or behaving. They are able to appreciate the whole picture and not be trapped into taking sides.

The fourth dignity, *inscrutability,* is remaining-in-nowness. Warriors let go altogether of their own logic, beliefs, and ways of doing things. At this stage, warriors overcome the boundary between themselves and the world and identify fully with other people and with earth, the weather, the forests, the sky, and the elements.

These four qualities are symbolized by four animals. Meekness is symbolized by a tiger, who walks through the jungle with every hair of his body alert. He keeps close to the ground and is not easily seen. He is sleek, supple, well-groomed, and vibrant with life. Perkiness is symbolized by a snow lion. The snow lion lives at the higher levels of mountain ranges. He has a long turquoise mane that blows in the breeze as he leaps joyfully from peak to peak in the fresh mountain air. Outrageousness is symbolized by a garuda, a bird that breaks out of its shell full-grown. It flies in space without ever needing to land, soaring beyond all limits and boundaries. From its vantage point above the earth, it sees all that happens with complete clarity. Inscrutability is symbolized by a dragon. He lives in the elements of earth, water, wind, and heat. In the autumn he lives in the mists, and in the spring he lives in the rains. He sinks into the bowels of the earth in winter, and he rises to cause thunder and lightning in the summer.

The four animals had their origin at least as far back as Taoist China and are probably even more ancient than that. According to Robin Kornman, Shambhala warrior and Chinese scholar, "Perhaps the most accurate view is that Central Asian mythical lore is internationalist. It arises from the culture of the Silk Route and combines into one civilization everything that merchants encountered as they journeyed in their caravans from West to East." The Silk Route was the caravan route stretching all the way from the Middle East to China that was followed for hundreds of years by merchants who exchanged culture and ways of life along with their merchandise. The Sufi poet Rumi, who lived in Turkey at the Western end of the Silk Route, suggests:

Think that you're gliding out from the face of a cliff
like an eagle. Think that you're walking
like a tiger walks by himself in the forest.
You're most handsome when you're after food.

Spend less time with nightingales and peacocks.
One is just a voice, the other just a color.

The four animals are more than merely symbols of the qualities. At later stages on the warrior's path, these animals become helpers and guides in the warrior's action. By contemplating the qualities of these animals, by feeling his way into them and trying to see the world through their eyes, the warrior understands the four qualities in a profound way.

The Dorje Dradul says of the four qualities,

Although everyone has some experience of these expressions of energy, unless there is actual discipline and awareness applied, there is no fundamental sense of going forward in your life, and the four dignities are buried as part of your habitual pattern rather than becoming a path toward egolessness. So fundamentally, the four dignities must be connected to the path of warriorship. In fact, they are an advanced stage on the path. The warrior is able to realize the four dignities only after he or she has developed an unshakeable conviction in basic goodness and has seen the Great Eastern Sun reflected in the experience of the sacred world. At that point, the warrior is plugged into a source of energy that never runs down.

Student warriors, still going steadily step by step through the gateway of fear to emerge fully from their cocoons, are fundamentally at the level of meekness. However, warriors at any stage on the path can see the seeds of all these qualities in their everyday life. The qualities build on each other, so that a warrior who has developed the quality of perkiness has not renounced or gone beyond the quality of meekness. It is not like learning math in school, where once you have "covered" algebra, you hope you never hear the word again. Meekness, the quality of being thoroughly grounded and open, is learned—or relearned—and used again and again. Furthermore, perkiness is a natural outcome of the warrior's accomplishment of meekness, and outrageousness is a natural result of accomplishing perkiness. In this sense, all the dignities are already contained in meekness, just as the teenager is already contained in the youngster, and the mature person in the teenager. The dignities do not have to be strived for; they are not some kind of credential. They simply characterize the natural development of the warrior as he or she practices mindfulness and awareness and continues on the path. Our path is not only to go deeper inward but to open outward as well, finding our place in the world and our interconnections with everything in it, indeed with the whole cosmos.

Being Meek Like a Tiger

Once you feel some confidence in letting go of the cocoon, you may start to feel meek. Once you experience basic goodness intensely, you may feel a little impoverished by it. But this meekness and impoverishment alert you to new possibilities. The cocoon is all puffed up with hot air. Whether you're overconfident, extroverted, and inflated, or depressed, withdrawn, and shrunken, you believe in your cocoon with a tremendous self-importance. But when you see through the holes in these imaginary beings and begin to know yourself more clearly, that arrogance no longer makes sense. You can smile at your pompous strutting and self-righteous complaining. This is an aspect of meekness.

Meekness is not the same as timidity. On the contrary, it means becoming less intimidated by who we are. We have touched our basic goodness, so that failing to please others or come up to their expectations does not make us as anxious. We can let go of our striving to fulfill our parents' and teachers' ambitions for us—or at least what we have imagined those ambitions to be. We can let go of any shame or guilt we carry from something we believe we did wrong long ago. We can tell what is genuine and what is not, and we need not rely on other people's confirmation or judgment for it. One eleven-year-old girl sat in a Shambhala training discussion group for nearly an hour listening to the adults puzzling over basic goodness. After a while, the group leader asked her whether she wanted to say anything. "It's easy," she replied. "Basic goodness is knowing the difference between what's fake and what's real."

With the mindfulness and meekness of the young warrior, we stay low, close to the ground, like a tiger in the forest—connecting its paws with the soil, watching, feeling, moving, with heightened awareness. The tiger is dignified but cautious. The tiger can move quickly as well, but with tremendous precision. Meekness is neither cowardly nor shrinking. It is feeling the hairs on your back stand on end, having your ears alert and open in all directions, smelling the electricity in the air, watching, waiting. We use all our senses, we listen and look and touch our world with interest and inquisitiveness, and we stay mindful in the moment. Stay alert, like a frightened doe, your nerves sensitive like bruises. Then suddenly, without *you* doing anything, a crack will appear in the cocoon and you can slip through.

So we go step by step, always on the edge. If we use a harpoon to snare a butterfly's cocoon it seems like overkill. If we peek out too far, the energy return can overwhelm us. If we fall off the edge, we may go back to sleep in the cocoon, we may become deaf and blind or overwhelmed with energy too hot to handle. There is a danger of not being able to take the sharp and newly penetrating points. So in order to continue our journey through the forest to the brisk clear air of the mountain top, which is the next step, we need to stay on the edge of mindfulness and join our mind with our body one hundred percent. That way we can connect ourselves to the world and begin to open up to it.

Mindfulness and awareness are the basic tools with which we continue on our journey into warriorship; synchronized mind-and-body is the vehicle; and fear is the stepping-stone and the gateway. In order to leap into space, however, we need our connections to the real world of earth. The quality of *meekness* helps us maintain that connection of mind and body, and of body-mind to earth. When you recognize that you have reached the moment to step out of your cocoon once again, if you put on a mask, raise false confidence, and pretend to leap, you will just be knocked back again: You always need *meekness*.

The journey of warriorship will not necessarily be a short one. It does not have some end-point at which we can say, "Thank goodness, now I am out of the cocoon and I don't have to bother with mindfulness any more." Again and again we find ourselves wrapped up in our cozy imaginary life. And when, for the thousandth time, we see this and feel our good warrior's heart, then it's up to us to step into the brightness and uncertainty of the world free from deception. There is no trick to this, no gimmick, no technique. No one can do it for us, neither therapist, nor spiritual teacher, nor even our best friend. Each time we take a step on the path, we claim our human heritage, the possibility of living joyfully without barrier or pretense.

 ## Suggestions

1. Mindfulness of Body

This exercise can help you to become mindful of the inner sensation of your body and to join mind and body together. A good time to do this is after sitting practice. Sit on a firm chair without leaning back, or on a stool. Plant your feet on the floor firmly, and place your hands on your thighs. Feel the sensation of your feet pressing on the floor. Feel the living warmth of your feet—feel it from the inside. Without losing your mindfulness of the sensation in your feet, move your attention up your shins and calves. Again keeping that sensation in your calves, move through your knees and into your thighs, hands, and forearms.

Move your mindfulness up your torso and upper arms to your shoulders—keeping the sensation in the previous parts as you go along. Move up through the back of your neck, over the top of your head, down your face and chest, and into your heart, coming to rest there. Have a sensation of your whole body as one harmonized unit. Hold that sensation for as long as you can—perhaps a few minutes.

After you have done this exercise, you may decide to remember to do it from time to time during the day. When you do remember, choose a part of your body—any part, your right forearm for example—and notice the inner sensation of that part. Keep the mindfulness of this inner sensation for a few moments while you continue your other activities. Notice any change in your perceptions.

2. Mindfulness of Action

Choose an ordinary action that you often do. It can be anything, but keep it simple. While you are doing it, be mindful of every detail. Maybe you choose cutting an apple. The first thing you do is prepare your space. Set down the cutting board; look at the details of the wood, how the grain goes, and how the previous cuts have marked it. Feel the texture of the apple, how it smells, how the colors of the skin subtly shade into one another. Feel the sensation of your arm moving to pick up the knife, your muscles tensing as you grasp it; feel its weight, look at its shape and sharpness. Hear the crunch of the knife as it slowly goes through the apple. See and smell the juice; feel your mouth starting to water. Keep going—the details you can notice are endless. When you notice that thoughts or the sound of someone talking has taken away your mindfulness, simply return to your activity of cutting, just as in sitting practice you return to the breath.

3. Mindfulness of Speech

Choose a favorite poem. Read it out loud to yourself.

Now read it aloud again, paying attention to each vowel and consonant, to each syllable and word and phrase. Speak each distinctly and precisely. Read slowly, word by word. You can definitely exaggerate. Sit up straight while you are doing this.

Feel the difference between the two styles of reading.

Read it out loud one more time. This time don't exaggerate the precision so much, but keep it in mind. Speak with a dignified, uplifted body.

Now have a friend listen. Repeat the poetry readings in both your usual manner of speaking and in the slow, precise way. Feel that both your readings are communications to your friend.

You can try this exercise in daily life. When you remember to, pay attention to how you are speaking without trying to alter anything about it. Pay attention to the quality of what you are saying, the loudness or softness, the speed, the tone, the feeling in what you are saying, and the meaning you are trying to convey. Now try to be mindful of your speech, and speak more precisely, as you did in the reading exercise. Do you feel any difference in what you are saying or in how it is being received by the person you are talking to?

4. Awareness of Space Around an Object

Choose an object you find particularly beautiful and care about. Put it somewhere free of clutter, against a plain background. Spend some time looking at the details of it. Let yourself appreciate its lines, its color, its texture, its quality. Now soften your gaze, relax your focus, and see the space around the object. You might notice an energetic quality to that space. Notice how you feel about the object and any change of perception when you relax your focus.

When you think of it, you can do this exercise on the spot, with anything your gaze falls on. First just look at the object in your usual focused way. Then, as before, soften your gaze, relax your focus, notice the details of the object and the space around it, and notice any change in your perception of and feeling about the object.

5. Awareness of Space in the Environment

The point of this exercise is to begin to realize the richness of the space around you and how it communicates with you. Go outside into a field or garden, or if you live in an apartment in the city, go to a park. Stand in one spot, pay attention to your breath for a few moments, and then pay attention to the sensation of your body. Now notice the space around your body, and extend that awareness to include the space in your environment. Stay there for a few moments, letting your awareness go out into the space, and notice how you feel. Do you feel threatened, refreshed, agitated, nourished, healed? You don't have to put a name on how you feel—just notice how you feel, but if you do find it easier to give it a name, that's okay. Move to a second spot, and repeat the exercise. Do the same at a third location. Notice the difference in how you feel in each space as you move from place to place.

CHAPTER 8

Gentleness, Fearlessness, and Genuine Heart

The world that we encounter beyond the cocoon is full of challenges. Once we open ourselves to it, something new can always appear to press our emotional buttons, rouse our habitual reactions, and challenge us to be mindful warriors and not mindless cowards. Painful points can come about, not just because we are more sensitive to the world but because we are more sensitive to our own reactions. It takes daring and courage to be genuine, to stay on the path of warriorship, to stay with the sharpness and awkwardness of who we are and how we are. In this chapter we will learn the tools of gentleness and fearlessness that we need in order to work with our emotional reactions and discover the genuine heart of the warrior that lies within them.

While we are still in the cocoon, we relate to the energy of our communication with others as an "emotion." If the emotion is too intense, too real, we're likely afraid of it. This emotional energy may feel threatening if it hurts simply because it hurts; or it may feel overwhelming because it's so delightful and passionate. It may feel painful because it is unfamiliar and "scary," and we get confused trying to "figure it out." We are afraid of losing control, of having our mask stripped. We narrow the emotional energy of our relationships and communications, we fix it and diminish its power. Then we give it a familiar name like *anger, passion,* or *depression.* Alternatively, we conceptualize it— thinking "it won't work out," "it's not practical," "it's not what I had in mind."

Gentleness, Fearlessness, and Genuine Heart

We may eventually become afraid to *feel,* truly and deeply. We may resist the energy, try to escape it, or react defensively to it, which creates further pain. We may become lost in our emotions or try to repress them. We may lose sight of the fact that without emotion nothing moves us.

Challenges of the Heart

Our emotions are our energy. They propel us along the path of warriorship. If we act out our emotions mindlessly, however, they dominate us as if something foreign were possessing us. When, for example, you feel anger rising and just let it blaze up, you may think, "I am really angry." By losing your mind to anger, you have lost contact with yourself and your energy. You have shifted your focus from the pure energy of anger to the "I" who thinks it is angry. Your idea that "I am *really* angry" takes over, and you may make a habitual response of shouting, hitting, throwing things, or storming away and stewing in a dark rage. The Vietnamese Buddhist teacher Thich Nhat Hanh says, "In expressing anger, we might be practicing it or rehearsing it, and making it stronger in the depth of our consciousness. Expressing the anger to the person we are angry with can cause a lot of damage."

Those who practice warriorship in the world often find themselves reacting with volatile emotion to small events that previously they would have brushed off insensitively. You may feel embarrassed by this, or thrown off balance. Who is this person? you may wonder. In fact, that's what happens when we let ourselves feel. When an associate is late meeting you for an appointment, anger and resentment might flare up as if from nowhere. You might feel surprising new flames of passion when meeting an old friend. You might feel deeply depressed over a seemingly small setback at school or work.

When you open your eyes and heart, you will find that the world is an unlimited source of sharp points. Being a warrior does not mean that everything will go evenly and smoothly. We are not trying to anesthetize ourselves—quite the contrary, we are trying to feel the world as it is, without a plastic skin to protect us. "If you want to follow the doctrine of the One," wrote Seng-ts'an, "do not rage against the World of the Senses. Only by accepting the World of the Senses can you share in the True Perception." The difference between the warrior and the coward lies in their attitudes toward the sharp points: The warrior pays attention to them and eventually can be delighted by them; the coward covers them over or runs from them.

As you see your cocoon more clearly, in the light of basic goodness, you will start to *want* to be genuine. Warriors are willing to get out of the cocoon, even though stepping out is frightening. When we see our masks, we also see the possibility of giving them up and of relating to the world directly, with gentle bravery and perhaps a touch of playful bravado. We can begin to see challenges as little electric shocks that wake us up, or like the fresh, cold smell of melting snow in early spring that clears the staleness of the city from our lungs and head.

This is the edge upon which you will find yourself over and over. One foot is in the cocoon and one foot is out—which way do you want to go? It's up to you. Stepping out is not necessarily a big deal. It need not be a struggle. It may be just a fleeting, almost imperceptible, insight about your cocoon—perhaps of stubbornness or grasping. If you can catch them, you can choose to acknowledge such insights. This is where the practice of mindfulness and awareness is essential—you slow down and become precise enough to be able to catch brief cracks in your defenses, then relax and open enough to acknowledge them.

When you experience the world outside the cocoon, you might feel very vulnerable, and small things can get to you. To function without your usual barriers of mindlessness and numbness can feel horribly embarrassing at first, since you feel the raw energy of your own emotions and the emotions of others. Each time you let go of your self-centered concern, you feel the sharpness, the real uncertainty and chaos of the world. You are more sensitive, immersed in something almost too real. This isn't always pleasant. All the things that you took for granted are no longer so automatic. You may feel naked, touched by energies and feelings that seem overwhelming and that you lack the skill to handle.

This experience is different for everyone. You may listen to other people and hear them for the first time. You may find that people you know are quite different from the way you always thought of them. You may realize how strange your husband or wife really is to you; or you may realize that there is some truth in the criticisms that your boss or teenage child makes of you. The affection your friends show may feel a little too intense; friendships may seem not to flow so smoothly as you look at your friends with fresh eyes. You may see more clearly the aggression and manipulation of your colleagues at the office.

Tom, a newspaper editor, seemed in a state of shock in a group discussion after he had been practicing for a few months. "Nothing is working anymore. I feel awkward and loud. I see how I boss people around, but I don't know how else to do my job. I see people being brutal to each other, and I don't know how to stop them. How *can* I go to work without my masks? What's wrong with masks anyway? I feel as if I'm being turned into a wet rag." Everyone else in the group nodded in sympathy. They too were having a rough time.

We want so much to be free from pain rather than face the simple truth of our life. But warriorship training isn't intended to make you feel good continuously. You're not doing something wrong if you sometimes feel pain. Your life is bound to feel more painful at times—perhaps a great deal more painful—as you begin to wake up to who you really are. When you sit too long with your legs tucked under you, your leg can go to sleep; as it wakes up, you get a prickling sensation as feeling returns to it—"pins and needles"—that can be quite painful. When you go to the dentist and get a shot of anesthetic, your jaw goes to sleep; as it wakes up and feeling returns, it can be very painful. Like feeling physical sensation return to a sleeping limb or jaw, waking up to who you are, *feeling* who you are, can be prickly and painful.

Sara, another group member, told us, "I had tried to be a good, loving friend to Joseph for two years. One day I looked at him and realized that I didn't really like him and didn't want to be with him. I just felt numb around him and always had. This was really a shock to me. I didn't want to hurt him, and I felt sad both for him and for myself, but our relationship was a sham. I knew I had to end it, but I would try to do it kindly. I realized that I had known this for some time but simply couldn't face it before. Now my feeling of wanting to be genuine is stronger than my fear of being honest with Joseph or my fear of being alone."

The warrior's journey is neither easy nor comfortable. Any spiritual teaching that tells you otherwise is not telling you the whole story. If a spiritual teacher tells you only about all the joy and wisdom you are going to find, you will be bitterly disappointed as the real challenges of the spiritual path dawn on you. Ease and comfort make up the armor of the cocoon.

The newfound warrior's heart is tender and inexperienced. We feel different and aren't sure exactly how to handle the world from which we've always tried to hide. One student, Peter, told a group, "Mary, my lover, and I had a fight. I realized that one of my masks was putting on a good show of being loving toward her. But I was not actually showing her, or myself, my tenderness. My show of loving was actually *covering over* my heart and saving me from the possibility of being hurt. I realized that I could be really genuine with her only if I was able to face the fear of showing my softness. For the first time in twenty years, I cried—from relief as much as from sorrow."

Gentleness

Stepping out of the cocoon begins with an attitude of loving-kindness. Fear has pushed us into a silent tantrum, and the way out begins with being kind and loving to ourselves. We *can* trust the basic goodness of the world and ourselves and others; we *can* let ourselves feel love and kindness. We don't have to break aggressively through the walls of the cocoon with a battering ram. We can gently face our fear of the unknown and step out softly, although abruptly. My daughter used to have terrible temper tantrums when she was three years old. She would fall down on the floor and kick and scream. The tantrums were frightening, and any attempts to talk her out of them, or even hold her, were useless. There was nothing we could do but sit by her and wait quietly. Finally she would scream, "Mama, get me out of here!" and let her mother hold her with love and kindness until she calmed down. We need to treat ourselves that way. As a text of Shambhala says, "That mind of fearfulness should be put in the cradle of loving kindness."

We need to accept, just as they are, the difficult situations and challenges that stir our emotions. Emotions are not things that we can possess or that can possess us. They are patterns of energy linking our bodymind with the world. The key to warriorship is to become aware of emotional energy as it arises, and of the fear as well as the softness and tenderness that accompany the emotion. Let go of the fear, refuse to hold on to the energy as "my anger" or "my passion," and you can feel the raw, unfiltered energy of connection. This is the warrior's challenge—to be open to and even go toward painful situations with curiosity, courage, and gentleness.

Where there is intense and painful emotion, there is also tremendous living energy. As Thich Nhat Hanh says,

When we are angry, we are the anger. When anger is born in us, we can be aware that anger is an energy in us, and we can accept that energy in order to transform it into another kind of energy. When we have a compost bin filled with organic material which is decomposing and smelly, we know that we can transform the waste into beautiful flowers. . . . We need the insight and non-dual wisdom of the organic gardener with regard to our anger. We need not reject it or be afraid of it. We know that anger can be a kind of compost, and that it is within its power to give birth to something beautiful.

Gentleness, Fearlessness, and Genuine Heart

When you open to your emotional responses with gentleness, you can let them be there without trying to cover them over or manipulate them with a story line about how you really feel. If you feel angry, forlorn, impatient, or any other intense emotion, then really *feel* the energy of anger, forlornness, or impatience. Make friends with it, listen to it, and let it tell you what it has to say.

Gentleness is not weakness or seductiveness but the flexibility to let go and open up to the world. We nourish it in our attitude of kindness to our own wild thoughts and crazy emotions during sitting practice. True gentleness is letting go of our self-conscious attention on ourselves while nurturing and caring for ourselves and others. We can stop attempting to control, let our bodies relax, and let ourselves feel soft and gentle and spacious.

The Shambhala teachings consider gentleness to be the quality of the Mother principle. Every one of us, woman or man, has experienced the accepting, nourishing, and caring qualities of someone who embodied the Mother principle for us, and we carry that impression within our body and mind. Each of us has the capability to open up to ourselves and others in the same way, with kindness and without judgment. In a discussion of working with anger, Thich Nhat Hanh writes, "Awareness can be called upon to be a companion for our anger. Our awareness of our anger does not suppress it or drive it out. It just looks after it. This is a very important principle. Mindfulness is not a judge. It is more like an older sister looking after and comforting her younger sister in an affectionate and caring way."

Fearlessness

Fearlessness is the quality of the Father principle—the fierce protective quality that dares to engage enemies. On the path of warriorship an enemy is anything that threatens genuineness and authentic living. Our main enemy is our own servitude to the cocoon world. Enemies are our own harshness, cowardice, and laziness. They threaten to steal our awareness and cast us back into the cocoon. Enemies threaten our communication and connectedness with the world. Most of all, they are *solemn*. But our fearlessness brings humor that can sweep away that solemnity as a fresh breeze blows the dead leaves out of the yard.

Once I sprained my toe and could hardly walk, so I parked my car outside the post office in a fifteen-minute spot. Rain was pouring down. When I came back from the post office, the car wouldn't start. I hobbled to a phone booth about fifty yards away, getting soaked in the process, and called for help. I returned to the car, cursing, to wait for a tow truck. After a few minutes I felt a shadow over my left shoulder. A policeman was banging on the window, glowering at me. After I explained that the car would not start, he pointed to another parking spot a hundred feet away and helped me push the car to it in the rain.

I climbed back into the car drenched and fuming. I looked across at my twelve-year-old daughter, who had been sitting inside. She was looking at me with amused concern. "Why are you so irritated?" she said. For a moment this made me even more irritated. I did not deny my irritation to her but felt its energy more intensely and directly after her remark. Suddenly I saw the whole episode from my daughter's perspective, and it was as if a bubble burst—poof! My daughter and I smiled at each other, and the tow truck driver found us cracking up with laughter.

Gathering your strength and fearlessness—and humor—in the face of a difficult situation will enable you to remain steady. This steadiness is the firm ground for maintaining awareness as you experience intense emotions, so keeping you from being swayed by your own reactions or the reactions of others. With this steadiness, the ups and downs of life will not forever knock you off balance. Steadiness enables you to open up with curiosity and gallantry to the unpredictable world around you. We really have no idea what will happen tomorrow or even in the next five minutes. Our whole life could change in a flash, but even then we need not lose our warrior's awareness altogether.

Remaining steady as emotions arise enables us to stay present with them without trying to change them. It takes courage to be fully present with our own emotional energy and the energy around us, whether the feeling is anger, sorrow, or passion, or a nameless mixture of these. It takes courage not to turn away from an emotion or try to diminish its intensity. But if you really stay with your anger, your passion, or your jealousy and ask of it, "What do you *really* want?" you may find that it is pointing in an altogether unexpected direction. As Liu Wenmin says, "To be able to be unhurried when hurried; to be able not to slack off when relaxed; to be able not to be frightened and at a loss for what to do when frightened and at a loss: this is the learning that returns us to our natural state and transforms our lives."

Fearlessness brings the capacity to listen to emotions without overreacting. When we are fearless, we do not dread what might be coming or hope for something better than we have. Habitual reactions such as blame, resentment, or exaggerated expectations give way to gentleness and patience toward our lives and toward the world. The world feels bright and rich and our eyes can open to the meaning and humor in even the small and simple things that happen to us, even though the world still has many thorns and we feel their sharpness more intensely.

When you can feel the energy of your emotions without being overwhelmed by them, you can listen to their insight and wisdom. Pause long enough to feel the world and hear what it is telling you. Let the space of awareness enter into your heart. In this way, you become more sensitive and open to the subtleties of the world.

An upsurge of emotional energy can be transmuted into insight if you slow down and remain aware of each stage of arousal precisely as it occurs. The Dorje Dradul pointed out several stages in relating with emotions, based on the Vajrayana Buddhist tradition. The stages are analogous to seeing, hearing, smelling, and touching the energy as if the emotion were coming closer to you.

As the emotion first comes into your awareness, you may have a sense of distance from it as if it were an external object. As the Dorje Dradul says, "In the case of seeing the emotions, we have a general awareness that the emotions have their own space, their own development." Then as you now get closer to it, you can feel the "pulsation" of the energy as when you hear the vibration of sound. If you stay with the energy, as it gets closer still you can appreciate it, feel its flavor, and realize that you can handle it, as if you were smelling and tasting a good meal and felt ready to eat it. Finally you can touch the emotion; you feel the reality of the energy, the "nitty-gritty of the whole thing." You realize that you *can* relate with your emotions, that they are not particularly crazy but just surges of energy. You can bite into them, digest them, and make them a part of you. At that point there is no separation between you and your energy.

The process of going all the way through your fear of emotional energy and relating thoroughly with it in this way is the process of transmutation, analogous to the medieval alchemists' transmutation of lead into gold. The alchemists did not get rid of the lead—they changed its appearance and its quality. The transmutation of emotions is the same. "There is fear that emotion might become too much, that we might fall into it and lose our dignity, our role as human beings," the Dorje Dradul wrote.

Transmutation involves going through such fear. Let yourself be in the emotion, go through it, give in to it, experience it. You begin to go toward the emotion, rather than just experiencing the emotion coming toward you. A relationship, a dance, begins to develop. Then the most powerful energies become absolutely workable rather than taking you over, because there is nothing to take over if you are not putting up resistance. Whenever there is no resistance, a sense of rhythm occurs.

Emotional energy does begin with genuine insight. Anger arises because of our sharpness of intellect—we actually glimpse something that is out of order in our world; but, when we see something wrong in the world, instead of trying to destroy it with our anger, we could let go of our self-righteousness and use that energy to try to correct the wrong. Passion arises because our senses are so wide open and we so appreciate another person, a flower, or even a gold watch; but instead of trying to seduce what we appreciate, we could take delight in our sense perceptions and create works of art. Envy arises when in our gut we feel the richness of our world; but instead of wanting to possess what others have, we could ourselves feel enriched by the sacredness of the world.

The Open Heart
Is Sad and Joyful

By opening ourselves to the world, we allow more energy to become available to us. We are awakened and called by the energy of our world. Because we are working from basic goodness and accurate insight, we connect more directly with the world without barriers of fantasy about how we would *like* the world to be. We connect our insight with the world around us in the energy of relationship, which is vibrant, intelligent, intense, and real. It has a direction and intention of its own. Experiencing it directly can lead us more deeply into the richness of the world. When you stay in tune with your own heart and feel its quality without judging it or impulsively reacting to it, you will discover beneath all the emotional highlights a deeper, tender, more constant feeling. At the core of the heart is a sense of profound, unwavering sadness and joy that comes from being truly open to the world and responding deeply to it.

Recently, I directed a Shambhala Training Program in France. It was a ten-day residential program, and the fifty participants were from all over Europe. In addition to talks, discussions, practice, and mindful walks in the surrounding forest, we all had to help care for the children, prepare the meals, deal with finances, clean the dishes and toilets, and do all the rest of what is needed to keep a community going for ten days. The habitual ways in which people keep separate from each other, without really feeling the struggle of each other's existence, did not quite work here. The participants felt very stretched, tired, and irritated, as well as inspired and opened.

Halfway through the program, a young woman came to see me. She launched into a series of complaints about how irritating it all was. She didn't know why she had come—or why she had borrowed money to come; she thought the people were being mean to each other. Then she started to cry, saying how hypocritical she felt at the difference between all the wonderful things we were studying and how people actually behave most of the time. She said she realized how she had put her irritation onto others—blaming them— but that the problem really started in her.

I felt so much loving-kindness coming through her pain and irritation, and so much longing for the group to live kindly together. Perhaps this was the first step in building a good human society, we speculated. Then people could be honest with each other, see their hearts more nakedly, and be gentle with themselves and others. Finally she told me that she was afraid of what would happen when she went back home after the program, afraid that she would just close up again.

So often in Shambhala Training Programs, in therapy groups, and in contemplative retreats the participants express a longing to love, to be kind and gentle to others and give to them—as well as a fear of this very kindness and giving. Many people weep, feeling that they are not ready, feeling the huge gap between what they want to be and what they are, feeling *bad*. Yet caring and longing to give are in that very heartbreak. The perception of each other's basic goodness is already there.

Beth, an unmarried mother and businesswoman, told another training group, "I was sitting at dinner with my eleven-year-old daughter. She was chattering on about school, and I was ignoring her, feeling irritated and preoccupied, as I often do at dinnertime. Funnily enough, on this occasion, I was thinking about the cocoon, which I had just heard about the weekend before. I glanced at my daughter, and suddenly I *saw* her cheerful, eager face. It was as if the whole room suddenly popped up like a cutout from a pop-up book. I heard my daughter's voice, listened to what she was saying, and felt her excitement about what had happened at school that day. It really touched me. It broke my heart to realize how I love her, and how I so often forget that she is a real human person."

Everyone longs not merely to receive but to give. Everyone longs to love and to be loved—not just in the romantic or sexual sense, but in a deeper sense.

We all have compassionate, caring energy in our hearts. We are all capable of sympathizing with *some* other being, whether it be human or animal. We *can* feel the joy and pain of another being, in the clarity of our heart. This is our pain: that we know we can love, but we think we do not know how to love or who to love. We are afraid to love even ourselves.

When we see that others feel the same way, it breaks our hearts. From our broken hearts, our hearts of sadness and longing and joy, we can look at others and feel their heart of sadness and longing and goodness. Then we feel our direct connection with them. We feel that their heart is our heart, that there really is no difference between their longing and our longing. While seeing and feeling such longing and kindness—and fear—sometimes people shake and weep so hard that it seems as if the whole cosmos were crying through them. At the same time, we might feel tremendous joy, as if the cosmos were laughing through us because this complex feeling is, at last, close to the truth.

Sadness is a feeling of aloneness. Feeling joyful, you want to share your joy with others, but you cannot really fully share it, because joy reveals itself only through experience. The only way others can share joy is to discover it themselves in their own intimate and personal experience, in their hearts. The only way you can share your joy is through your presence and your relationships, through communication of your genuine connection with others. However much warriors may want to help others and give them something of the joy and refreshment that we have found on our path, we know that they have to find their own way. We can guide them, but we can never do it for them.

Jennifer understood this profoundly during the second weekend of her training program:

There are so many stories, so many ways in which the teachings and practices have touched my heart and changed my life. Perhaps the most memorable occasion happened during the second time I attended a Shambhala training weekend, four months after I had attended my first. I had missed the Friday night talk; instead, I went to a party with my husband, Richard. Late that evening he told me that he had had an affair with another woman. Neither of us had had an affair before this time, though I had been in and out of love with various men over the previous couple of years. I was devastated when he told me.

We went to the program on the Saturday morning. The day was intense for me; everything was very one-pointed. I experienced a great deal of rage. Alone, after the Saturday night talk, I made the conscious choice not to shut Richard out, to see him as he was rather than as I wanted him to be.

Sunday was much the same as Saturday, but with more of a broken-hearted quality. Then, while I was sitting on Sunday afternoon, I began to have a sensation of falling. I knew that I was right there, but the sensation of dropping through a tunnel was very vivid. It felt bottomless, with nothing for me to grab on to. I was terrified, crying. I had an impulse to run from the room, but I held on, knowing that I would be having an interview with the director soon. Finally I was escorted into the interview room. The director looked at me and asked what was going on. I described what was happening. Then I asked her if this was the "suffering" I had heard of in the Buddhist teachings. She leaned forward in her chair and said, "No. It's warriorship." I asked her if I would have to live like this all the time. She pointed to a picture of the Dorje Dradul and said simply, "He did."

I returned to my sitting cushion, the weekend continued, and then it ended. And life goes on, with all of its ups and downs. But something happened in that moment, when I had sought reassurance and had found, instead, my own sad and tender heart, my own dignity. There's no turning back.

Our open heart is joyful because it loves, but it is also sad because it sees the tremendous struggle of others to be genuine and true. We know that it is a lonely struggle, and we long to help them, but all we can do is nourish their own dignity and courage. We cannot take the journey for them. My daughter went through the Shambhala Training Program and was so enthusiastic that she volunteered to coordinate programs. Each time she came home from a program, I felt overjoyed at her joy, but at the same time I felt a piercing ache of sadness. At first this bothered me a great deal, and I thought about it. Why would I feel sad that my daughter had discovered this path, a path that I myself love so much and that I have seen so many people benefit from? Gradually, I became accustomed to feel this sadness, even though I could not explain it. Perhaps it was a sadness at seeing her heart and true intelligence blossom, knowing that her life was not going to be ignorantly blissful, but would perhaps be genuinely full. Perhaps it was seeing her growing up and changing so beautifully.

Sadness and joy are the heart's responses to change. The sadness of an open heart has nothing to do with depression, or self-pity, or self-indulgence. Everything is changing around us all the time. In that sense everything is dying. We ourselves are changing and dying, as is everyone we love and everything in the world of beauty and grace. We cannot hold on to our lives or ourselves as we are now and try to stay that way. We are changing, our lives are changing. This is the beauty of life, the joy and sadness of it. Joy amplifies all the pain of the setting-sun world, making the contrast more acutely felt. Avoiding freshness and change itself causes pain. Even the path of warriorship may feel like an oppressive challenge, such that the student is like a mother who must respond to her baby's cry again and again, no matter how tired or preoccupied she may be.

Pointing to the place of sadness in the warrior's path or any spiritual path was one of the most profound teachings of the Dorje Dradul. So much spiritual teaching and systems of therapy nowadays are oriented toward finding contentment, joy, love, wisdom, and all the other wonderful things. Sometimes they seem like another version of the inalienable right to the pursuit of happiness. People who feel genuine sadness are told that they are sick. Psychologists list sadness as one of the symptoms of clinical depression, and the latest wave of self-help books label depression—and by implication sadness—as one of the most common diseases of our time. Perhaps people just feel genuinely sad that their lives feel so empty, that the society they were born into is such a mess, and that they and others are suffering so much. People feel this kind of sadness for others, often without being aware of it. It is the sadness of knowing the world of the setting sun and its contrast with the possibilities of the Great Eastern Sun.

Once at an advanced Shambhala Training Program in New York I was asked to give the first talk in place of the Dorje Dradul, who had just recovered from a lengthy illness. I prepared as thoroughly as I could at short notice and I went in to see him to go over my notes just before leaving for the talk. After I read them to him, he said, "I think there is something missing—sadness." This hit me with a jolt. He seemed to be talking about much more than what I was going to say that night. He was talking about what was missing in our society altogether—a sense of genuine sadness, not anger, or righteousness, or despair, but sadness for our real plight and the horrifying danger human society is in. I have always remembered that moment.

An open heart realizes that the human heart *is* sad when it is genuine. Early American blues and Spanish flamenco—songs of love and separation of any time and place—reveal a sadness that is less an expression of depression or misery than of the depth of the human heart. In the best of these songs there is always something timeless and beyond the personal drama. It rings true to us, and we feel glad. The root of the word *sad* is the Latin *satis,* which is also the root of the word *satisfied*. So sadness is related to being completely full, completely satisfied. When I eat dinner with close friends—not at a "dinner party" but at a genuine feast of friendship—a sense of sadness often dawns as the evening wears on. It comes from the feeling of fullness and quiet joy that is present in the atmosphere, and because in being together in this way a hint of the inevitable parting is always present.

Sadness is often accompanied by tenderness, which in turn brings an open heart and genuineness—and this is profoundly joyful. Joy and sadness are inseparable. People cry at weddings or out of sheer joy when they are happy. We feel quiet, soft, tenderhearted joy when we are sad and thoroughly in touch with ourselves. Holding a newborn baby—whether it be human, animal, or even a tree sapling—brings joy at the new life blossoming but at the same time a certain inexplicable tender and sad heart. Sadness *is* joy, and joy *is* sadness, and if you try to avoid one, you will never experience the other. "Experiencing the upliftedness of the world is a joyous situation," the Dorje Dradul said. "But it also brings sadness. It is like falling in love. When you are in love, being with your lover is both delightful and very painful. You feel both joy and sorrow. That is not a problem; in fact it is wonderful. It is the ideal human emotion."

Joy lifts you "out of yourself" and off this earth toward heaven. Sadness makes you feel your presence on the earth, with all others who dwell on it. The path of Shambhala joins heaven and earth—joy and sadness—which in any case are inseparable. Joy-sadness is the genuine feeling of the human heart. Its tenderness is always there, beyond all the self-centered emotional upheavals that sway us this way and that. You discover the genuine heart when you journey through the world carrying the warrior's weapons of gentleness and fearlessness.

With Open Heart We Perceive
the Details of the World

With the genuine heart of sadness and joy, we see, hear, smell, taste, and touch the details of the world around us without being caught up in them, fascinated by them, or repelled by them. We discover that we are in a bright and rich world that perhaps we never quite saw before. D. H. Lawrence beautifully describes this plunge out of the cocoon into the world in his poem "Escape":

When we get out of the glass bottle of our ego,
and when we escape
like squirrels in the cage of our personality
and get into the forest again, we shall shiver
with cold and fright.
But things will happen to us
so that we don't know ourselves.
Cool, unlying life will rush in,
and passion will make our
bodies taut with power.
We shall laugh, and
institutions will curl up
like burnt paper.

The freshness is like stepping out into a cool but sunny day after having been cooped up in bed with the flu for a week; or like arriving by boat at a majestic Norwegian fjord in the early morning, the sun glinting on the mountaintops and reflecting off the deep blue water—after setting out the night before from the smoggy, polluted London docks. Going canoeing on the lake or walking in the mountains on a weekend, getting away from the noise and pollution of the city, or just walking in the park early in the morning before the traffic and bustle has begun reminds us of this wholesomeness and delight.

When we experience the world in its details, with open hearts, we feel ourselves to be immersed in a living, spacious world rather than in the static claustrophobic dead world of our fearful minds. We become artists in everyday life. As the Dorje Dradul said, "Artistic vision is having the clarity to fall in love with what you see." Each detail begins to have its own place and meaning. We may see a rock, lying on the path surrounded by ferns that have sprung up in the overnight rain, as a nuisance to be kicked out of the way, the ferns as weeds to be chopped down. Or we could appreciate the way each fern has grown so delicately around the rock, each having its place, the whole being gentle and harmonious.

When you look at a peony, you first see the whole flower, its color and shape. As you keep looking, you see the petals and veins and stamens and pistils. When you look more closely still, you see the segments and shading in the petals, until you begin to feel the vastness in those details. To see the vastness by looking at one thing in its details is to see its sacred connection to space and to all other things. A thing becomes illuminated because of the space in and around it. If you go to an old junk shop and find a valuable antique vase on a shelf surrounded closely by hundreds of other objects—in front, in back, and all around—you probably don't see it very clearly. But if you take that same vase upstairs and put it in a spacious room, on a pedestal, with special lighting, the sacredness of the vase becomes apparent. The space around it illuminates it, and you can experience its beauty.

When you see an object illuminated by space, when you see with your heart, the object actually communicates back to you. When you cherish something, it glows. It tells you where it belongs and how you should present it, because you see it so clearly. Then when you follow its magical instructions, you create a work of art. This is creativity, art in everyday life, the inspiration of the genuine heart of sadness and joy.

 ## Suggestions

1. Thoroughly Tasting Your Emotion

When an emotion arises, notice what happens in your state of mind. You can experience its energy directly if you pay particular attention to the intense and sharp feelings, catch moments where there is a shift or crack in the energy, see the spaciousness of the situation, remain steady and feel rather than manipulate the energy to fit your particular idea of it. At what stage do you give the emotional energy a name? Once you name it, see how you create an elaborate story line about how you feel, why you feel that way, who "made" you feel that way, and so on. Perhaps you feel sad because you're missing an ex-lover. The energy of sadness arises, and you quickly name it "loneliness." Then you start to analyze why you're lonely and why the person is gone. You think you still want to be with the person, which makes you feel even more forlorn. Then you feel the person rejected you, and you start to get resentful. Your mind takes off in all kinds of ways and escalates the situation until you're feeling thoroughly miserable and hopeless. Whether it is loneliness or another emotion, just notice the whole process as it arises, as you name it and as you create your story.

The point is not to try to intensify the emotion or otherwise manipulate it, but simply to be aware of it as it arises and as far as you can as it develops all the way through. You might choose to practice awareness of an emotion such as the "elation" you feel when you meet an old friend, rather than the loneliness of missing someone. I do not suggest that you try to dig up old, hurtful feelings or linger longer than usual on emotions that arise. Just apply awareness to whatever emotion arises and continue to be aware as it passes away. Making an effort to apply awareness in this way is itself an expression of your basic goodness. That effort may itself change your experience of the emotion so that you do not experience it with quite the habitual heaviness or grasping. Whatever does happen, touch it, feel it, and let it go.

2. Accepting Negative Emotions

At a time when you are feeling anger or depression or some other "down" emotion, try to notice any additional feelings of judgment that you put on top of the emotion. When you feel depressed, for example, do you feel bad about feeling this way, on top of the depression? Try instead to look at the emotion as an expression of your basic goodness and health. How might you react to the emotion differently if you did not judge it as "negative"? This additional layer of negativity is what the Dorje Dradul used to call "negative negativity," saying that "this secondary, commenting kind of intelligence of double negativity is very cautious and cowardly as well as frivolous and emotional. It inhibits identification with the energy and intelligence of basic negativity." Can you see the depression as pure energy and let yourself feel it wholeheartedly, without judgment? Without condemning yourself for feeling "depressed" and thereby making yourself feel even worse, can you find the genuine sadness in your depression? Can you look at your sadness fearlessly, without extra comment, be gentle toward it, and appreciate its wisdom?

3. Stepping Out of the Cocoon

Lie on the floor, and pull your body into a tight ball, with knees pulled up to your chest, arms clasped around them, head bent over your knees—the classic fetal posture. Close your eyes tight, and feel black space all around you. Keep your body tense. Feel the tension in your whole body, starting with your feet and working up through your head. Stay like that for a short while. Without opening your eyes, gradually relax, trusting that the world is good. Let yourself be born out of your cocoon. Slowly unfold into a sitting posture, still on the floor. Now abruptly open your eyes. Breathe out. Feel the fresh air on your raw skin, and feel the space. Look around you, at one thing at a time. Look closely— see space and light around what you are looking at. Take your time. Feel the goodness of what you see.

4. Radiating Loving-Kindness

The purpose of this practice, derived from the Buddhist tradition, is to develop the energy of *maitri,* or loving-kindness, and radiate it to others. (In this description I have borrowed from Mirko Fryba's *The Art of Happiness.*) It is best to do the practice after a period of sitting, while you are still on your cushion. Try it only after you have some familiarity with the basic mindfulness practice.

There are several steps to it.

1. First reflect on your understanding of the basic goodness of yourself and others—the universal, unconditioned basic goodness. Let your mind just rest in that openness for a moment.

2. Recall a situation in which you felt content, free from hostility, ill will, and stress—in which you felt well-being and happiness. Imagine this situation as vividly and clearly as you can. Recall where you were, the people involved, what you were doing, and so on. Take a few moments to establish the scene firmly in your mind. Now turn your attention to the physical sensation in your body as you recall that situation. Feel that sensation—its warmth, vibration, color, however you feel it. Now give it a name—"happiness," "well-being," "contentment"—whatever feels right to you.

Still paying attention to that feeling of bodily well-being, let the details of the remembered situation fade. Just stay with the overall mood and the feeling of well-being. As you stay with it, allow yourself to feel it intensely. Allow the feeling of well-being to increase, thinking, "May I be happy" or "May I experience well-being," or whatever name you have given the positive feeling that you generated.

3. Think of someone who is alive today with whom you have had a good relationship, toward whom you feel kindly and who has been kind to you. (It is better at first not to choose a lover or a parent. Begin with someone with whom you have a basically positive connection, whom you can quite easily wish well without getting caught up in strong emotions.) Hold the image of that person vividly in mind. Recall the feeling of happiness that you generated in Step 2. You may particularly experience this feeling as focused in the center of the chest—the "heart center." Feel that you are radiating that good feeling from your heart center to the person you are thinking about, thinking, "Just as I wish happiness for myself, may _____ be happy."

4. When you feel some familiarity with radiating *maitri* to people toward whom you feel positive, you can try radiating it to people to whom you feel neutral or with whom you have had negative encounters. Again, recall the image of that person, radiate well-being toward them, and think, "May _____ be happy," or "May _____ experience well-being" (or whatever). Don't force it—be gentle, and stop if you begin to feel that you are not being genuine.

5. The final step is to radiate *maitri* without a specific direction. Again, generate the feeling of happiness and well-being in yourself. Now let that feeling radiate out in front of you, behind you, to both sides of you, above and below you. Without losing the feeling of well-being in your own body, focused slightly in your heart center, just feel it extending out into the space all around you. As it radiates out, let it touch whatever beings it encounters, whether they be humans, animals, plants, or the earth itself. As you radiate well-being, think, "May all beings enjoy happiness."

Just as the sitting practice of mindfulness is practice toward developing mindfulness in daily life, so the sitting practice of developing *maitri* is practice toward developing *maitri* in daily life. When you have practiced *maitri* in sitting and feel some familiarity with it, you can begin to practice it in daily life as well. When you are with someone toward whom you feel kindly, and who has positive feelings toward you, quietly recall the feeling of well-being that you generated in your practice, and radiate that feeling to your friend. Move on to radiating *maitri* in more difficult situations when you feel ready.

CHAPTER 9
Letting Go

Trust

Feeling and opening your genuine heart of sadness is the key to letting go of your preconceptions and your interpretations of the world. By letting go, you leave your familiar and snug world behind, at least for a moment, and relax into the sacred and strange space of the real world. To do this, you need to have basic trust. Basic trust is not trusting *in* something but simply trusting. It is very much like breathing. You do not consciously hold on to your breath or trust in your breath, yet breathing is your very nature. When you breathe out, you trust that the next breath will come in—you don't think about it, or wonder about it, you trust. When you take a step, you trust that the earth will support you. When you eat, you trust that your stomach will digest the food. This is basic trust.

To be trusting is your basic goodness; trusting not only the basic functions of breathing, eating, and walking, but the sacredness of your whole world. Such trust grows as you step over the threshold of fear again and again and discover that the world beyond your fear is supporting you.

Your basic trust relaxes you and lets you *be*. It is simple, unremarkable, ordinary experience, but at the same time it is very powerful; it has a quality of fulfillment. Like the vast, profound, blue sky that is free from clouds yet accommodates everything, from the small white fluffy clouds of a summer's afternoon to the violent cumulus of a thunderstorm, you let yourself be with whatever you are feeling.

But trust can be even more basic. Even when your body is not working according to your idea of "health," you can still trust your fundamental well-being. Usually we don't experience this level of trust except in life-threatening situations, but it is a basic state of mind that is always there for us.

The story of the scientist Ivan Pavlov illustrates this level of basic trust. Early in the century, before the time of antibiotics, Pavlov was dying of a massive systemic infection. He lay in the hospital close to death, and the doctors could do nothing for him. He quietly asked his assistant to go to the riverbank where he used to play as a boy, fill a pail with warm mud, and bring it to him. The assistant discreetly brought the mud to Pavlov who spent a long time kneading the mud as he had done as a child. The fever broke, and he recovered. Pavlov trusted his intuition that he needed to play with the mud; he trusted his memory of being contented by the riverbank as a child; he trusted his body as he lay there kneading the mud, being with the mud. Simply put, Pavlov trusted his world.

Doctor and author Larry Dossey reports another story of basic trust. In July 1989 six men made a trek across Antarctica. One of the men, Keizo Funatsu, became separated from the others in a blinding snowstorm. His only chance for survival, he knew, was to bury himself in the snow and wait to be found. He had dug a pit and settled in. "Very few people have that kind of experience, lost in the blizzard," he later recounted. "I said to myself, 'Settle down, try and enjoy this.' In my snow ditch I truly felt Antarctica. With the snow and quiet covering me, I felt like I was in my mother's womb. I could hear my heart beat—boom, boom, boom—like a small baby's. My life seemed very small compared to nature, to Antarctica." The next morning Keizo heard his teammates calling his name, and he stood up, unhurt, joyfully shouting, "I am alive!"

Dossey comments, "Completely covered with snow, Keizo Funatsu had realized that to do *anything* would have meant almost certain death. He had simply to be, not do. . . . There is an aspect of experiences such as [this] that runs counter to the modern belief that real change requires robust effort. . . . [It] was an attitude of watching, waiting, silence, and emptiness—ways of being, not doing."

Many people who experience sudden breakthroughs in health, Dossey continues, "frequently speak of an inner attitude of accepting the universe on its own terms—not dictating what ought or should happen—in spite of the dreadful circumstances they are enduring at the time. . . . This is not a self-effacing, passive, giving-up stance; it is one of attunement and alignment with what they perceive to be the inherent rightness of all that is."

Your moods—elation, depression, boredom, whatever—are all trustworthy. You don't need to regard some as healthy and good and others as bad and unworthy. Depression, or a dull, numb state of mind, is just as trustworthy as elation. It is hard to trust our moods because we so rarely allow ourselves to experience them fully. Usually when we are happy, we want it never to end and we are simultaneously afraid of losing it. So we try to hold on to our happiness, which keeps us from experiencing it fully. When we are bored, we usually try to entertain ourselves because boredom is empty and threatening. When we are depressed, we don't accept that it may be an intelligent response to the situation at hand, but instead consider it unpleasant, something to get out of. These moods tend to become threatening because we *perceive* them as threatening. If we try to deny or get rid of a mood, it only becomes stronger. But if we allow it to *be,* by realizing that the mood *is* trustworthy, then we truly make friends with it. We can allow ourselves actually to feel fully. We don't need to check constantly on whether we are feeling the right thing or not.

Constantly checking up on yourself implies that you have a lack of trust in your genuine being. It cuts you off from the world. To develop basic trust, you have to give up wondering how far you have come and how far you can go. It means giving up measuring yourself against your own expectations or others' achievements. It means giving up assessing yourself against any standard at all, even your own.

To trust is to be free from the doubt of "being in two minds" about something. Fundamentally you *are* of only one mind, so you *can* be fundamentally free from doubt. Basic trust is unconditional—there is no polarizing *distrust.* When you trust, you drop the good-versus-bad, perfect-versus-imperfect tug-of-war that conditions your view of yourself and the world. You don't look to a belief system for confirmation or condemnation. You trust whatever occurs at any given moment, because you have discovered that you yourself are profoundly trustworthy. A well-known and much loved Zen text, called "On Trust in the Heart," begins:

> *The perfect way is only difficult for those who pick and choose;*
> *Do not like, do not dislike; all will then be clear.*
> *Make a hairbreadth difference, and Heaven and Earth are set apart;*
> *If you want the truth to stand clear before you, never be for or against.*
> *The struggle between "for" and "against" is the mind's worst disease.*

When we trust profoundly, we relax our iron grip on ourselves and our own viewpoint. We see other sides of issues. We see conflicts and successes from other people's point of view as well as our own, and we see our own lives within the larger scope of society. In turn, we see our society within the context of the global community, and we feel the place of humans on earth in the context of all of life and of the life of earth itself.

This change of viewpoint is very similar to the experience that many astronauts have reported. Soaring way above, they see the whole planet Earth, alone and fragile. They see the continents, the major mountain ranges, the oceans and weather patterns. They see no lines or colored patches delineating nations, as appear on globes and maps. Rather, they report a profound sense of the unity of life on earth and of their interconnectedness with all beings on the earth. For many astronauts, this new vision has transformed their lives.

''First Thought'' Is Best Thought

When we trust, we can perceive with a genuine open heart, whatever occurs *at that very moment that it occurs,* fresh and unstained by the clouds of hope and fear. The Dorje Dradul used the phrase "first thought, best thought" to highlight that *first moment of fresh perception,* before the clouds of judgment and personal interpretation take over. "First thought" is "best" because it is not yet covered over by all our opinions and interpretations, our hopes and fears, our likes and dislikes. It is *direct perception of the world as it is.*

The moment of first thought has also been called *nowness,* because it occurs only right now. You cannot hold on to first thought—you can only touch it and let it go, again and again. The only time you can do it is *now,* and *now,* and again *now.* You have to do it, and do it, and do it. You can discover "first thought, best thought" by relaxing into the present moment in a very simple way. Perhaps you are sitting in an airport looking down from a balcony onto the crowds milling around below. Suddenly your inner chatter stops. You are right there for a *moment,* and you actually see and hear. You see the pattern of motion; you hear the hubbub of voices and machines; you have a sense of timelessness and completeness: "first thought, best thought."

You may also discover this moment when you are suddenly shocked. Perhaps you have had the experience of slipping on ice. Without any thought, your whole body and mind become unified to prevent a fall. At that moment you feel completely alive and present. Afterward, you may get a sudden rush of adrenaline and say, "Whew, that was close," but the energy and wakefulness linger for a while.

Although we call it "first *thought,*" it is not necessarily a thought that comes in words. It is the very first inspiration, however it expresses itself to us. It may be just "aah!"—a sharp gasp as we come around the bend on a mountaintop and see the valley laid out below. Then, of course, we may start thinking second and third thoughts, such as, "Oh my, isn't that beautiful," or "How stupid that I didn't bring my camera."

The same is true for experiences that are not so beautiful, as Shambhala student Julie discovered. "I was speeding down the highway, and my mind was several miles ahead, thinking of my little boy, who would be wondering why Mommy was late picking him up at school. Suddenly, on the side of the road I saw a car that had been sliced in two by a lamppost. A woman was lying on the ground beside the car. I couldn't tell whether she was alive or dead. She was surrounded by firemen and curious onlookers. All my thoughts of being late and what my child would think of my being late and how fast I must drive and how much traffic there was melted into a pure blankness in the horror of seeing such an accident. Although I did not dwell on the vision, for some time afterward my perception was extremely clear and sharp."

"First thought" is a translation of the Sanskrit term *pramana,* an important term both in the Buddhist psychology of perception and in the Shambhala teachings. *Pra* translates as "highest," "best," or "first"; and *mana* means "mind." A flash of direct perception of color or sound, according to masters of the practice of mindfulness, is immediately (within a sixtieth of a second or so) followed by a mental recognition of that direct perception. *Pramana* refers to that very first moment when the mind recognizes the direct perception. That thought is a direct response to the perception; it is pure and accurate and unadorned by interpretation. Therefore, it is the best thought. Afterward it is elaborated in a proliferation of conceptualizations and interpretations, again very quickly, carrying consciousness further and further away from that initial direct perception. Normally, in the cocoon, we live in our interpretations, completely out of touch with our perceptions.

We do not have to be advanced practitioners of mindfulness to see the interpretive process at work. It is happening constantly. All we have to do is pay attention mindfully to how our inner chatter responds to everything we see, hear, smell, taste, and touch and how it interprets the world to fit its version. When we let go of those interpretations, we experience first thought and perceive the world directly, without the filter of language. First thought is the fresh open state of mind that Zen teacher Suzuki Roshi calls "beginner's mind."

The first moment of awakening in the morning can be an opportunity to notice "first thought" because the mind is not yet caught up in the daily routine. We rarely catch the actual moment when we awaken from sleep, but sometimes you may experience a kind of blank in which you don't even remember where you are or who you are. This moment might be frightening or joyful, but you will have a vivid perception of the room around you, a moment of first thought. Second thoughts quickly follow: You feel "I," you think "Who am I? What am I?" and suddenly—there you are. Your name comes to mind, your profession, family, debts, and so on.

I have particularly had moments of fresh perception while taking photographs. A photograph can capture the vivid first moment of experiencing something, just as it is, but first you, the photographer, must open your mind and see: the afternoon sun glancing off a bright yellow-green moss-covered rock in the middle of a clearing in the pine forest; a long horizontal bulbous cloud, dark with rain, yet brilliantly lit underneath by the evening sun; white mist over the bay, through which the faint outline of an island, a boat, and a lone seagull suggest something out of nothing; a pile of steaming brown cow dung surrounded by yellow dandelions. In order to capture these moments, you look through the viewfinder not only at the objects themselves but at the light shining around and within them. Afterward, when you put the camera down and look at the ordinary world, it suddenly seems bright and vibrant too.

When you take a photograph, just before you click the shutter your mind is empty and open, seeing without words. When you stand in front of a blank sheet of paper, about to make a painting or do calligraphy, you have no idea what you will produce. Maybe you have some plan for the painting or you know what symbol you want to calligraph, but you don't know what will appear when you actually put brush to paper. What you do out of trust in open mind will be fresh and spontaneous. Opening to first thought is the way to begin any action properly.

The same process happens, very fast, at every moment of our lives. Whether we are artists or not, we can experience any moment as first thought. We have to touch first thought again and again. Practice of warriorship does not promise that you will reach an ultimate point where you don't have to pay attention anymore. At the moment when you are about to make *any* gesture, before you actually do it, you can trust and open to "first thought, best thought." When you are about to drink a glass of water, do you just reach for it and grab it and swallow it down? Can you practice a moment of first thought, clear perception, as you reach for the glass; and again as you touch it; and again as you lift it; again as you move it toward your lips; and again as you taste the water on your tongue? When someone speaks sharply to you, do you immediately fire back, or can you touch a moment of first thought before you respond? Likewise, when you go about your daily business, make coffee, go to work, use the copier, attend a meeting, walk down the street, eat dinner, have an argument with your partner or make love, if you would open to first thought, each of these occurrences in your life *could* be fresh and direct. Too often we ignore first thought—we think it is too silly or outrageous. We have to be daring to catch first thought and follow it. First thought can guide our lives when we trust.

First thought is sometimes called "sudden glimpse." To have a "sudden glimpse" means, on the path of warriorship, to catch a glimpse of fundamental basic goodness, our true nature, the awakened state of mind. Awakening to our genuineness is not getting into some continuous state of "wisdom" or "joy," where we feel good and don't have to exert effort anymore. Rather, waking up is making continual effort to catch first thought, again and again glimpsing who we genuinely are. It is like trying to catch sight of a comet in the night sky—you can see it only with your peripheral vision. If you try to focus with your normal way of looking, you lose sight of it again. If you think you have caught first thought, you have already lost it—that is why you can have only a sudden glimpse of it.

The practice of the warrior is to touch first thought in a sudden glimpse again and again, acknowledge how quickly it passes into second thoughts— then let go of second thoughts and again touch first thought. As the Dorje Dradul used to say, "It's manual labor." There is no shortcut, or quick fix, for the warrior. If you keep practicing in this way, gradually you will become more accustomed to first thought. You will recognize it more easily. Like the memory of someone you love who has departed, first thought will be present as soon as you remember it, and the flavor of it will rub off onto your life.

Ugyen Tulku Rinpoche describes the practice of sudden glimpse this way:

The only way to really acquire all the great qualities of enlightenment is to repeat many times the short moment of recognizing mind essence. There is no other method. One reason for short moments is that because there is not stability right now, the recognition of awareness doesn't last for more than a brief moment, whether we like it or not. By practicing many times, one gets used to it. It is not that one is doing something conceptual like meditating on an object or keeping a thing in mind. We simply need to recognize naked awareness, to allow for a moment of the awakened state of mind. It is not like we have to create something.

This poem celebrates first thought:

First thought provokes laughter
Because it is so shocking
And maybe embarrassing
First thought grips you in its teeth
   and won't let go
until you scream second thought
First thought is clear
Trust the clarity
no second thought
CUT
STOP

First thought is always outrageous
You want to disown it
"Did that come from me?"
"I didn't do it."
But second thought says "You did.
Maybe they'll lock you up"

But maybe first thought is not so outrageous
Then you feel like a genius
Maybe you'll get an award
"I am so good
I captured first thought."

Real first thought is the thunderbolt on the head
The iron clap of the dralas' power
If you listen to the silence you can hear it
   loud and clear
But not with the ears

First thought is the baby
the first tiny connection
you can make with your world
that is baby first thought
before we get to the bigger ones
A "glimpse" we call it
But that's too silly—
We can call it love

First thought is the only thought
It is the rain in the rainforest
It is the sky in the universe
It is the heart in the outrageous love you
*   can't even admit to yourself.*

Letting Go of Second Thoughts

The key to capturing first thought is letting go. Letting go includes letting go of memories of past successes and failures, old wounds, and beliefs about the world. It is not easy to do. Our habit is to hold on to what we think we know. It takes practice and bravery to step forward openly into this moment, this new situation, without relying on memory and all the rest of the baggage, especially if we feel resentful or hurt. If we are remembering the past, we are reacting to it, living in it; we are not living in the present, *now*.

We try all kinds of ways to hold on forever to the significant moments of our lives. We take photographs, we write journals, we go over the moment again and again to fix it in our memory. Sometimes it seems as if the memory is more important than the moment itself, just because it does seem more fixed. We can remember and relive the memory in our minds over again, whenever we wish, although usually the freshness has gone. What made that moment so special has gone and we can't get it back.

Anthony tells a funny but poignant story about refusing to let go:

Last night was a Saturday night and, being a nonwork night, I stayed up rather late. I forgot to reset my alarm clock and the damn thing went off as if it were a working morning. I woke up out of a deep sleep and blindly thrust out to turn the alarm off. It was one of those "twilight zone" experiences. I'm sure you've had the experience of suddenly waking up and not knowing where you are, what day of the week it is, what you have to do this day, and so on.

What was really interesting for me is that a few days earlier, I had had a good fight with my wife. One of the ways I react to being hurt is to go into my "silent treatment" behavior, which I suppose is a type of passive-aggressive approach. Well, when I got up so suddenly, I actually found myself trying to remember, along with the above-mentioned things, if this was a day I still had to maintain my silent treatment. What a riot! This struck me right between the eyes in terms of "letting go."

A warrior must be willing to let go of even his beliefs and insights, no matter how profound they are. Otherwise, these preconceptions become traps, and we will find ourselves living in concept, caught in the webs of logic and reasonableness that we have spun. We created the idea of a good life—now we have to live it, but maybe it is not so good. We thought we had managed to avoid discomfort, but maybe we have not. Some of us may live a fairly easy life until we die; others may be confronted constantly with terrible challenges and horrors. Yet we all *are* confronted with challenges if we open our eyes and see them. The more willing we are to let go, the more challenges come to us that put us on the spot. Each moment of our lives is a moment of letting go, letting some part of us die, so that the next moment can be born afresh. We all are confronted with a challenge at the moment of physical death, and at that time our philosophies are of no use to us at all; they count for nothing at that unique moment of nowness.

Someone I knew had been a Buddhist practitioner for many years. She had received all the empowerments to do the advanced practices. Then she discovered she had a brain tumor. As she came closer and closer to death, she became more and more grasping, unwilling to let go of her life peacefully. Her anxiety focused on which practice she should be doing and how to "die properly as a Buddhist." Her Buddhist philosophy seemed to have become a millstone rather than a guide and she died without letting go of this burden. In the Buddhist tradition, this kind of attachment is called the "golden chain," when religious beliefs become yet another thing to grasp and cling to. Any spiritual or psychological teaching or therapy, including the Shambhala teachings, can become a golden chain.

Letting Go

As Seng-ts'an says in "On Trust in the Heart":

Clinging to this or to that beyond measure
The heart trusts to bypaths that lead it astray.
Let things take their own course; know that the Essence
Will neither go nor stay;
Let your nature blend with the Way and wander in it free from care.

A leaf falls and floats gently to the ground, twisting and turning as it falls, catching the sunlight. It falls and falls, slowly turning, finally coming to rest on a patch of moist green moss crossed by sun and shadow. If we watch that leaf with a sad, gentle heart, we may feel profoundly connected to it. It is in itself neither beautiful nor ugly, and it does not belong to us. It is just a leaf falling. We can see it falling and we can appreciate it, but we can't possess it or our experience of it. This is true of everything in life. Our children grow up from bouncing playful toddlers to intensely loving and hating adolescents, but we can never possess them, no matter how much we love them and want to think of them as "our children." When we do not try to possess our children, we can delight in them as they grow into being who they are.

We have to let go. There really is nothing else we can do, not because of any moral law, not because the teachings of Shambhala or any other teaching or therapy says so, but simply because the past has already gone, and if we cling to what has gone, we cannot be fully with what is here now. If we cling to the beauty or joy or horror of the past, then we cannot feel the beauty and joy and horror of the present moment.

In sitting practice, we begin to let go when we practice letting go of our thoughts and our heavy emotional patterns. We let go of a little bit of this and a little bit of that, and each time, we feel relieved and unburdened for a moment. But letting go must go deeper than this. We have to let go of trying to possess the world altogether, of trying, in a sense, to possess our own lives.

In the current economy, or in any economy, we don't possess our own security; we may be unemployed, all our savings running out. We do not know how long our health will last, however healthy we feel at the present. We like to think that we have control over our lives, and that we have important choices to make, and in some ways we do. But in the context of a larger vision, we do not have such definite control and the choices we make may not be the ones that really determine how our life goes. When we let go of all these hopes and anxieties, we are left naked. We respond to whatever situation we are in from our tender and vulnerable heart, not from the hard knot of certainty.

In his poem "Thursday," William Carlos Williams expresses the sense of letting go:

> I have had my dream—like others—
> and it has come to nothing, so that
> I remain now, carelessly
> with feet planted on the ground
> and look up at the sky—
> feeling my clothes about me,
> the weight of my body in my shoes,
> the rim of my hat, air passing in and out
> at my nose—and decide to dream no more.

We do not know the depth and breadth of our world and we cannot know all the answers, or even all the questions. When we open our minds beyond our cultural myths and theories, we realize that the universe is mysterious; we have no idea what is really true. We can only trust our basic intelligence and the sacredness of the world. This can bring a sense of great joy and relief—we don't have to pretend to know all the answers anymore. We feel the boundary of our familiar world, and we do not fear that which is outside of it—that which is strange to us. The sense of strangeness may make our hair stand on end, as when we hear a strange sound while alone at night. Yet that is the truth about life—it is quite strange, though it can be cheerful.

The strange but real world is trustworthy because it is always present and, so long as we are genuine, it always responds to us. As long as we do not interpret that response in terms of success or failure, it always gives us a way to go forward. Instead of working so hard to get everything in your life just right, you can profoundly trust and let go. When you learn to let go further, you can let the intelligence of basic goodness determine the course of your life, as it does in any case. It brings great relief and joy to be able to let go in this way. In a videotape telling about her walkabout with the Australian Aboriginals, Marlo Morgan says that each morning they would wake up at dawn and dance and sing with delight and humor, like young children. Even when there was no food or water to be seen for miles around, at least as far as Morgan could tell, they would sing, "Oh what a wonderful day it is today, what shall we do," as if they had never seen the sun rise before and had not a care in the world. Because they were able to let go, they had an intimate love for every plant and small insect that lived in that desert and an intimate relationship with the dralas of the land. They never went without food and water, and when they found enough for the day, they would spend the rest of the day playing together, having ceremonies, and celebrating the beautiful sacred world they loved so much.

The Joyful Snow Lion

The image of the warrior who has leaped out of the cocoon, trusting and letting go, is a snow lion. In Tibet, snow lions are traditional symbols of creatures who manifest delight in the world, who pounce and leap around from mountaintop to mountaintop. They are fun-loving, inquisitive, and awake. They see everything and are always cheerful because they have no doubt or obstacles. They symbolize disciplined energy because they always enjoy leaping from peak to peak, much as the warrior enjoys leaping from first thought to first thought. They have basic trust in their capability because their minds and bodies are always in harmony. Snow lions have the meekness of the tiger but without any self-consciousness. They symbolize action—mindfulness in action. Like snow lions, warriors who have had the bravery and willingness to become genuine enjoy their lives and their world, enjoy their challenges, and welcome the fear of difficult situations. They take delight in facing difficulties head-on and seeing what happens.

Old doubts may attack you, in the form of second, third, and endless thoughts, and they may try to pull you back to the more familiar, stale world. The playfulness of the snow lion is really more seductive and leads you to look more inquisitively at the world—to go out into it rather than spending energy to ward it off. As you go into the world, it suddenly shows its true self—its basic goodness. When you look at someone with appreciation and admiration, suddenly they manifest that. It's the same with the world.

We can be like the white snow lion, leaping around the peaks and boulders of the highlands, its body taut with power. We can feel invigorated and joyful because we know we can never again fall back into total depression and go to sleep like the setting sun. We know how to free ourselves from second thoughts. We are care*free,* but not care*less.* Our basic discipline of mindfulness is continuous, and our minds are beginning to open. We can see larger vistas of the world. We can be energetic and care for people. We can leap into the brilliant and rarefied space of the sacred world. Then the real magic happens: Because you appreciate the world, it appreciates you.

Letting go is relaxing and appreciating the ordinary but magical world we live in. Unless it is based on cultivating gentleness and fearlessness and on having the discipline of mindfulness and awareness, however, letting go can be sloppy and aggressive. The Dorje Dradul comments:

> Letting go is more than just relaxation. It is relaxation based on being in tune with the environment, the world. . . . For example, a professional race driver in an auto race can drive at two hundred miles an hour on the race track because of his training. He knows the limits of the engine and the steering and the tires; he knows the weight of the car, the road conditions, and the weather conditions. So he can drive fast without it becoming suicidal. Instead it becomes a dance. . . . For the warrior, every moment is a challenge to be genuine, and each challenge is delightful. When you let go properly, you can relax and enjoy the challenge. . . . Letting go is not based on getting away from the constraints of ordinary life. It is quite the opposite. It is going further into your life, because you understand that your life, as it is, contains the means to unconditionally cheer you up and cure you of depression and doubt.

Let go of even the *idea* of letting go—that is the point. Trusting your world is the key. If you *try* to let go, you'll get stuck in the Chinese finger puzzle: Your fingers get trapped, and the more you try to free them, the more stuck they get. You can only let go, and then your fingers will slide out. This is the catch-22 of letting go: You can't let go if you try, and you can't let go if you don't try. The only solution is to take a chance and jump off the cliff. Your parachute is your trust in basic goodness. If you don't trust, you won't jump in the first place. You can't let go unless you trust that you'll be caught on the way down. That's why you have to be brave. You have to be a warrior.

As a warrior, you can be brave like the astronauts, who attach themselves to their space-ground by little cords and float out into the dark and limitless void, with no "real" ground below to catch them. They escape their terror by doing their work completely with one thought, on the spot. Their bravery comes from first thought, letting go of second thoughts, and then paying attention to detail. They find their ground in first thought. If they lose this awareness, they have no more thought.

Letting Go

People look for intensity in danger: racing cars, rock-face climbing, bungee-jumping. They try to intensify their experience and hope for the best. When your life is on the line, you feel real and alive. But you don't have to be quite so dramatic to be a Shambhala warrior. You can put your life on the line at every moment in the ordinary world, without creating theatrics, by letting go of your self-made interpretations. When your energy is free to dance and play, it can create real drama. The best actors in the world are gentle and soft—they don't try to crank something up but let the energy through.

Letting go is by no means the same as repressing or trying to "get rid" of painful emotions, like the false idea of "detachment," in which you become distant and unfeeling. On the contrary, you let go of the *barriers* to feeling. You go *into* your feelings, with gentleness and fearlessness, rather than becoming more detached from them. You let go of the crusts of habitual responses that cover the heart's deeper feeling of tender sadness and genuine caring. When my daughter was fifteen, like many teenagers she went through a period of anger and pulling away from her family. Things got more and more tense for several months. Whenever I asked her what was going on with her she would say, "Dad, trust me, *please*. I *need* to do this."

The only way to keep in touch with her was to practice letting go. Over and over again, I had to let go of my anger and fear so that I could see her as she was. I had to let go of thinking of her as my little girl and thinking that I had to keep track of her every move. I did, in fact, trust her. I felt glad that she had the daring to branch out and experience a larger world, and trusted that she would come through it strengthened. I became extremely angry at times, however. Beneath the anger I could feel sadness that our relationship was changing irrevocably as well as joy that she *was* growing up. Though she was going through such a difficult time, she *was* handling it with grace. Nevertheless, the anger and fear would rise up again and again along with vague images of her getting into some unknown, terrible trouble. Again and again I would have to practice letting go of these images and respond to what was actually happening.

To let go of our uptightness and self-centeredness, our righteous anger, our feeling of being victims, our phony optimism, or whatever our habitual second thoughts may be, far from trying to be detached from them, we have to *feel* these things, touch them, hold them. *Then* we can let them go.

Letting go takes energy—you can't be mushy and sweet about it. It is fearless warriorship as well as gentle warriorship. To practice letting go, you have to *capture the moment of holding on*—holding on to your past, your depression, your passion, whatever—holding on to your cocoon. The moment that you realize you are holding, first stay with it, continue to hold, and acknowledge that you are holding. Hold, and then you can let go. Surrender—give it up, give it all up. Hold, intensify that state of mind, let go, and relax. That is the precise action of the warrior.

The warrior's practice that we have been describing in the previous chapters is about *letting go* all the way through: letting go of the cocoon and opening up to energy and space. Before we go on, it might be helpful to summarize briefly the journey we have mapped out so far. First, we looked directly and honestly at the cocoon, feeling its hardness and brittleness, and feeling how it cuts us off from our own living energy and the living energy of the larger world. The basic nature of the cocoon *is* clamping down, closing up, trying to feel small and hard—all this out of fear of energy and space. The cocoon *is* a hard knot of space and energy frozen in our muscles, frozen in our feelings, and frozen in our thoughts. The only way to break out of that frozen space is to see it, to feel the intense energy of fear that makes it up, to use that energy to leap into the fear, and to ride the energy as fearlessness.

At each stage of the journey, we let go of another hard layer of the cocoon and open further. As awareness develops, we begin to feel the space of our environment and the raw energy of our emotions. As we let go of labeling and trying to control our emotional energy, we uncover the deeper feelings of joy and sadness of our hearts. When we let ourselves feel our hearts and discover our basic trust, we have the possibility of letting go into first thought and nowness. We are able to relax into a vaster sense of space and to feel greater energy swirling through our being without needing to suppress it, control it, or spew it out all over the place. We are able to contain the energy in the large space of our mind-heart. We are ready to go a step further—to rouse ourselves to meet the energy of the world all around us and to attract that energy to us so that we can help others.

 ## Suggestions

1. *Trusting the Sky and the Earth*
Go out to your garden, or to a park or a field. Lie down on the earth, on your back, legs slightly apart, arms straight out from the shoulders, palms up. Relax your body step by step, from the top of your head down to your feet. Feel

yourself dissolving into the earth. Feel the earth supporting you and sustaining you. Now stand up. Stand firmly on the bare earth, with your feet spread apart—about the width of your shoulders—arms relaxed by your side, as if you were a solid oak tree. Imagine you are putting roots deep down into the earth. Let your body relax profoundly. Feel the solidness and reliability of the earth. Let it support your weight and carry you. Now feel the sky above you. Feel the openness and spaciousness of the sky. Feel the energetic, living quality of the space above and around you. As you stand there, feel the strength of your head and shoulders, as if you were reaching up from the earth to the sky. Feel your body joining the sky and the earth, like that solid oak tree.

2. Discovering Perceptions and Interpretations

Sit in a public place, like a café or a waiting room. Remember your mindfulness and awareness practice. Let yourself slow down, and look around with open eyes and ears. Pay attention to details in the environment—colors, shapes, objects, people. What is the first detail that catches your eye in each person you see? The tattered red jacket on that young man, with an eagle imprinted on the left shoulder? The whimsical expression in the right eye of the elderly woman drinking coffee? Notice how quickly you have a feeling about the first detail: "That jacket is dirty and ugly." "What's wrong with her eye?" Notice the vivid detail and your interpretations, but do not judge either of them.

Next notice everything around you of a particular color—blue or red or the color of your choice. Do you just see the color as color, or do you label it immediately with your second thought: blue—it's a hat; blue—of the sky; bluebird. Try to see just color, without naming the thing.

Now walk down a street, observing everything on the street as much as you can. See if you can just see without naming each thing you see. Notice how your thoughts take off from a simple observation and immediately start a whole interpretation and story line about it. See if you notice the momentary gap between what you see and what you think—your interpretation of the simple perception.

3. Playing with "First Thought"

Place a blank white sheet of paper on a table in front of you. Let your mind settle by practicing mindfulness of breathing for a while. Hold a Magic Marker a foot or so above the paper. (A jumbo marker would be good.) Relax your mind so that you're looking at the blank sheet of paper and your thoughts are quiet. You are going to make one dot on that sheet of paper with your marker, but you don't know exactly when and you won't try to control it. Sit there with your arm poised, marker pointing down, ready. Wait. Suddenly—your arm goes down, and the dot is made. Notice the moment the mark appears: "first thought, best thought."

4. Practicing Letting Go

Hold both of your arms out in front of you, relaxed, bent at the elbow, your hands open and palms up. Clench your fists tight. Gently open your fingers until your hands are completely open again, as if you were offering a small gift to someone or letting a butterfly fly away.

Now clench your fists again. This time, clench them as tight as you can. Feel the muscles in your arms and shoulders getting tight. *Quickly* relax your grip, and open your hands completely.

Do this again, and clench even tighter. Think, "Tighter, tighter, tighter," for thirty seconds. Now suddenly open your hands; think, "Let go." As you let go, you might let out a little sigh or a soft "ahh."

Do this again. This time, notice your state of mind as you clench tighter and let go.

If an emotion arises that comes from your cocoon, such as jealousy or resentment, imagine that you are holding the emotion in your clenched fist. Hold, tighten, let go.

Finally, imagine that you are holding in your hand your most valued and precious possession. Hold, tighten, let go. Now hold on to your most dearly held belief—hold, hold tighter, let go.

5. Letting Go of Dark Feelings

Recall a situation that you recently experienced that made you feel fearful, tight, and claustrophobic—that evoked dark feelings. Imagine the situation as if it were in front of you now, on a movie screen or in a bubble of light. (You can imagine that the bubble is a soap bubble and that the situation you are contemplating is projected into it like a holograph, if this helps.) Examine the scene clearly in full color. See all the people taking part in it, hear what they are saying, feel what you felt in that situation. Let yourself relax with gentleness toward the situation.

When you have established the scene and recalled your feeling for it clearly, pop the bubble of light so that it shatters into many tiny pieces of colored light. You are not harming any of the people in that situation, just popping the situation itself. Let all the pieces of the scene go free, along with your heavy dark feeling about it. Enjoy the dance of energy and color that it creates. Notice the contrast between the darkness and heaviness of the original scene and the joyfulness of the dancing flashes of light. It might even make you laugh.

6. Sending and Taking

This exercise is an extension of the exercise on developing *maitri* in Chapter 8. It is based on the Buddhist practice called "sending and taking." In it, we send well-being to others and we accept their pain into ourselves, using the breath as a vehicle. While doing the *maitri* exercise, you may have found that as you radiated kindness to others, you began to think of all the pain in the world—the suffering of others in less fortunate lands, or the suffering of a friend that is sick. This exercise will help you to work with the sadness of realizing others' pain. Usually we try to keep pain away from us, so that we might remain happy ourselves. This practice is based on the fundamental fact that we are interconnected with each other and cannot separate ourselves off from the pain and troubles and stresses of others.

The exercise is very simple: Having practiced the development of *maitri* for a while, you can radiate *maitri* on the out-breath.

On the in-breath, open yourself to admit the pain and sadness of the world. Allow into your being the suffering, anxiety, stress, and darkness of all those trapped in the setting-sun world. Let yourself feel the sadness of all this. After your breath comes in, simply let go of that suffering. Transfer your attention to your feeling of well-being. On the out-breath, breathe out basic goodness, well-being, health, and benevolence from your heart to others and the environment.

This practice is a recognition that you really are not separate from others, that the pain of others is your pain, that you cannot generate well-being in yourself unless you are willing also to work with the pain of others. You cannot truly isolate yourself and pretend that the sadness of the world does not affect you. So you allow the sadness of others to come into your being without putting up barriers, just as your breath naturally comes in if you do not try to stop it. In exchange, you give away well-being.

This practice can be difficult—you might experience a great deal of resistance to letting in pain. It might make you feel quite claustrophobic. However, you do not get stuck on your sadness, because it is just for one breath. Then on the out-breath, you relax and breathe out goodness again. Likewise, you cannot get stuck on your joy, because on the in-breath, you allow sadness into your heart again. This is a good practice to help you realize the inseparability of sadness and joy, since your in-breath and out-breath are really all part of one breath, which is part of the atmosphere that we all share. It is better, though, not to try the practice until you feel some relaxation and familiarity with basic mindfulness practice and the practice of radiating *maitri*.

This practice is effective and quite magical in helping you to let go of your self-centeredness and open your heart to sadness and joy and to actually care for others. It is quite different from the exercise, sometimes suggested in self-help books, of drawing in goodness from your environment and giving out your pain and bad feeling. As the Dorje Dradul said to a group of Shambhala students, "Give your sanity to the world; keep your neurosis to yourselves."

CHAPTER 10

Raising the Energy of Windhorse

Through the practice of Shambhala warriorship, you can learn to arouse and attract positive energy and radiate that energy to others. Through your practice of awareness, and through your sad and tender heart, you experience sounds, sights, and energies to which you were insensitive before, and a more direct connection with others and with the environment. With this kind of relaxation and openness, it is possible to tune in to the living reservoir of energy that exists all around you and within you, all the time. In the Shambhala teachings, this living energy is called *windhorse,* and it is the manifestation of basic goodness. It is powerful and dignified like a horse; forceful, swift, and unpredictable like the wind. When you step out of the cocoon, you can ride on this energy; if you feel hopelessly stuck in your cocoon, connecting with windhorse can help lift you out.

Wind represents the brilliant living energy all around us and within us. It has a meaning very close to the Chinese term *chi.* According to *The Encyclopedia of Eastern Philosophy and Religion, chi* literally means "air, vapor, breath, ether, energy." It is also "a central concept in Taoism and Chinese medicine. In the Taoist view, *chi* is the vital energy, the life force, the cosmic spirit that pervades and enlivens all things and is therefore synonymous with primordial energy." The use of the term "wind" to symbolize universal living energy is common to many peoples throughout the world. It suggests forces that normally can be observed only by their effects.

The Navajo believe that every visible object in the world has an invisible aspect that is called "Holy People." There are Mountain People, Star People, River People, Rain People, Corn People, and so on. These Holy People are symbols for the consciousness within all things, which Navajo call the "Holy Wind" (nilch'i). In humans this invisible aspect is called "the Wind within one" (nilch'i hwii'siziini). According to the Navajo, these "Holy Winds" are not at all distinct; all are really part of One Wind and the living energy of Wind flows in and out of even the most apparently solid objects.

The *horse* represents the fact that humans can ride on the energy of wind. It is not merely an abstract philosophical idea or sentimental religious belief but can be an actual experience available to all of us. The grace and power of the horse gave early peoples the ability to travel great distances—it was as close as humans came to flying, before the airplane. The horse is often a sacred symbol representing, according to the Dorje Dradul, "any wild dreams that human beings might have of capturing a wild animal. If any human beings would like to capture the wind, a cloud, the sky, if anybody would like to ride on mountains or dance with waterfalls—all of those are incorporated in the symbol of the horse."

Describing *windhorse,* the Dorje Dradul says,

Raising windhorse [is] raising a wind of delight and power and riding on, or conquering, that energy. Such wind can come with great force, like a typhoon that can blow down trees and buildings and create huge waves in the water. The personal experience of this wind comes as a feeling of being completely and powerfully in the present. The *horse* aspect is that, in spite of the power of this great wind, you also feel stability. You are never swayed by excitement or depression. You can ride on the energy of your life. So windhorse is not purely movement and speed, but it includes practicality and discrimination, a natural sense of skill.

The energy of windhorse is recognized universally, even when it is not called by that name. A connection with windhorse is the basis of charisma. Many cultures speak of this energy. In Arabic, for example, it is known as *baraka,* "a kind of charisma or spiritual electricity, because it is a kind of power that seems to energize those who receive it, even when they return to secular lives and mundane tasks."

Mihaly Csikszentmihalyi, former chairman of the department of psychology at the University of Chicago, has spent a lifetime studying experiences of windhorse, although he calls such moments "optimal experiences" or experiences of "flow." In these experiences, people report, their lives seem, at least momentarily, fulfilled. Csikszentmihalyi interviewed thousands of ordinary people in a wide variety of different occupations for his studies.

One of his interviewees, a dancer, described her experience of dancing thus: "A strong relaxation and calmness comes over me. I have no worries of failure. What a powerful and warm feeling it is! I want to expand, to hug the world. I feel enormous power to effect something of grace and beauty." Another dancer said, "Your concentration is very complete. Your mind isn't wandering, you are not thinking of something else; you are totally involved in what you are doing. . . . Your energy is flowing very smoothly. You feel relaxed, comfortable and energetic."

A rock climber commented, "You are so involved in what you are doing that you aren't thinking of yourself as separate from the immediate activity." Another climber said, "One thing you're after is the one-pointedness of mind. You can get your ego mixed up with climbing in all sorts of ways and it isn't necessarily enlightening. But when things become automatic, it's like an egoless thing, in a way. Somehow the right thing is done without you ever thinking about it or doing anything at all. . . . It just happens. And yet you are more concentrated."

These remarks capture the characteristics of windhorse: the synchronization of mind and body, so that thoughts are not separate from action; the feeling of relaxation and calm combined with a sense of power; the joy and warmth toward others; and the loss of the sense of a separate watching self.

Csikszentmihalyi's work demonstrates that such moments of genuine warriorship are not rare or limited only to the most accomplished but occur in the lives of many. *Whether they occur by chance or through our own effort depends on whether we train.* Csikszentmihalyi emphasizes that the important element in bringing about "flow" in one's life is the mastery of consciousness:

> How we feel about ourselves, the joy we get from living, ultimately depends directly on how the mind filters and interprets everyday experience. Whether we are happy depends on inner harmony, not on controls we are able to exert over the great forces of the universe. Certainly we should keep on learning how to master the external environment, because

our physical survival may depend on it. But such mastery is not going to add one jot to how good we as individuals feel, or reduce the chaos of the world as we experience it. To do that we must learn to achieve mastery of consciousness itself.

Just before he died, pianist Artur Rubinstein was interviewed by Mike Wallace. Wallace asked whether, given the modern belief that mind is just the brain, he was sad that his wonderful talent would be entirely lost when he died (a strange question indeed!). Rubinstein replied that he knew nothing about death or the brain. He knew, however, that whenever he played, something tangible reached out from him and touched the audience, lifting their spirits. Through that "something" he felt that he communicated directly with the audience. Rubinstein was clearly not talking merely about the physical propagation of sound through air. He was describing the power of windhorse.

Windhorse need not be restricted to special moments of optimal experience of enjoyment and fulfillment. It is an energy that you have probably already experienced many times, before hearing about windhorse. Windhorse does not discriminate between presidents and bank clerks, between men and women, between paupers and millionaires. Windhorse is available to you whenever you remember to connect with it, even in the darkest moments of fear and depression. It can be roused by anyone who is willing to let go of ego-centered concerns and open to it with bravery and humor. It is rare, however, to know how to rouse this energy spontaneously and increase it. "Raising windhorse" is the practice of deliberately opening to this energy and rousing it in your own being.

Try this now: Slouch down in your seat, hunch your shoulders so that your heart is restricted, look at the ground a few feet in front of you, and stay that way for a few moments. How do you feel? Probably not so good. Now sit up straight, do not lean against the back of the chair, and raise your gaze, looking forward and slightly upward. Imagine that something is pulling up gently on the top of your head, so that your head, shoulders, and torso all feel strong and uplifted. Stay this way for a few moments. Has your mood changed? Do you feel more positive, rather than depressed and downcast? Alternate between these two postures a few times, and you will really feel the difference in mood that they induce in you. The uplifted, positive, and energetic feeling of the upright posture is a taste of windhorse.

You have to be brave to raise windhorse. You cannot do it if you prefer to stay in your cocoon; in that case the energy can feel sharp and threatening.

Raising the Energy of Windhorse

Certainly windhorse has no concern for the ego's comfort. It is best not to try to raise windhorse before you feel that you have a good understanding of mindfulness and awareness practice.

When you are not afraid of the energy, you can raise windhorse on the spot, in a flash. It does not take time—you don't need to prepare for it. Wherever you are and whatever your state of mind, at that very moment you can raise windhorse. Windhorse is your source of power, and when you raise it, you find your sacred space. From there you can go out and meet the world. Whatever your circumstances, when you raise windhorse and connect to the energy-power bank of the world, you can radiate goodness and caring from your heart to others.

It is important to trust that the place where you are at the moment, both physically and in your state of mind, is a good and workable place to raise windhorse. There is no need to think you should be doing something else or going somewhere else that might be a better place. Trust that wherever you are and whatever you are doing is appropriate. *Now* is the best moment—it is the only moment we have.

Nor do you need to reject your mood, whatever it may be—frightened, elated, bored, anxious, curious, uncertain, or confident. If you feel obsessed with concerns about your past, about old injuries, about current moods and tendencies, you can let those worries be just as they are for now. Perhaps you want to raise windhorse because you are in a frightening physical situation, or are facing a difficult job interview, or are about to meet with an angry boss or ex-lover. Perhaps some intense fear or doubt has arisen that threatens your confidence and you want help with your anxiety. That is precisely what the practice is for, so there is no need to try to hide from your fears.

To enable you to feel something of the quality and energy that comes from raising windhorse, I suggest a simple exercise that uses your intuitive feeling and creative imagination. The practice of raising windhorse can be passed on only by personal instruction, not through a book. One cannot fully convey the magic of a genuine practice in writing because it is living energy that must be passed on, not merely an idea. It is the same with any practice, from sitting to healing to playing the guitar to learning to light a campfire—the living human wisdom is learned directly only from a living human. However, doing this exercise with open mind and heart can help you to raise windhorse in a direct and natural way.

Raising Windhorse

A kneeling posture, which comes from the Japanese traditions of spiritual warriorship, is helpful for raising windhorse. Sit back on your heels, toes flat on the floor, and rest palms on your upper thighs with your elbows out. If you cannot manage this posture, however, sitting on a meditation cushion or a straight-backed chair is fine for this simple feeling-visualization exercise.

Before you begin to raise windhorse, acknowledge the wisdom of your heritage—its seriousness and power as well as its humor—and your place in this heritage. This practice was not made up by the Dorje Dradul or concocted to complement the latest psychological trend for isolated individuals seeking personal fulfillment. We are part of a great company of warriors, stretching back and forward in time. Past warriors may even be watching us raise windhorse, encouraging us.

Raise up your physical posture. Feel your head and shoulders strong and uplifted, as if they were reaching up to the sky. Make your spine straight and taut like a bowstring, but not so tight that it becomes stiff. Keep your chest soft and your heart open. Imagine and feel that you are surrounded by a bank of living power and energy all around and above you. Feel its energetic quality. It has depth and richness, it vibrates. It is a feeling of the profound *quality* of all things. It is loving and full and has great affection for the earth and all that exists, but it is also razor sharp and cuts all aggression and hatred.

To help you visualize it, you might feel that the energy has a slightly golden hue, like the sky at dawn, although it is basically colorless. It is living energy— warm and quivering. It is particularly strong in front and slightly above you, as if you were looking up at a master warrior who is sitting on a platform and gazing down at you with an expression of warmth and affection, yet sees you just as you are, with sharp and uncompromising wakefulness. Visualize that the energy is descending and enveloping you. It is very real. In the vast space all around you is unlimited living power and energy that you can call down *because you are a part of it.*

As you feel the energy descending, raise yourself up toward it—raise your posture, your energy, and your humor, as if you longed to go toward that energy. Raising windhorse has been said to be a person's wakefulness meeting the wakefulness of the universe. Feel your good heart that is affectionate, tender, and kind. You don't need to get solemn and religious about this. Raising windhorse is actually a way to lighten up. Now feel (imagine) that the energy and power around you are ripening and becoming overwhelming. Let your mind and heart go into that energy. There is no preparation for letting go. Let go, as you have learned to let go of your thoughts in sitting practice. Let go of your feeling of separateness, of dwelling in your body, of any inadequacy or psychological impoverishment. Just let go. *Abruptly.*

As you let go, feel that you are riding on waves of energy. Your body cells are not separate from the cells of the air around you, and the air cells around you are not separate from the energy cells of the power bank of energy that is descending and enveloping you. You are connected to the world. Feel that you are connected to and not separate from this ocean of energy. The energy is real, you can open to it and allow it into your system. You are not conjuring up something; rather, you are opening to what is already there and allowing it to open you. You may feel that you are "just imagining it," but this energy is real. You feel it in those sudden, unexpected moments of openness that happen in sitting practice or in daily life. And through your intuitive feeling and imagination you tune in to it.

Raise yourself up and cut any doubts and hesitations. You can feel like a king or queen of your world because you are at the center of your world. Wherever you are, feel *that* as your sacred place, your sacred palace. Whether you are in the middle of the street, in a one-room apartment, in an expensive home, on a factory production line, or at home with your parents, that place is sacred and the center of your world. In it, you are the monarch.

As you sit in your sacred palace, touch back on your own genuine heart. Imagine and *feel* that you are a monarch with a broken heart—confident and joyful, as well as genuinely sad. You can radiate goodness and benevolence from your broken heart and bring healing and caring to others. From your broken heart, you can love and cherish and take care of others, who are your fellow kings and queens. You can expand your experience of the energy that descended and entered you. Forget *yourself* and ride the waves of energy, and expand out and out, radiating kindness as far as you can. This is the key point of the whole practice: cutting your own aggression and fear, to receive the benevolent energy of the cosmos into your own heart and radiate that positive feeling to others.

We have described doing the practice quite slowly, but it need not take long at all. You can do it quickly, if you are in a tight spot and want to raise windhorse in a hurry.

We will summarize this exercise of creative feeling and imagination in a short verse that you can read aloud; or you can record and play it back so that you can follow it as you listen:

Feel a power-energy bank all around, descending enveloping opening.
Feel love so full and affectionate and energetic.
Feel the quality of your world.
Feel the vast space, power, and energy.
Feel uplifted and raise yourself up—your posture, as well as your humor.
Feel your tender heart and affection.
Now you can feel the energy ripe and overwhelming.
Let go into it. Abruptly.
Feel you are riding on waves of energy.
Actually connect your body cells with the air cells and energy cells,
so you feel not separate from the world.
Raise yourself up and cut all thoughts of impoverishment.
Feel like a king or queen of your world.
Feel like you live in your sacred palace.
Feel like you can love and cherish and take care of your fellow kings and
    queens.
Now expand your experience of energy further and further.
You can do this on the spot, in an instant, if you are not afraid.
Then you can go out and meet your world
from your source of power and sacred space.

The Experience
of Raising Windhorse

Raising windhorse is not at all a solemn practice. When the Dorje Dradul first introduced the practice to a group of trainee Shambhala teachers, he had been mentioning for some weeks in advance that we would do it, and an intense anticipation had built up. When the day came, we went into his sitting room to receive it in groups of five. Those who had not yet gone in waited outside in the hallway. Perhaps we anticipated a big zap! As each group came out, those in the hallway were quite perplexed to see many of the trainees chuckling or quite openly laughing. When we finally entered the sitting room and received the practice ourselves, it seemed brilliant, yet simple—almost silly to complicated minds that look for something pretentious.

I first experienced the practical effect of windhorse in 1978, a few months after we learned the practice. As vice-president of the Naropa Institute, I led the

staff who were working on its accreditation candidacy with the federal accrediting agency. The initial team of examiners had visited for four days and made its
report, which began, "The Naropa Institute has to be seen to be believed!"

We had to respond to the report in front of a prestigious and imposing
board of examiners in Chicago. For many nights before our trip, we had stayed
up into the early hours of the morning preparing our documentation. The
afternoon before we were to leave, we went to the Dorje Dradul's office. There
we practiced with him the Shambhala warrior practice known as executing the
Stroke of Confidence—a formal way to raise windhorse with brush, paper, and
ink that we will describe in Chapter 12. We spent an hour there, and the
windhorse in the room became so thick it was almost tangible—a sense of
tremendous energy and humor. As we left, he gave us a huge smile and said,
"Remember me," which I took to be a reminder to rouse the windhorse that
we had shared that afternoon. That night, after another few hours of preparation, I was so wired with nervous anticipation that I stayed up the rest of the
night and listened to all nine Beethoven symphonies as well as the Beatles and
Janis Joplin. I was still wide awake as the car drove up to the front door to take
me to the airport.

One of dozens of groups being examined, we arrived at the O'Hare Hilton
Hotel in Chicago, where the meetings were being held. We had rented a hotel
room in which to rest and prepare, and we had a few hours to wait. We were
exhausted. All of us had minor psychosomatic stomach or head problems. The
long hard work of so many people at the Institute now seemed to depend on our
performance, weighing heavily on our shoulders. We spent those few hours flat
on our backs.

When the time came for the meeting, we knelt on the floor in warrior
posture and raised windhorse together. (We forgot to lock the door, and just as
we were about to raise windhorse, I had a comical image of the maid coming in
and seeing four grown men kneeling on the floor with their hands on their
thighs and elbows jutting out.) Again I felt the swirl of energy and delight, just as
we had roused it in the Dorje Dradul's office the previous afternoon. It was so
powerful that it was almost intoxicating—so much so that after we visited the
men's room, we took the wrong exit and landed in a janitor's closet, myself
leading and the rest of the team piling in behind me. We almost collapsed with
laughter right there among the brooms. We were having a great time for a
bunch of men in their thirties about to go into a very serious examination.
However, I felt very strongly that because we had raised windhorse, we would
be able to ride the energy rather than be overwhelmed by it.

As we entered the examination room, we were shown to our seats by the chairman of the examination team that had visited the Institute in the spring. He was there to support our application, but he looked as anxious as I had felt during the days of preparation. Around the huge oval table sat about a dozen men and women who looked very imposing—heavy-duty academics and pedagogic bureaucrats. They were friendly, however, and seemed genuinely curious about us and our Institute. In spite of our tiredness and nerves, we were all quite relaxed, joking with the examiners and rising to all their challenges. After the interview was over, we were amazed at the confidence and sharpness that we had expressed in the meeting.

The meeting had been a success, and the Institute received candidacy— the truth is we did deserve it. We were quite sure that our success was due in no small part to the fact that we came into that meeting with windhorse—soft yet confident and with a sense of humor—and were able to ride the energy of our nervousness. We heard that for some years afterward some members of the accrediting agency were quite unhappy about our candidacy and felt that we must have somehow bamboozled the visiting team and the examiners. Perhaps we did overwhelm them: We had the force of a sincere mission and a vision of a beneficial organization propelling us—and windhorse. Now after twenty years, the agency points to the Institute as an example of their forward-looking vision in accrediting a college that is taking a leading role in providing education that can inspire and nourish students academically as well as in their life journey.

Any kind of challenging situation, whether large or small, is an opportunity to leap through hesitation and raise windhorse. Ted, a project engineer in the Bay Area of California, says, "I try to remember to raise windhorse just before I enter the door where I work. My work is often hectic and demanding. During my drive to work, I cannot help thinking about what I have to do that day and often get quite worked up about it. Taking that moment to raise windhorse just before I go through the door cuts all that thinking and anxiety, and I go in with a fresh mind."

Sally tells a dramatic story of raising windhorse in an intense and challenging situation.

I have been involved for the last year or two in an unpleasant and complicated neighborhood court action involving a family of drug users and their impact on the neighborhood. Since my long marriage ended in divorce because of my husband's drug use, and he sometimes obtained drugs through these people, the whole situation was intensely charged with fear and grief for me. The situation also has dramatic overtones of race and class, and because of various complications, it has been tried both in small claims and in superior court.

I had to make a written declaration about these people and the drug situation in the neighborhood, which is ongoing and complex, then read it aloud in court. During the time that I was involved with this case, I had given a lot of thought to what I honestly could and couldn't say. I sweated blood over my declaration, so that it doesn't say anything that isn't whole-heartedly true. It took considerable persistence just to get my declaration written and march my body into the courtroom, because I was dreading having to speak.

My goal in this whole situation had never been to "get" this family. They are people who have lived near me for most of our lives, and I know that whatever excesses of behavior their addiction drives them to, they are fellow human beings. In a strange way, I felt that I was on the side of the people we were suing because I did not hate them, as did some people in the neighborhood association, and that in certain ways, I had more respect for the difficulty of their situation than did their own lawyers. I know that addicts are unable to control their behavior and suffer themselves from what they do.

While I was watching others testify, I experienced hot and cold flashes in my arms and hands. When it was my turn to testify, I was the last witness for the day, and it was almost time for court to adjourn. When the judge finally called my name, I raised windhorse as I stood up and walked over to be sworn in.

My testimony was filled with moments of silence. The words seemed to come out of emptiness rather than some story prepared in advance in my brain. I could feel that the opposing lawyers wanted me to indulge in some kind of emotional display so that they could discount my testimony, yet the structure of their own arguments worked against them. Because they were invested in my behaving in a particular way, I discovered, they were having a hard time evaluating what I was actually saying.

I found that by acting simply and clearly, I was able to see and avoid the traps the lawyers were attempting to lay to discredit me, and I was able to give my testimony in a straightforward and effective manner. During this whole time, there was a tremendous sense of spaciousness and attention in the room. I felt a kind of relaxed presence in the situation as aspects of the testimony kept shifting and revealing themselves differently. Perhaps the most important part for me was that I was able to honestly discuss my addict husband's association with these people without disparaging him, myself, or them, despite the lawyers' attempts to push me into some type of emotional outburst. I spoke clearly and made my case well, and I felt that I was heard.

After the judge dismissed me and adjourned court for the day, I rode down in the elevator with a couple of my neighbors who had also testified. They thanked me for my testimony and told me that I had discussed things no one else brought up in this case. My arms and hands were still tingling. Outside the sun flashed on the lake. I sat in my car in the parking garage for a while, letting my body settle down before I drove home. I felt peaceful, relieved, and finished.

It can be particularly helpful to raise windhorse at times when you are feeling especially oppressed—by tiredness or resentment or feelings of blame and unworthiness. Such times come to you no matter how many years you have been following a path of warriorship. At those times you feel your oppressed mood as solid and unchanging, as if you will always be trapped in this oppression. You try to analyze your depression, your doubt about yourself, and your fear of what is to come, trying to find the root of these moods, to trace these things back to earlier wounds. This does not seem to help at that very moment, although that work on yourself may be helpful at another time.

If you raise windhorse when you are in a mood like this, you may not feel that it has changed much. Yet raising windhorse has made a slight gap in the solidity of your mood. If you do it again and again, you may actually feel your mood shifting slightly. You discover your mood was not permanent after all. This slight shift, this slight breeze of windhorse, can begin the process of cheering up and rediscovering your bravery.

There is magic to windhorse. This "four-legged miracle" gives you the strength to leap from cowardice to bravery. As when you have slipped on a patch of ice your awareness is suddenly completely *there,* windhorse, too, abruptly cuts through daydreams and scheming. The energy of windhorse opens a gap in your steady stream of setting-sun thoughts and brings you to the present moment. It might feel as if you were intoxicated or suddenly shocked, as if you had come face to face with simple wisdom that does not need words.

Raising windhorse is not a gimmick, however. You cannot expect a dramatic outcome from any particular instance of it. Indeed, the immediate effect you experience may surprise you. You may feel bored or as if nothing has happened at all. You may continue to feel afraid, even though you might also be inspired. Sometimes you might even feel heartbroken. You might be surprised that raising windhorse has the effect of making you feel humble, almost shaky perhaps, yet strong. It is not necessarily a dramatic experience, but it is powerful. This state of being can influence your world.

Susan, an actress for many years, says that the first time she raised windhorse, she felt a tremendous shock, as if she were being physically wrenched open, her heart exposed. She felt:

I was empowered to be queen of the whole world, I had such confidence. But at the same time I felt a terror of experiencing that confidence without the mask. I felt confident but open and vulnerable. It reminded me very much of acting. There I could take on the role of a queen or some extraordinary character and feel comfortable settling into the power of that role. In the context of the play I felt empowered to experience and communicate the reality of that character. But raising windhorse at first is terrifying because it is not a temporary role you are exploring, as in acting. It is the direct and shocking experience of genuineness.

The ups and downs of the experience of the practice are not really significant. The downs do not imply that you have somehow done the practice "wrong." If you raise windhorse regularly, particularly whenever you feel trapped in your cocoon, then gradually you will begin to feel that something is penetrating and accumulating in your system. Raising windhorse is a practice that comes from the world of sacredness. If you continue to do it, the first small pinprick in your cocoon is joined by many others, and the walls become thinner. Gradually, it becomes easier to step out into the world of sacredness and the Great Eastern Sun. However frightened you may be by outside circumstances or by your own emotions, however deeply stuck in your cocoon you may think you are, the powerful energy of windhorse is always available to you.

CHAPTER 11

Inviting Dralas

In Chapter 3, I described the dralas as patterns of living energy and wisdom in the world that you can connect with when you open your mind and heart. When you feel the boundlessness and depth of your own experience you realize that the energy and wisdom of the world is not fundamentally separate from your own energy and wisdom. In this chapter we will discuss how you can begin to connect in practice with the drala energies of your own life and environment. To connect with the living energy of your world you have to let go and leap out of the dead world of your cocoon. You must be willing to step beyond any ego-centered concerns about your own welfare or survival. The practices of mindfulness and awareness, and raising windhorse, are therefore the basis of connecting with dralas. Through these practices, you gradually let go of your cocoon more profoundly and develop a sense of egolessness.

The Dorje Dradul writes:

Training yourself to be a warrior is learning to rest in basic goodness, to rest in a complete state of simplicity. In the Buddhist tradition, that state of being is called *egolessness*. Egolessness is also very important to the Shambhala teachings. It is impossible to be a warrior unless you have experienced egolessness. Without egolessness, your mind will be filled with your self, your personal projects and schemes. Instead of concern for others, you become preoccupied with your own "egofulness." The colloquial expression that someone is "full of himself" refers to this kind of arrogance and false pride.

Experiencing egolessness does not mean that you have reached a permanent state in which you have *no* ego, even if that were possible or desirable. Rather, it means that you see the impermanent, discontinuous nature of your ego. When you have a sense of egolessness in your being, living in the world is not a struggle but a dance. You are capable of opening to first thought, a sudden glimpse of wakefulness, to *nowness*. Only in the gap of *nowness,* between thoughts, between things, or between events, can the dralas enter.

The Japanese word *ma* conveys this sense of a gap in which the dralas may dwell. *Ma* is "the natural distance between two or more things existing in a continuity," writes Arata Isozaki, as well as "the natural pause or interval between two or more phenomena occurring continuously," "a place where life is lived," and "the way of sensing the moment of movement."

Gina Stick, a graphic artist and architectural designer, worked closely with the Dorje Dradul especially on developing an approach to visual arts based on the Shambhala teachings. She speaks of *ma* in her M.A. thesis, "Dwelling in Oriental Architecture":

Gap is not vacant; gap refers to the moment between discursive thoughts or events, without which there is no room for them [the dralas] to enter. . . . The deity is that which is quintessentially real: to provoke it is witnessing the truth of the moment, which can only be experienced *now.* Gap as *ma* is the moment of *nowness,* which is the only time in which the deity exists and can be perceived. The kami [the dralas of the Shinto tradition] always dwell *now* and are never past or future. To witness them, man needs to synchronize the time of himself with the time of the deity and provoke the moment of nowness.

Ma as a temporal principle refers to reality as an unceasing sequence of events. An event is a break in a continuum of time, in the same way as sacred space is a break in the continuity of space. Both are required to contact the kami.

The dralas descend into empty places in space or in time. It is in the *ma,* the gap between two things that are somehow related in space, or two connected events in time that the dralas enter. A small opening in a rock can have an intense living quality; a moment of silence is often called "pregnant" for good reason. With this understanding it becomes clear how to invoke dralas into our life: whatever creates a gap in our thoughts, a sacred space, a powerful object, a moment of sudden recognition of connection, an auspicious coincidence—if we are present to these places and moments, we may encounter dralas there.

In an essay called "The Eloquent Sounds of Silence," author Pico Iyer says, "Silence, then, could be said to be the ultimate province of trust: it is the place where we trust ourselves to be alone; where we trust others to understand the things we do not say; where we trust a higher harmony to assert itself. . . . In love, we are speechless; in awe, we say, words fail us."

To Connect with the Dralas You Need Honesty and Bravery

You need honesty to meet the dralas. You cannot connect with the dralas if you are living in deception, especially self-deception. If you are not telling the truth to yourself about who you are, what you feel, what you long for, and what you fear, then you breed confusion. You propagate a foggy cloud around yourself, and the dralas will not be interested in you. On the other hand, when you uplift yourself with care and affection and honesty, then the dralas are there already. You can cultivate them, but you do not have to invent anything. You have to have bravery to live without deception, to be genuine, to care for your world and go out to others genuinely. Yet this is the only way to connect with the dralas. A Zen koan puts it: "A monk asked Hui Chung of Nan Yang, 'Why do I not hear the teaching of inanimate objects?' Hui Chung replied, 'Although you do not hear it, do not hinder that which hears it.' "

You also need bravery to be unafraid to go forward into what seems strange. It is in the unfamiliar, the strange—and not the habitually familiar—that we find reality. Invoking the dralas is not necessarily pleasant or comforting. There is energy there that we cannot grasp, manipulate, or subdue. When some people first hear about dralas, they become quite frightened or highly irritated. They feel that they are being introduced to more than they bargained for, as if some primordial memory were being awakened in them. It is not just the thought but the almost tangible *energy* of that memory that comes alive and seems threatening. When we take part in group ceremonies to invoke the dralas, we often have a powerful feeling of unreality in the space—that is, a feeling of unreality in relation to the conventional reality of the setting sun. We have to be brave to let go into that; then we discover the magic of the sacred world. According to the Dorje Dradul:

> You might think that something extraordinary will happen to you when you discover magic. Something extra-ordinary does happen. You simply find yourself in the realm of utter reality, complete and thorough reality. . . . True magic is the magic of *reality*, as it is: the earth of earth, the water of water—communicating with the elements so that, in some sense, they become one with you. When you develop bravery, you make a connection with the elemental quality of existence.

Extending yourself out to meet the dralas, allowing a gap in your time and space, could be symbolized by the garuda, a mythological bird that bursts out of its shell full grown—suddenly and completely *there*. Its color is brilliant red, with a golden hue. It looks like a condor with its huge wingspan and its hooked beak and fierce expression, while its wide-open, piercing eyes look as if they could see to the limits of the sky and beyond. Almost never flapping its wings, it glides effortlessly for vast distances, never needing to rest or to find a landing ground. It has no reference point on earth, so it has no bias or stance. It never measures how far it has gone or how far it could go. It just flies on and on, without ever looking back to see where it came from.

Even though she can fly, the garudalike warrior never departs from the tiger's meekness and genuine decency and the uplifted discipline of the snow lion. A warrior who can fly so far above the cocoon of the setting sun could be called "outrageous," in the sense of going beyond boundaries, not being limited by conceptual barriers or fears of any kind. The garuda's outrageous shriek penetrates the heart of the setting-sun world. It is like a sword that is always sharp, and even the thought of sharpening it would make it dull. Because it flies so high, it never gets trapped in narrow valleys that only have one way out. The garuda has no need to hope or expect anything; it is completely beyond poverty or fear of making a mistake.

The garuda is always first thought because it never has a second thought. It is not caught by logic and is not always looking for the next thing. It has no plans or schemes in mind but always acts from the open space of basic goodness. The garuda is shocking, outrageous—its redness and fierceness and its shrill piercing voice stop the mind like a thunderbolt. If you saw it in front of you, you would gasp. There is no limit to how far it would go. It doesn't even care. It is free from all restriction, flying in the upper atmosphere.

You can ride on the back of the garuda if you are very brave. You can hitch yourself to its wings and soar and fly in the rarefied atmosphere with no doubts or obstacles of any kind. You can look through its eyes and see the past, present, and future. You can expand your world and your vision as if you were an astronaut looking at the earth. You have *big mind,* if you can see the whole picture, if you let yourself feel the energy of the garuda, flying on first thought, fresh and free, without mundane constraints holding you in your cocoon.

Dralas Ride
on Auspicious Coincidence

To invoke the dralas, you have to pay attention to everything. You especially need to pay attention to the patterns in your life. When you pay attention to your simple but subtle experiences, you are connecting with the dralas. When something sudden happens in your life, it cuts through your habitual daydreams, and if you pay attention, it wakes you up. It might be just a flash of color abruptly calling your attention in the sunshine; it might be the sudden sound of a siren a block away; it might be a brief moment of silence in a roomful of chattering people. Or it could be a forceful turn of events in your life—losing a job, or finding a job that you did not expect; hearing of the death of a friend; a tree falling on your house; someone insulting you out of the blue; a check arriving in the mail—anything. If we pay attention to these things, we can hear the dralas.

We can open to the dralas if we are willing to listen to our intuition and give in to it. Perhaps we have a strange feeling that a friend is in trouble and needs a call from us; we sense uncomfortably as we are driving that all is not well at home. We may feel a sudden urge to begin a new form of artistic work; an intuition that we should form a business partnership or seek a friendship with a relative stranger; a desire to tell a new friend private things though we feel embarrassed. We should pay attention to these intuitive feelings.

Simple experiences like this may not seem to have much to do with dralas. But it is precisely that intuitive insight, that sense of knowing without knowing how we know, that is the inner ear with which we can hear the dralas. When we feel a longing that goes altogether against any rational reasoning, we can decide to have the courage to follow our longing. When we feel a slight tug—maybe to take a walk down a particular street, perhaps to talk to a stranger, or possibly to take a day off work to sit and gaze gently out of the window—we should be alert to how things unfold. We should follow these longings. We can hear the dralas, if we are willing to listen.

Sometimes I have ignored a fleeting, perhaps strange thought in a meeting, only to find later that it would have been tremendously helpful if I had spoken it out loud. Or something just didn't feel right, but I did not voice that feeling because I could find no "rational" ground to support it. Yet at times when I have followed my intuition, it has made a difference, changed the tone of a meeting, brought new energy and inspiration—and maybe been necessarily irritating as well.

I used to be quite down on myself because I always wanted to take time to make decisions or start a project, while around me colleagues rushed around excitedly and seemed to get a lot more done. Gradually, however, I have learned to appreciate waiting. There always is an auspicious moment for accomplishing something, I have seen, and it is better to wait for that time than to charge ahead—but, of course, you have to be ready when the time does come, otherwise you will again miss the moment. Being on time, the right time, is the key, but usually we miss the time. We feel such pressure to accomplish something that we are unable to stop and listen to our feelings.

Some years ago, I was in the middle of a very difficult dispute within an organization of which I was a director. I had written a first draft of an angry and outspoken letter that I intended to circulate. When I turned on my computer to write the final draft, the screen came on for a moment and then fizzled out—the power supply had failed. I was in too much of a hurry to wait the week it would take for the computer to be fixed, so I actually bought a new computer—such was my anguish and speed. Later, it seemed that sending the letter had not been helpful overall—although it did clarify the issues for some people, it only hurt others. Only much later did I realize with something of a shock that, in the broken computer, I had received a very clear message to wait. From that time on, whenever something unexpected interrupts my activity—and this happens surprisingly often when I am in a rush—I always let it slow me down to pay attention to what I am doing and why I am doing it.

Sometimes we have a feeling that this day is a good day to get things done, or that it is a good day to wait and do nothing. Anthropologist Alton Becker told a story about being in Java when a friend of his, who was a very reckless driver, ran over a small child playing on the village street. The child was not killed, but Becker's friend was devastated. He noted the day on his calendar and told Becker, "Never again will I drive on this day." Becker said, "You mean this date of the year?" His friend replied, "No, *this* day." Javanese understand the cyclical nature of time and the sense that days have qualities that repeat and can be felt.

When we slow down and pay attention to what is happening *now*, then we begin to see coincidences in our life—strange, unexpected connections between events. Coincidences shock us when we pay attention to them. They create a momentary gap in our minds, through which we can feel the presence of dralas, for dralas ride on the vehicle of meaningful or auspicious coincidence. In Tibetan the word meaning "auspicious coincidence" is *tendrel,* and *tendrel* also means a link in the chain of cause and effect. It conveys the idea that what appears to be coincidence actually has interconnected causes—that is why such coincidences intuitively *feel* meaningful to us even though we do not *know* how they came about. All coincidence is meaningful, though we cannot possibly see the causal reasons for everything that happens to us. Some coincidences are so clearly meaningful that they strike an uncanny chord in us. The meaning of the word *coincidence* is actually a "falling together." Dralas are connected with being on time, on the moment of *nowness*. When we are *on time,* not chasing ahead or lagging in the rear, everything seems to fall together. For a moment we do see the larger picture, the web of many cooperating causes and effects, in which our lives are immersed.

When you listen to people's stories of how they came to a path of warriorship, or how they came upon a particular career for which they have great passion, or how they came to marry a person who has brought great depth to their lives, you will usually hear the sounds of the dralas at play in the fields of coincidence. If you look back over your own life, you may find the dralas have been at work, riding on coincidence, long before you heard about them. As we pay more attention to the details of our lives, these coincidences appear to happen more often. It may be that we are noticing what has always been happening to us, or it may be that our care and attention are beginning to attract meaningful energy—the energy of dralas.

I first came to America from England in 1965 because of auspicious coincidence, thus embarking on my long winding journey to Shambhala. I was trying to decide whether to make a career change from physics—the subject of my doctorate—to molecular biology, which was all the rage then. It was a rather dangerous leap to make at the age of twenty-five. I had a longing to do it, but not so much because of my interest in biology. I did not really understand the longing. I felt that I *had* to do it, but I was afraid to take the plunge. I was wandering along the street trying to make the decision when I came upon a traffic jam. Right there, stopped in front of me, was the bus to the biology laboratory. Without further hesitation, I stepped on the bus, rode to the lab, and told the director I wanted to make the change. Within a few months I was on my way to America. I had planned to return to England in two years, but I lingered on aimlessly, kept in America by a series of smaller but still significant coincidences. Then in 1970 I met the Dorje Dradul and understood why I was there. Looking back, I can see how my yearning for a genuine spiritual path determined all those decisions that brought me to the States and kept me there.

When we pay attention to them, such coincidences can point to the way to live in the sacred world with harmony. We begin to feel the magical quality of the most ordinary happenings in our life, things we have taken for granted as "just" cause and effect. We can begin to see how extraordinary it is, though also very ordinary, that flowers appear in the spring because we planted bulbs in the fall; that water boils when we turn on the gas; that the screech of a crow wakes us from a daydream. We begin to understand how ordinary it is that an old friend calls the day after we dream of him; or we have a strong sense that someone we have just met will be very important to us—and later this proves to be true. The world is profoundly trustworthy. When we trust and participate fully in the way the world happens, then the dralas may join us.

The Dralas Are Attracted to Places and Objects We Care For

The sense of place is extremely important. Some dralas are connected with space and the elements, while others are attracted to particular places. Some places seem to have more power than others. There are magnetic spots, or power spots, on the earth where the drala energy can be felt almost as if it were tangible. When you are open, you can discover these places and take care of them. Some people can actually hear the hum of the earth at such spots. There are such power spots wherever you look. If you raise windhorse and then look at a hillside on the opposite side of the valley, your eye will naturally gravitate to particular spots where the energy of the hill is concentrated. It is as if the landscape had nerves running through it and these spots were the nerve centers.

Animals naturally find the power spots of a place—cows in a field tend to congregate around them, deer sleep on them, birds land on certain trees. Many of these places have very healthy vegetation, sometimes lots of wildflowers. Ancient monasteries and churches were often built on these places. Such spots can be places of healing and power, exuding tremendous energy. They are places where we can invoke the dralas. We should literally find our spot and sit on it. It would be a good place to build a house, to sit and be healed, or just to sit.

Sacred places have the power to evoke energy in us that can change our perception. We enter a different quality of time—drala time, or dreamtime, as the Australian Aboriginals call it. Artist and anthropologist Robert Lawlor, who spent thirteen years with the Aboriginals, writes that dreamtime stories extend

> a universal and psychic consciousness not only to every living creature but also to the earth and the primary elements, forces, and principles. Each component of creation acts out of dreams, desires, attractions, and repulsions, just as we humans do. Therefore the entrance into the larger world of space, time, and universal energies and fields was the same as the entrance into the inner world of consciousness and dreaming. . . . Every land formation, and creature, by its very shape and behavior, implies a hidden meaning; the form of a thing is itself an imprint of the metaphysical or ancestral consciousness that created it, as well as the universal energies that brought about its material manifestation. . . . One cannot consider the visible and invisible worlds separately.

Paul Devereux has spent thirty years investigating sacred places and sites of sacred monuments, such as the Avebury circle in England. Devereux explains that the ancient peoples who built the stone monuments, like indigenous peoples today, see the earth in two ways: they see the ordinary physical earth, the only one "civilized" people see, and simultaneously they see the "spirit earth," or the earth as the dwelling place for dralas.

Devereux found confirmation of this twofold perception of place in work with many present-day indigenous peoples—the Australian Aboriginals, the Kalahari ¡Kung, the Kogi, and many others. He quotes anthropologist Paul Wirz, who, working with the Marind-anim of New Guinea, saw that power spots, the places of *Dema* or drala, had the ability to transform perception:

> In most cases such spots have a striking outward appearance in consequence of some strange or unexpected aspect. In them occur unusual land forma-

tions, chasms, uplands, swamps with sandbanks or gravel deposits fresh or salt. Curious noises may be heard in them. . . . Occasionally people catch sight of strange apparitions, the *Dema* themselves, rising out of the earth, though mostly such visions are but fleeting and uncertain.

The physical and "spirit" earth are two aspects of the *same earth*. We, too, can see the earth with new eyes if we are willing to open and to care enough. A majestic outcropping of rock; the small group of ancient trees standing on a patch of high ground; a quiet pool in the middle of a forest fed by a series of waterfalls—all can be places for the dralas to arrive. We can invite the dralas into specially reserved, protected spots—we can create *ma* intentionally. In Japan, for example, the countryside is filled with small shrines to the kami, placed at such power spots. Every garden and home has at least one shrine marking the power spot of the garden. The shrine is not elaborate—it can be nothing more than a rope or a group of rocks marking off an area—or it can be a small wooden dwelling with an opening for fresh flowers. As Matsuoka says, "The *kami* makes an appearance, then vanishes. Rather than not know at all where the *kami* might make its temporary appearance, our ancestors took to demarcating an 'area of *kami*' [*kekkai*] by enclosing a particular space with a twisted rope thus sanctifying it in preparation for the visit of *kami*. There might be nothing within the *kekkai* or perhaps just one tree or rock."

The dralas are attracted to an environment that is uplifted, elegant, and spotless. If we refine and cultivate our environment, we invite drala energy into it. You need not have an expensive home, but wherever you live, you can take care of it. You can keep it clean and uncluttered, maybe adorn it with fresh flowers, as if to welcome an honored guest. You could create a special space in your home—a special room, or simply a small corner of your apartment. You could place a flower arrangement there, and a calligraphy or picture. This can be your sacred place to practice in. If you take care of that place, simply going there can create a feeling of *ma,* first thought, and bring freshness into your daily life.

The dralas land on sacred objects. Just as helicopters can't land on the tops of trees, dralas can't land on piles of garbage. The dralas need a definite connection through which to channel energy. They are dots of focused energy. They don't just spew unfocused energy out into the atmosphere and hope it's picked up. Generalized dralas don't exist. There is no drala of everything. There are specific dralas: dralas of fountains, dralas of wind, dralas of weightwatchers—lots of them. So you need a specific drala-catcher, it could be a flower arrangement, a painting, or a rock—it could be anything with authentic richness and quality.

Everything in the world is sacred, but by cherishing things we bring out and nourish their sacredness so that it can be seen and felt. When an old woodcarving is left in the corner of an attic collecting dust and mildew, it seems like nothing—you might as well light a fire with it. But if you take it out and dust it and polish it and place it in an appropriate spot—one with space around it so it can be seen properly—you might discover that it brings great beauty to your home. Everything has drala energy associated with it, but caring for our possessions in this way makes the dralas manifest in the richness and authenticity of the world. We can take care of our belongings and have a proper place for each of them, and to do this we have to slow down and take time.

Treating our own bodies with care and affection also attracts dralas. How we dress, clean, and nourish our bodies affects our state of mind and our windhorse. We don't have to wear expensive clothes or eat extravagantly, but we can dress and eat with an attitude of respect and appreciation for our bodies. This includes a certain quality of formality. We lose our windhorse when we become completely casual. In photographs or paintings of previous generations, people may look *uptight* in their stiff collars and formal dresses. But they undeniably show uplifted head and shoulders and a lot of windhorse. Special scarves, lapel pins, or hats attract dralas—anything we wear around our head and shoulders that uplifts us and raises our windhorse.

When you care about something, you *take care* of it; when you care about someone, you *take care* of him or her. Your continued care for the objects and people in your life maintains the drala energy and keeps it contained. Otherwise it seeps out and the connection is lost. If you treat your world kindly and gently, with affection and appreciation, that makes a lot of room for the dralas to enter and remain. Dralas need space. They will not force themselves on you—they're too polite. They do offer themselves when they're attracted, but they go away if they are not received and the connection maintained. When we put loving, caring energy into something, its sacredness shines out and attracts further drala energy. If we take an attitude of loving care toward our objects and spaces, then dralas will come along and offer their energy as well.

Dralas Are Attracted to Passion and Wholeheartedness

True creativity—that is, creativity in which something genuinely new enters the human realm—comes from connection with dralas. Much that passes for creativity is actually new permutations and combinations of old ideas. This activity of manipulating old ideas into new forms can result in forms and things that are beautiful and beneficial to human society—but without being truly creative. A creative act is an act of inspiration, which literally means being "breathed into" by the gods.

Robert Grudin, who teaches writing at the University of Oregon, writes with insight on inspiration.

> The word "inspiration" originally meant a breath of divinity or transfusion of soul received from the gods by some deserving individual. The word now denotes the experience of a sudden insight that cuts across categories or otherwise leaps over the normal steps of reasoning. Though both these definitions are helpful, it is the ancient one, with its religious overtones, that seems to hold more psychological truth. To be inspired is to surrender one's mind to a new force, heedless and powerful. Experiencing inspiration is like leaving the world of effort and abandoning oneself to an irresistible flow, like a canoeist drawn into the main channel of a rapids, or a bodysurfer who catches a fine wave just below the crest.

Many artists—painters, musicians, poets, and writers—have said that at times they feel as if their work were created by an energy coming from beyond their ordinary state of being. Some say this energy feels almost like an entity using them like an instrument. Sometimes they refer to these energies that are almost entities as "divine" or "God" or "spirits," depending on their particular belief system.

For example, composer Johannes Brahms refused for years to talk about how he composed and only gave in to questions when he felt near to death. Then he said:

> All right then! I shall relate to you and our young friend here how I establish communication with the creator—for all inspired ideas come from God.

If I feel the urge to do some work, I turn to my creator. . . . Immediately afterward, I feel vibrations penetrating me. They are the spirit that moves the soul energies within, and in this condition of ecstasy I comprehend clearly what remains dark during my normal state of mind. These vibrations take the form of certain mental images after I have expressed that I want to be inspired to compose something that will uplift and advance humanity—something of lasting value. The finished work is revealed to me bar by bar when I find myself in this rare, inspired state.

I have to be in a semi-trance to get such result—a condition when the conscious mind is in temporary abeyance, and the subconscious mind is in control.

Richard Strauss described how, "while the ideas were flowing in upon me, the entire musical, measure by measure, it seemed to me that I was dictated to by two wholly different Omnipotent Entities. . . . I was definitely conscious of being aided by more than an earthly Power, and it was responsive to my determined suggestions." And Puccini said that the music of his opera *Madame Butterfly* "was dictated to me by God; I was merely instrumental in putting it on paper and communicating it to the public."

Poet Amy Lowell says, "Let us admit at once that a poet is something like a radio aerial—he is capable of receiving messages on waves of some sort; but he is more than an aerial, for he possesses the capacity of transmuting these messages into those patterns of words we call poems. . . . I do not hear a voice, but I do hear words pronounced, only the pronouncing is toneless. The words seem to be pronounced in my head, but with nobody speaking them." Novelist Thomas Wolfe wrote, "I cannot really say the book was written. It was something that took hold of me and possessed me. . . . It was exactly as if this great black storm cloud had opened up and, amid flashes of lightning, was pouring from its depth a torrential and ungovernable flood. And I was borne along with it."

The English poet William Blake wrote the poem *Milton* "from immediate dictation, twelve or twenty or thirty lines at a time, without premeditation, and even against my will." Philosopher Friedrich Nietzsche wrote,

One can hardly reject completely the idea that one is the mere incarnation, or mouthpiece, or medium of some almighty power. The notion of revelation describes the condition quite simply; by which I mean that something profoundly convulsive and disturbing suddenly becomes visible and audible with indescribable definiteness and exactness. . . . A thought flashes out like lightning, inevitably and without hesitation—I have never had a choice about it. . . . There is the feeling that one is utterly out of hand, with the most distinct consciousness of an infinitude of shuddering thrills that pass through one from head to foot. . . . Everything occurs quite without volition, as if in an eruption of freedom, independence, power and divinity.

Artists seem to be more willing than scientists to articulate their experiences of dralalike energy and their feelings that true creativity comes from letting go of self-centered ambitions and opening to a greater world. Yet some great scientists and mathematicians have also described their creative process as involving a connection with patterns of energy and inspiration beyond their mundane experience.

Albert Einstein, for example, said,

A person who is religiously enlightened appears to me to be one who has, to the best of his ability, liberated himself from the fetters of his selfish desires and is preoccupied with thoughts, feelings, and aspirations to which he clings because of their superpersonal value. It seems to me that what is important is the force of this superpersonal content and the depth of the conviction, regardless of whether any attempt is made to unite this content with a divine Being.

In another essay, Einstein referred to this conviction as the "cosmic religious feeling" and said, "In my view, it is the most important function of art and science to awaken this feeling and keep it alive in those who are receptive to it."

Einstein said that his creative insight came to him in "more or less clear visual and motor images," which form the basis of "rather vague play." He said that words did not seem to play any role in his creative process except later, when they were needed to communicate his understanding to others.

At the conference on "Humans in Nature" held at the Naropa Institute in 1991, the eminent physicist George Sudarshan said that, at the point of a substantial discovery, one feels not elation but "weak knees," that is, awe mingled with fascination. During these creative moments, Sudarshan said, one does not feel authorship but rather a sudden connection of mind and body. We do not create—we discover, we tune in. Suddenly, we are in a witnessing mode. This can happen in many daily-life situations where there is a sudden conjunction of oneself and one's environment.

The German mathematician Johann Friedrich Karl Gauss, who is considered one of the very greatest of mathematicians, struggled to prove a theorem for two years. "Finally, two days ago," he wrote, "I succeeded, not on account of my painful efforts, but by the grace of God. Like a sudden flash of lightning, the riddle happened to be solved. I myself cannot say the conducting thread which connected what I previously knew with what made my success possible."

We do not have to be geniuses or exceptionally talented to feel the inspiration of the dralas in doing work that we love. The people quoted here discovered how to be wholehearted about what they loved. It is passion and dedication, hard work and readiness to play, that prepare us for inspiration. When we take such an attitude toward one thing we do, it rubs off on everything we do. Doing something wholeheartedly, with genuine passion, attracts the dralas. The passion may be gardening, or woodworking, or writing, or composing music, or scientific research. It may be as simple as taking the dog out for a walk at daybreak each day, or cooking dinner for the family. Whatever it is, passionate and complete involvement engages the heart and mind and body in one activity. We are contained, not dribbling away our energy or entertaining ourself in halfhearted frivolity. We have a feeling of harmony and gentle power.

There are dralas of human activities such as cooking, composing music and poetry, farming, making furniture, and building a dwelling. Dralas like anything that has energy. They like anything that is loved and cared for and treated as sacred. When you put energy into something, the energy stays there. It is captured in the object: in your work of art, in the meal you cook, in the perennial flower bed you cultivate. The energy radiates out like a lighthouse beacon, attracting further energy—alias the dralas. It is literally the same principle as magnetism. Dralas are a form of energy as yet unknown to scientists—a union of spiritual/psychological energy and physical energy. The same principles apply to dralas that apply to all forms of energy—for instance, like attracts like. The positive energy of our care and attention attracts the positive energy of the dralas. It is like resonance: When you pluck a string on a guitar, the strings on a nearby guitar will resonate with the note you play on the first one.

The Dorje Dradul said, "The dralas are the elements of reality—water of water, fire of fire, earth of earth—anything that connects you with the elemental quality of reality, anything that reminds you of the depth of perception. There are dralas in the rocks or the trees or the mountains or a snowflake or a clod of earth. . . . Whatever you come across in your life, the dralas are there." The dralas are inconceivable but nevertheless real. They are attracted to power, to spotlessness, to windhorse, to passion, and to any focus of energy. They protect and help the flow of energy on the earth and in the sky and in the human heart. If you listen, you can always hear them. Dralas create thunder and lightning and earthquakes and fire. Dralas are the heat on a hot night. They are in the *qualities* of things.

Go outside to a place where you can see birds. Sit down, relax, and do sitting practice of mindfulness of breath for a few minutes. Now look at a bird. Look softly, with a gentle, unfocused gaze. Pay attention to the way the bird moves—particularly the changes of its motion, from perching to flying or sudden changes of direction. Try to feel that motion and that sudden change in your own body.

Hold a rock, and feel its weight pushing down on your hand. Try to squeeze it in your fist and feel its solidness and unyielding quality. Lie on the bare earth, let your body relax, and feel that you are dissolving into the earth. Let the earth support you and feel its solidness, feel that it carries you and cares for you; feel that you are a part of that earth and that the earth's solidness and realness are a part of you. Stand in the rain, feel the wetness and the way the water refreshes and cleanses. Hold mud in your hand, squeeze it through your fingers, and feel the way the water binds the earth together. Feel the blood flowing through your body, and feel your own wateriness. Lie on your back and look up at the sky. Feel the vast open space around you—let your awareness go out into the space, and feel that that space, as well as earth and water, is a part of you, and you are a part of it. This is the way—not by reading books—that you can experience the dralas of the elements. The Dorje Dradul encouraged Shambhala students to garden and to camp out. Once, while on a yearlong retreat, he decided to go for a drive in the country at four o'clock on a bitterly cold February morning. As we walked slowly to the car, a cold wind blew hail into our faces. By the time we arrived at the car door, I was shivering, irritated, and altogether not very cheerful. As he clambered into the car, the Dorje Dradul looked up at me with an amused but slightly cynical smile and said, "If people would like to relax, they should go camping."

I laughed and said, "To experience reality, sir?"

"Yes," he emphatically replied.

The sacred world is everyday-life-as-art in action. We can perceive dralas when we extend the artistic vision into ordinary life; when we *see* rather than merely look-at, *hear* rather than merely listen. This distinction between *see* and *look-at* is made by Frederick Franck in *Zen Seeing, Zen Drawing.* He says, "Merely *looking-at* the world around us is immensely different from *seeing* it. Any cat or crocodile can look-at things and beings, but only we humans have the capacity to see. Although many of us, under the ceaseless bombardment of photographic and electronic imagery that we experience daily, have lost that gift of seeing, we can learn it anew, and learn to retrieve again and again the act of seeing things for the first time, each time we look-at them." Franck quotes Rudolf Arnheim as saying, "Every child entering grade school in this country embarks on a twelve-to-twenty-year apprenticeship in aesthetic alienation. Eyes they still have, but see they do no more." Hui Neng, the Zen sage, Franck tells us, said, "The Meaning of Life is to See." Franck adds, "Not to look-at, mind you, but to see!"

And the Dorje Dradul makes a similar distinction.

Looking is your first projection, and if you have any doubt, then it might have a quality of tremor or shakiness. You begin to look, and then you feel shaky or anxious because you don't trust your vision. So sometimes you want to close your eyes. You don't want to look any more. But the point is to look properly. See the colors: white, black, blue, yellow, red, green, purple. Look. This is your world! You can't not look. There is no other world. This is your world. This is your feast. You inherited this; you inherited these eyeballs; you inherited this world of color. Look at the greatness of the whole thing. Look! Don't hesitate—look! Open your eyes. Don't blink, and look, look—look further. Then you might *see* something.

If you listen, you can hear the dralas, you can hear their love. Our eyes can see the patterns as well, but we focus too sharply. So first we soften our ears. Vision is habitual for most of us, but sound is unexpected: the call of the loon, the haunting lighthouse foghorn, even traffic that we have to put up with, the sounds of sirens and the horns of taxicabs. We can hear the most outrageous sounds if we listen. You can practice listening and hearing. Listen to tapes of whales and loons and hear their songs. Listen, and hear tap drip, cereal pop, sound of children's chatter. Go outside and listen. Listen, and hear frogs, electricity, energy snaps, the cries of pheasants making love in the bushes. Listen, and hear the patterns, hear the silence of rocks and trees and bountiful rhododendrons.

Invoking Dralas in Ritual

The dralas do not abide in one place; rather, they arrive and then depart in their own time, so for Shambhala warriors, waiting and repetition are important aspects of invoking them. Philip O'Connor, a British vagrant—a "tramp," or as we would say nowadays, a "homeless person"—wrote that in walking endlessly the roads of England he sometimes had an

> incomparable feeling . . . as though one were a prayer winding along the road; the feeling is definitely religious. . . . All hard nodules of concepts are softly coaxed into disbursing their cherished contents. . . . Maybe mental fireworks will gloriously light the mind—but quickly the world will attach the inner light to outer phenomena. . . . The speed of transit between inner state and outer appearance is a feature of tramping. . . . *Time* stops in such perceptions.

The different experience of time and place when he was alone in the landscape was apparent whenever O'Connor came in contact with townspeople. They would appear "terribly quick, jerky, and doll-like, with chatter to suit." O'Connor's insights were clearly the result, in part, of his own extraordinary openness and his confidence in his own way of being and perceiving. The slow, repetitive, and often boring nature of walking, however, probably had a lot to do with preparing him for these insights. These are precisely the qualities of much ritual and ceremony. Rituals are nothing like the shows that are put on for tourists—and often for anthropologists. Rituals can go on for days, can involve fasting and sleeplessness and endless repetition of spoken phrases, drumming, chanting, and dancing. A ritual can be simply paying attention to one's breath repetitively, over and over, perhaps for days and weeks, going through boredom and fear. Or a ritual can be practicing a skill—working with brushstrokes, wood-chisel cuts, or musical scales. Perseverance and repetition, with joy and humor and playfulness, not solemn religiosity, are key to invoking dralas.

We experience the sacredness of life when we regard each object and each act as a ritual act. When we go beyond the boredom of ordinary things, we discover real joy in them that comes to us from the object or act itself, rather than from the hopes and expectations we project onto it. Even the seemingly trivial aspects of life—the clothes you wear and how you wear them, the food you eat, or the mug you drink out of—can contribute to the overall sacredness of that life in a society that appreciates the inner meaning of ritual. Thus, there is no separation between sacred and profane; all actions in life become part of the sacred; all rituals become sacred rituals and ways to attract the interest and energy of the dralas.

Dralas are invoked in group rituals, in ceremonies, and in festival celebrations. Ritual is a profound and powerful way that societies maintain internal harmony as well as a connection with the nonhuman worlds on which they depend—the worlds of animals and plants, of mountains and lakes, and of dralas. Dolores LaChapelle, director of the Way of the Mountain Learning Center in Colorado, leads ceremonies and rituals to renew our connection with earth. Ritual, she says, "gives us new insight into truth. It is not something out there to be searched for, or worked towards, or fought for. Rather truth appears out of the interactions of all those present—human and nonhuman—during the time of the Festival itself. The more one enters into the play of the Festival, the deeper one penetrates into the truth." This view of sacred ritual dates all the way back to Confucius, who taught, according to Herbert Fingarette, that sacred ceremony is not a "totally mysterious appeasement of spirits external to human and earthly life. Spirit is no longer an external being influenced by the ceremony; it is that which is expressed and comes alive *in* the ceremony."

Ceremonies and rituals provide a gap in the normal flow of daily life for an entire group—a kind of group gap. Ceremonies are the observance of natural order, and their purpose is to align humans with natural events in order to contact dralas. As the Chinese say, nature creates ceremonies and humans observe them. Isozaki's observation that "Japanese festivals were ceremonies for summoning the spirits" is true of the festivals, ceremonies, and seasonal celebrations of all peoples who still have a connection with this dimension of their natural reality. Ruth-Inge Heinze says,

> Christians believe that, during the Holy Communion, Christ manifests in the host. Hindus know that, during rituals, their priests call the gods and these gods will manifest in the temple's statues. Other ethnic groups have rituals to evoke nature spirits (residing in stones, trees, mountains), they may also evoke deified ancestors or the "nameless" Divine, the life force per se.

Rituals bring group energy together to expand the atmosphere and transport the participants to drala time. It raises the windhorse of the group together so that those who are having trouble connecting can come along. It raises the awareness of the participants so that their perceptions are clarified and they can see sacredness in that moment. The powerful atmosphere of group windhorse attracts the dralas, and on it they can descend.

Indigenous peoples have not lost their heart connection to the cosmos to the extent modern people have. They can still communicate with natural elements and forces and with each other in a way that we lost long ago because we ceased to be open to them. Don Jose Matsuwa was a Huichol shaman who lived in the Mexican Sierra mountains. He died in 1992 at the age of 110. He visited New York and California twice. On the first visit he conducted a ceremony to bring rain to drought-ridden California—and rain indeed came. On his second visit he said:

The sacred feathers talk to me about why there has been no rain in this place [California]. In some places Tayaupa [the sun] burns your land, in other places Tayaupa's face is hidden. This place that you live in and many other places in your country suffer from drought, too much rain, shortages, many problems. There is a reason for this misfortune, for you have not been doing ceremonies, gathering together, thanking the earth, the gods, the Sun, the sea for your lives.

I see that many people here are so caught up in their own little lives that they are not getting their love up to the sun, out to the ocean and into the earth. When you do ceremonies, sending out your love in the five directions—the north, the south, the east, the west, and the center—brings life force into you. That love brings in the rain. As it has been since human history began, people are wrapped up in their little worlds, and they forget the elements, forget the source of their life.

You must study these things I am saying, and with understanding, your life will become stronger. . . . Then, one day, the sea will give you heart; the Fire will give you heart; the Sun will give you heart. And when you come to my village, I will know.

Matsuwa is teaching us the deepest form of ceremony: to open our hearts with love to the earth and the sun and the oceans, to the rocks and trees and animals, and then to receive back the heart and life-force that we so sorely need. We always feel fear and doubt when we are willing to open ourselves to such possibilities, but those of us on the path of warriorship at least know that we *can* let go of our little minds and go through the gateway of fear. We can open our hearts to the vast, profound, and strange universe, to the earth and to the heavens, to other animals, and to our fellow humans.

Like all great shamans and teachers, don Jose had a sense of lightness and humor as well as fervor and power. He discovered his main apprentice, Brant Secunda, after Brant as a nineteen-year-old was wandering in search of a Huichol village and got lost. He was saved from dying of thirst in the desert by a dream vision of one of don Jose's shaman colleagues. Afterward, Brant spent seventeen years apprenticing with don Jose. Their relationship, as well as the sacred way of life of the Huichol, is charmingly portrayed in a video, *Virarica, The Healing People*. At one point, don Jose, by then old and wizened, is lying on his back in the shade exchanging jokes with his young apprentice. Brant comments, "The Huichols laugh more than any other people I know. Happiness and sadness are the same thing, they say, only happiness makes you feel better. I remember don Jose saying, 'Nothing I have taught you is worth anything if you leave here and can't tell a good joke.' "

Smoke is very frequently used to invoke the dralas in groups. For example, in Native American traditions sweet-grass is burned and brushed over participants with a sacred feather in a purification ceremony called "smudging." The sacred pipe is smoked and passed around the circle in a ritual that confirms the peaceful connectedness of the people in the circle to each other and to all beings.

In the Shambhala tradition, groups invoke the dralas through a *lhasang* ceremony. *Lhasang* literally means "calling the gods." Dried juniper branches are burned on glowing charcoal. As the thick sweet-smelling white smoke rises up, the students chant a long invocation to the dralas. At the end of the chant, the student warriors circumambulate the smoke in a clockwise direction chanting continuously the warriors' victory cry: *"Ki, Ki, So, So: Lha Gyelo; Tak, Seng, Kyung, Druk: dYar Kye!"*

Ki, uttered very sharply and forcefully, dispels all negative energies. *So*, uttered more gently and with longing, invites harmony and calls on the dralas. *Lha Gyelo* means "victory to the gods," in this case the dralas. *Tak, Seng, Kyung, Druk* means "Tiger, Lion, Garuda, Dragon," the four animals that symbolize stages on the warrior's path. Finally, *dYar Kye!* has no literal meaning but is just a joyful cry of having accomplished one's objective. In Tibet this cry was often uttered when a group reached the top of a mountain pass after a long and difficult climb through obstacles of weather and bandits.

The Shambhala warriors walk around and around chanting and carrying pennants representing the four animals. They pass through the smoke anything that they wish to purify and energize with drala energy. The smoke passes over them, and they breathe it in. A tremendously powerful atmosphere of wakefulness—with a sharp edge—develops in these gatherings. One can feel the windhorse rising.

I have suggested in this chapter merely a few of the countless ways to invite the dralas to enter your life. The dralas will gather round with their energy, and help you to build your connections with other warriors and with the sacred world when you listen to your intuitive insight and to auspicious coincidence, when you pay attention to the elements and care for the earth, and when you regard every act as a ceremony and care for every object as a ritual object. They will gather whatever you undertake, when you do it with passion, wholeheart-edness, and concern for others' well-being. Finally, they will gather whenever you raise windhorse, whether you are alone or in a group. To make these genuine connections is the way to begin to build an enlightened society.

Dorje Dradul, circa 1981.

PART THREE

Authentic Action
in the World

CHAPTER 12
Authentic Presence

Many traditions have the understanding of the personal and cosmic energy we are calling windhorse and drala, and many different traditional practices can help us raise windhorse and invite the dralas, to make that miraculous leap into the sacred world of the Great Eastern Sun. All these ways require dedication, wholeheartedness, and awareness. Wisdom and the practices of warriorship are not made up on the spot to satisfy some temporary need. Wisdom practices arise out of the accumulated efforts of men and women over hundreds of years. Still, only your own awareness can make them fresh and up-to-date. Awareness is awareness of this very moment, *now*. Memory of the past and expectation or hope for the future all occur in the present moment, now. There is no other real moment but *now*. Awareness is *nowness*. By raising windhorse, you join *nowness* with the traditional wisdom of the great lineages of men and women who have practiced and accomplished warriorship, who have built good human societies, and in whose footsteps we aspire to follow.

Joining nowness and traditional wisdom has an analogy in the baking of a loaf of bread—the recipe comes from the trial and error of many generations. You inherited it from your great-grandmother and were taught by your mother how to use it, but *right now* it is up to you to follow the recipe and produce fresh, warm, sweet-smelling bread.

Further Ways to Raise Windhorse

Some Shambala warriors train in traditional Japanese practices that are still powerful for inviting dralas: *Chanoyu,* or tea ceremony; *Ikebana,* or flower arranging; and *Kyudo,* or archery.

In *Tea Life, Tea Mind,* master of Tea Ceremony Soshitsu Sen says, "A monk once asked his master, 'No matter what lies ahead, what is the Way?' The master quickly replied, 'The Way is your daily life.' This concept is at the very center of the Way of Tea. The principles of the Way of Tea are directed toward all of one's existence, not just to the part that takes place in the tearoom. In practice, the test lies in meeting each occurrence of each day with a clear mind, in a composed way. In a sense, even one's smallest action is the Way of Tea. It is this that makes it just as significant as when it began more than four hundred and fifty years ago."

The ceremony takes place in a clear and simple room, with maybe a scroll on the wall and a flower arrangement with only one flower in a place of honor. A pot of water is set to boil over a charcoal fire and gives a feeling of open space. (As a guest, I have had an extraordinary feeling of timelessness as that pot of water quietly boils and the steam goes up and the sound of water bubbling gently penetrates the air. It is as if that caldron of water had been boiling for hundreds and hundreds of years.)

Into this open space and timelessness come the guests and the host, who enters through a separate door carrying the tea utensils. The host prepares thick green tea in a lengthy and precise but simple ceremony. Sweets are presented. The tea is served and drunk—the strong bitter taste is quite shocking even when you are anticipating it. The bowls are examined. The tea utensils are cleaned. There is an atmosphere of wholehearted awareness. Everything is done with tremendous precision and sense of being there in the moment. The host and guests exchange a few words of appreciation with much bowing back and forth. The exchange between host and guests is genuine and full of sad and joyful heart.

The guests leave, the host packs the tea utensils and carries them away, leaving just the empty room and the boiling caldron. It feels so complete and full, yet a lingering poignancy remains, as if a whole lifetime had taken place in that simple ceremony. Now it is over.

Soshitsu Sen explains that the four basic principles of the Way of Tea, to be practiced in daily life as well, are harmony, respect, purity, and tranquillity. He says,

"Harmony" is the result of the interaction of the host and guest, the food served, and the utensils used with the flowing rhythms of nature. It reflects both the evanescence of all things and the unchanging in the changing. . . . The principle of harmony means to be free of pretensions. . . .

"Respect" is the sincerity of heart that liberates us for an open relationship with the immediate environment, our fellow human beings, and nature, while recognizing the innate dignity of each. . . . This principle presses us to look deeply into the hearts of all people we meet and at the things of our environment. It is then that we realize our kinship with all the world around us.

"Purity," through the simple act of cleaning, is an important part of a tea gathering—in the preparation beforehand, the actual serving of tea, and, after the guests have left, the storing away of the utensils and the final closing of the tearoom. Such actions as clearing the dust from the room and the dead leaves from the path all represent clearing the "dust of the world," or the worldly attachments from one's heart and mind. It is then, after putting aside material concerns, that people and things can be perceived in their truest state. . . .

"Tranquillity," an aesthetic concept unique to Tea, comes with the constant practice of the first three principles of harmony, respect, and purity in our everyday lives.

Kyudo, the Japanese art of archery, is another practice through which we can gather and raise the energy of windhorse. This very simple practice is well known to many through Eugen Herrigel's classic *Zen in the Art of Archery*. It originated as one of the main fighting methods of the samurai, but for six hundred years it has been taught, unchanged, as a practice for synchronizing mind and body and raising windhorse. The power of the weapon has been harnessed into the power to *overcome* aggression.

In kyudo practice, the archer stands only six feet in front of a large target, usually made of a hay bale. Hitting the target is not the point, although later you do shoot at distant targets. Steve Cline, a Shambhala student and kyudo instructor, describes making a shot:

First the practitioner assumes a solid stance like a tree whose branches extend naturally to heaven, but whose roots are planted firmly in the earth. The upper torso has a sense of upliftedness, as if a string were lightly pulling the head to the sky. When the *yumi* [bow] is fully drawn, the moment of release ripens naturally, of its own accord, as energy flows up and out from the *tanden,* the center of the body near the navel. The mind follows the path of the arrow, allowing itself to rest in the space. There is a sense of "lingering" like the deep resonance of a temple bell after it is struck.

Over and over he or she practices the apparently simple form: taking a stance like a vast oak tree, joining heaven and earth; raising the bow; pushing the bow forward and extending the string; holding that, hold, hold, and—release! It is said that it can take ten years just to learn to release the arrow properly. The buildup of intensity and the energy arising at the release feel very much like raising windhorse.

A master of this art, Shibata Kanjuro Sensei, is the twentieth in a family line of bow-makers and master archers for the Emperor of Japan. He came to North America first in 1980 to teach kyudo to Shambhala students, at the request of the Dorje Dradul. Had he stayed in Japan a few years longer, he would have been appointed a "Living Treasure of Japan"—the highest cultural honor of that country. In North America he was so impressed by the practice attitude of his students, compared with his Japanese students, most of whom now do kyudo only for sport or social advancement, that he returned again and again. He took up permanent residence in the United States in 1985 and has taught kyudo in North America and Europe ever since. His English is very sparse, and his appearance is fierce, with piercing eyes, bushy black eyebrows, and a deeply lined face like the mask on a Japanese samurai's suit of armor. Yet in ordinary activities, Shibata Sensei conveys a light humor and joy of life that is uninhibited even by his conventional Japanese manners.

When Sensei is in the dojo (practice hall), it is another story; there, he can display a fierceness that is awesome. On one occasion on his first visit to the United States, a student in the class (we were all beginners) missed the target and the arrow hit the wall behind with a loud *thwack.* We all started to chuckle, until suddenly we were stopped by a wrathful shout, *"No!"* Sensei explained with a fearsome glower on his face, "Kyudo—for *you.* Laughing at another—*not so good!"* Then he shook his head and broke out into a big smile.

Shibata Sensei exhibits a combination of humbleness and power. He emphasizes over and over again that "kyudo is *mind,"* slapping his lower abdomen (where, in this tradition, *kokoro*—which means something like "mind-heart-spirit"—is said to reside). By this he means that kyudo is practiced not for the competitive or sport aspect but as a way of polishing kokoro, letting go of negative emotions, confusions, and fixation on self, and rousing windhorse. As Sensei says:

> The ultimate goal of kyudo is to polish your mind. It is the same with *zazen* [mindfulness practice]. You are not polishing your style of shooting, but the mind. The dignity of shooting is the important point. Without the right mind, no matter how long you shoot, this dignity won't be gained.
>
> Rather than being a question of hitting the target due to good form or good style, if your mind is correct, you will naturally hit it. This is the case for anything that you do, not just kyudo. If you are always wondering about the target or the result, then nothing good can come of it. If you always look at yourself first, look at your own feet, your basis, then things will naturally go right.

Another practice taught in Shambhala to invoke windhorse is the practice of executing the Stroke of Confidence, or the Stroke of *Ashé*. This practice is something like calligraphy or sumi-e drawing in spirit, although there are further depths of meaning to *Ashé*, which originated as a *terma* of the Dorje Dradul as I described in Chapter 3. The practice was recognized by both the Dorje Dradul and Shibata Sensei to be identical in essence to kyudo. It is outwardly very simple: standing or kneeling in front of white calligraphy paper, with a bowl of black ink and a calligraphy brush, the warrior makes one stroke down on the paper.

There is first the empty sheet of paper. Then there is the first dot when the brush first strikes the paper, followed by the stroke down. Then the brush is lifted off the paper. The blank sheet of paper symbolizes the beginning, before anything has happened. It is the empty canvas of an artist, before he or she knows what to paint. It is the target in kyudo. It is the open sky, clear and very big, able to accommodate the entire earth, sun, moon, and stars, a peaceful sunrise or a violent storm. It mirrors the mind and heart that is open to all possibilities. It may be the openness in your mind just before you say something to a friend but are not sure what. It may be the moment of silence just as a meeting begins or just before you leap down a ski slope. Yet your mind is not completely blank because you have the intention, perhaps even the longing, to say or do something. You wait to make a first connection with reality—first thought.

The stroke of *Ashé* is the warrior's weapon—a two-edged sword that cuts all aggression and hatred and, at the same time, cuts itself so that no sense of self-importance or self-righteousness remains, no idea that you are a victor over something or someone. When you do the stroke wholeheartedly, you have no separate sense of self. The stroke cuts through your conceptual thoughts and cloudy emotions, joining your mind and body, and opening a crack in the cocoon. When, as a Shambhala warrior, you execute the stroke, you first open your mind to feel the solid earth beneath you and the energy of space around and above you, and you recall the vision of the Great Eastern Sun. Then, you abruptly make the first dot, which symbolizes first thought, followed by the stroke down, which symbolizes unconditional confidence. At the end of the downstroke you pause, letting go of any thoughts of having accomplished anything, any lingering ego fixations. Then, as you abruptly lift the brush from the paper you open your mind further to the energy and magic of windhorse that can enter through the gap in the cocoon.

When practices such as tea ceremony, kyudo, or the stroke of *Ashé* are passed on properly and fully there is always a transmission of the energy and inner meaning of the practices beyond the words. This is true of any spiritual practice. Experiencing the atmosphere and flavor of the practice, and learning the details firsthand, is as important as hearing or reading the words of instruction. For the student to be able to receive the complete transmission, he or she needs to have had some experience of mindfulness and awareness, some practice in letting go of self-centeredness. Without that grounding in gentleness and genuine caring for others, and without proper instruction, to attempt the practices may create confusion and do more harm than good.

In the Shambhala path of warriorship, intensive residential retreats allow groups of warriors to open to awareness, to raise windhorse, and to execute the *Ashé* stroke together. Participants live together, studying, practicing, and doing all the necessary daily chores such as cleaning and preparing food. All the usual emotions of a group of people living and working closely together arise intensely, so it is fertile ground for drawing out fear and aggression, as well as for discovering joy and confidence. There is an atmosphere of dignity and upliftedness as well as relaxation and humor—amidst considerable feistiness and occasional chaos. It is the seed of establishing an enlightened society.

The students practice sitting as well as raising windhorse and executing the *Ashé* stroke. They study the central texts of the Shambhala teachings—the main text presents the meaning and symbolism of the stroke of *Ashé* in detail. They practice individually and execute the stroke together as a celebration of sacredness and Great Eastern Sun vision. The liveliness and one-pointed atmosphere in the room during these group sessions can be electrifying. Sometimes the stroke is done in turn while students stand in a large circle. As each person does one stroke, watched intently by all the others, the windhorse moving around the circle is almost visible.

There are parallels to the practice of the *Ashé* stroke in the Chinese and Japanese understanding of the brushstroke in painting and calligraphy. According to François Cheng:

> In the eyes of the Chinese painter, the execution of the brush stroke is the link between man and the supernatural. For the brush stroke, through its internal unity and its capacity for variation, is one and many. It embodies the process through which man returns in painting to the original gestures of creation. (The act of executing the stroke corresponds to the very act which draws the One forth from chaos, which separates Heaven and Earth.) The stroke is simultaneously breath, yin-yang, Heaven-Earth, the ten thousand existents, while at the same time taking on the rhythm and secret instincts of man. . . .
>
> According to this, the art of painting is not a mere description of the spectacle of creation; it is itself creation, a microcosm whose essence and function are identical with that of the macrocosm. . . .
>
> The Ink in impregnating the Brush endows it with a soul; the Brush in making use of the Ink endows it with spirit. . . . Man possesses the power of formation and of life; if not, how would it ever be possible to draw from Brush and Ink a reality having flesh and bone.

A renowned calligrapher once told a Chinese emperor, when asked how to hold the brush, "If your mind [*kokoro*] is correct, the brush will be correct. This holds true for any of the Ways. If one's mind is crooked or warped, so will be one's technique. When a calligrapher writes 'no-mindedly' in the here and now, the brush strokes are vibrant; if one is distracted or full of delusion, the lines will be dead no matter how well they are constructed."

A similar understanding of making a primordial stroke is expressed by the Sufi poet Jalalaudin Rumi in "The Name":

Do you know a word that doesn't refer to something?
Have you ever picked and held a rose from R.O.S. and E.?
You say the NAME. Now try to find the reality it names.
Look at the moon in the sky, not the one in the lake.
If you want to be free of your obsession with words

and beautiful lettering, make one stroke down.
There's no self, no characteristics,
but a bright center where you have the knowledge
the Prophets have, without books or interpreters.

The stroke of confidence is not a stroke of calligraphy, nor does it derive from traditional Chinese painting. Rather, it is a practice that was received afresh for our time by the Dorje Dradul. As such, because it embodies the timely, living wisdom of the Shambhala teachings, it is a particularly powerful and magical practice. It is a specific way to rend the setting-sun veil that normally prevents direct experience of sacredness and windhorse. When asked on one occasion what the stroke symbolized, the Dorje Dradul replied, "One." His questioner continued, "One what?" "One with everything" was the succinct answer.

Raising Windhorse
Gathers Authentic Presence

The practice of raising windhorse is cumulative and gradually gives rise to *authentic presence*. This is a translation of the Tibetan term *wangtang,* which literally means a "field of power." On the Shambhala path of warriorship, authentic presence grows in your system as your genuine confidence matures and you are able to open yourself again and again to the energy of windhorse. Authentic presence develops in a simple cause-and-effect process from letting go of ego fixation, of obsession with yourself and who you are, and of grasping for power and possessions. All *you* have to do is to raise windhorse and let go. This letting go must extend to letting go of your concerns about your progress along the path of warriorship. Then the dawning of authentic presence is as automatic as action and reaction.

Authentic presence is easier to point to by example than to describe. However, it is not a mysterious or especially rare quality. We have probably all met people with some degree of authentic presence, at least in an outer sense. They have a simple smile and genuine cheerfulness, combined with a seriousness that approaches sadness. Yet they also have a sharp edge: they have cut through pretension and learned to live humbly and directly, and their presence challenges others to be without pretense as well.

Such people often need tremendous discipline in their chosen way of working in the world. Yet they have modesty and humor. They sparkle with rare liveliness and spirit. They may be well-educated people in positions of high visibility and great power, or they may be completely anonymous, ordinary people with little formal education. One of the people in my own life who had authentic presence—though I did not think of it as that at the time—was Amy, the woman who came to clean my parents' house when I was a teenager. Another was an elderly, partially deaf physics teacher in my high school. Mr. Godfrey had been a bomber pilot in the Second World War, but he could not quite get the hang of teaching teenage boys—he did not know how to terrify them. So he was a laughingstock among most of my classmates. Yet amid the rather brutal atmosphere of an all-boys school, he radiated kindness, quirky humor, and wisdom. Amy and Mr. Godfrey had both let go of self-centeredness and genuinely seemed to care for others in a way that was unique in my world at that time. I loved both of these people, and in their simple words and kindness their genuineness and authentic presence had a strong effect on my life.

Nancy Wake Forward, an Australian, was a young journalist in Europe before the Second World War, fun-loving and enjoying the high life of Paris. On a trip to Vienna, she saw the degrading treatment of the Jews and determined to become involved in the French Resistance movement. "Back in Paris," she says, "I would think of all the chaos in Germany. But what could an inexperienced girl like myself do or hope to achieve when so many brilliant, well-informed men had failed to make an impact on the outside world?" Her involvement in the Resistance began slowly, smuggling documents and helping downed Allied pilots. Then she trained in London and became a secret agent and saboteur. The Nazis dubbed her the White Mouse (the title of her autobiography) because she was so hard to find. She was one of the most decorated women of the war.

On one of her many escapades, Forward traveled through German lines on a stolen bicycle with no license and no identity cards to fetch a radio transmitter. She cycled three hundred miles in seventy-two hours and had to be lifted off her bike when she returned. She recalls, "I got through German lines because I looked innocent and polite, you see. They were holding up everybody. I went through with a little string bag on the end of my bicycle with a couple of leeks or carrots, and I was just a little housewife." When asked if she was ever afraid, she replied, "Never. Why should I be afraid of a situation? Afterward you might say, 'Ah, that was a close call.' But your reaction has got to be good. If you're going to be frightened you'll never get away with anything."

She kept her sense of humor through all this. Recently she told a reporter, "I'll tell you something absolutely wonderful. Some fans in New South Wales want to name a race horse the White Mouse. I was thrilled pink. The woman says the horse is very naughty and I said she takes after me. Don't you think that's gorgeous. Lots of funny things happen to me, so I don't lead an uninteresting life."

The authentic presence of an accomplished warrior has the power to benefit many people. It comes from a profound letting go of inner grasping after personal gain. It is a field of power that we recognize in the subtle radiance of genuinely wise leaders. Men and women of authentic presence are characterized by simplicity and humor, not burdened by holding a lot on their minds. Their presence can at times be powerful to the point of seeming majestic. At other times they can be unpredictable or wrathful or even appear quite foolish or petulant, like a child.

Maya Angelou, author of *I Know Why the Caged Bird Sings,* strikes all those who meet her as a person of great authentic presence. When she speaks, from the minute she takes the stage, the audience—which often numbers thousands—is electrified by her power. Yet somehow she is able to establish what feels like personal rapport with each of them. Angelou tells how she was raped when she was seven, and for five and a half years after did not speak at all. "I was a giant ear," she says. She went on to become a singer and dancer, playwright, poet, and author.

During her talks, she can be completely uninhibited, frequently breaking into spontaneous song, dance, and poetry. The large hall throbs with her energy. She says, "People always recognize the truth no matter how it is spoken," a statement of which she herself is a vivid illustration. People are moved to tears by her full, radiant, "tell-it-like-it-is" presence. Yet it is beyond ordinary charisma or mere celebrity. It is clear that she has done plenty of work on herself, which she characterizes as "trying to be a Christian." She says that her response to people who say they are Christians is, *"Already?"*

When someone once asked her how she got from her impoverished background in rural Arkansas to where she is today, she said simply, "By being grateful." Her confidence is as strong as her humility, and she talks about confidence as one of the most important virtues: "With confidence, you can do anything; without it, you can do nothing."

Fame has little, if anything, to do with authentic presence, although some people with authentic presence do become famous in spite of themselves. The Christian contemplative and writer Thomas Merton and the physicist Albert

Einstein are two people with authentic presence who became well-known in spite of their lack of interest in fame and fortune. Like Thomas Merton and Albert Einstein, the Dalai Lama, though famous, has retained a deep humility and feeling of being one with the ordinary people of the world. He exhibits tremendous authentic presence and has transcended the bounds of the religious and cultural traditions he came from to go directly to the hearts and needs of people.

The Dalai Lama, leader of the Tibetan government in exile and Nobel Peace Prize winner, has shown the most extraordinary bravery and compassion since he led a few thousand people out of Tibet to escape the Chinese purge in 1959. Since that time he has seen the beautiful land of Tibet abused, turned into an industrial wasteland, and used as a nuclear dump. He has seen the sacred places desecrated and cherished teachers of Buddhism imprisoned and tortured. He has never expressed hatred or even resentment toward the Chinese perpetrators of this horror, but he has never lost heart and never given up working for the return of his people to their land. Yet the Dalai Lama has also gone far beyond dwelling on the misfortune of his own people. He has traveled the world showing concern for suffering in every country to which he is invited, bringing together religious leaders, politicians, and scientists in the spirit of ecumenicism. He always expresses an attitude of loving-kindness and encourages people of all persuasions to overcome fixation on the rightness of their particular views and traditions over others and to work together in harmony.

Some years ago I spent a week visiting the Dalai Lama at his residence in Dharmsala. I was with a group of six scientists who had been invited to discuss the mind and life sciences with the Dalai Lama. The Dalai Lama constantly radiated friendliness, and the room was filled with a feeling of heartfelt warmth between all of us. Yet within that friendliness, the Dalai Lama also demonstrated an extraordinary sharpness of intellect. He often leapt ahead of the scientist who was making the presentation and asked a question to which the reply would be, "Your Holiness, that is *exactly* the next experiment that the scientists did." I left feeling uplifted and nourished by the insight and kindness that had filled that room.

In *The Sword of No-Sword,* John Stevens describes the life of one of the greatest Japanese Zen sword teachers of modern times, Yamaoka Tesshu, who lived from 1836 to 1888. Like the Dorje Dradul, Tesshu was a remarkable poet and painter as well as a master swordsman and renowned teacher of swordsmanship. In the last eight years of his life he produced more than a *million* works of painting and calligraphy. Stevens says of these works, "Many were obviously dashed off in a frenzy of Zen enthusiasm; still, there is no trace of stagnation or a taint of constructed characters. Wonderfully constructed, his paintings too are a joy to contemplate, and has anyone brushed better Zen cartoons? As a master of *sho* [calligraphy], the highest of all art forms, Tesshu's calligraphy is indeed that of an ascending dragon."

The "ascending dragon" is an allusion to one of Tesshu's paintings that shows a dragon soaring to the top of Mount Fuji in a flash, while a snail slowly creeps up the mountainside but also reaches the peak in the end. Tesshu's inscription calligraphed on the painting was:

> *If this snail*
> *Sets out for*
> *The top of Fuji*
> *Surely he will*
> *Get there*

Here are a few of the many other poems Tesshu composed:

> *Perfect when clear*
> *Perfect when cloudy*
> *Mount Fuji's*
> *Original form*
> *Never changes*

> *If your mind*
> *is not projected*
> *into your hands*
> *even 10,000 techniques*
> *will be useless*

> *Against an opponent's sword*
> *assume no stance,*
> *and keep your mind unmoved;*
> *that is the place*
> *of victory.*

> *Self-centered thoughts*
> *are reflected as*

clearly as in a mirror;
let others see them
and you will be making a fool of yourself

"No more sake for you"
(my doctor declared)
but look at how tattered my sleeves are—[i.e. my body is all worn-out
    and ready to go]
pour me some, please;
fill my cup again and again.

Tesshu, like the Dorje Dradul, shocked the conventional society of his time by his love of sake, or rice wine. Stories of his sake-drinking exploits and his sense of humor were legion. On one occasion, when Tesshu was drinking with his companions, they dared him to try to ride a horse so violent that no one could get near it, let alone ride it. According to Stevens, "Tesshu walked straight into the horse's stall, grabbed it by the tail, and started yanking. 'Look out, you madman!' the others yelled as they headed for cover. To everyone's surprise, the animal no man could tame meekly followed Tesshu out of the stall and stood at bay in the middle of the stable."

Tesshu served in the imperial household for ten years, and because of his freedom from corruptibility, he was deeply trusted by the emperor. A fellow minister once said of him, "He doesn't need fame, fortune, status, or even life itself—how do you deal with such a man."

Tesshu established the Muto Ryu (no-sword system) school of swordsmanship. According to Stevens:

Tesshu insisted that no-sword swordsmanship was ultimately pure spirit. Near the end of his life Tesshu's movements were extraordinarily supple and he could defeat an opponent without even touching him. Students had sore spots on the places where Tesshu had merely pointed his sword at their bodies.

A week before his death, Tesshu called all his trainees together for a final practice session. Tesshu told them, "I'm dying. My physical strength is gone. I am barely able to stand. Not a trace of competitiveness remains. I'll now prove to you all that Muto Ryu swordsmanship is a thing of the spirit. If any of you displays the slightest reserve today, the Muto Ryu will perish with my death."

Without regard for Tesshu's terminal illness, one by one, eight or nine disciples came forward and attacked him ferociously. The first student attacked, and just as he was about to bring down his sword with all his might, he was spun around and crushed to the floor by a tremendous force. Yet Tesshu had not physically touched him. The other students went flying in the same way. Tesshu proclaimed, "This is the sword of no-sword."

Tesshu was renowned and popular. There was a constant stream of visitors to his home. "Callers included those who merely wanted to borrow money or to have some petition presented to the emperor," Stevens says, "but most came for instruction and counsel, and not a few hung around just to absorb a bit of the tremendous energy radiated by Tesshu's presence. . . . Despite the constant crush of visitors, Tesshu's door was always open and all were received with courtesy."

Yet his popularity was of no concern to him. "Whenever Zen attempts to win converts or compete with other sects," he said, "its true spirit is lost. Nothing I have done was for the sake of popularizing Zen. . . . If just one person carries on the right transmission, I will be satisfied."

Tesshu appears to have been a man of unyielding determination, uncompromising bravery, wild humor, and great kindness. There are many parallels in his life to that of the Dorje Dradul. Like the Dorje Dradul, he was a man of authentic presence, a master warrior.

Warriors of authentic presence often do not fulfill the usual image of a holy man or woman. They are not bound inwardly by conventional understanding, to the extent that their contemporaries might consider them unorthodox or too outspoken. They have no need for secrecy or privacy, no need to hide their real humanity behind a veneer of specialness or holiness. Yet however outwardly unconventional *or* gracious their appearance, they have given up grasping for personal comfort, and so without pretense or needing to crank anything up, they constantly radiate loving-kindness.

When he was a young man in Tibet, one of the Dorje Dradul's main teachers was the "crazy saint," Khenpo Gangshar. Reginald Ray, author of *Buddhist Saints in India,* describes Gangshar in this way:

As a young monk, the Khenpo was renowned for his scholarly training and rigorous, indeed faultless, observance of the vinaya [monastic rules]. At one point, however, he became extremely sick, was given up for dead, and finally passed away. His corpse was laid out in a small room. Some time later, he suddenly and most dramatically revived, leaping up and throwing open the shutters of the tiny cell where he had been put.

From that moment on, he seemed to have become an entirely different person. He took a female consort, renounced his vows and behaved in a bizarre fashion. He was said to be able to tell people's inner thoughts immediately by just looking at them. Many who met him found his attainment self-evident and became disciples and devotees. Others were troubled and embarrassed at this strange behavior, were uncomfortable in his presence, and criticized and avoided him.

Nor are examples of such warriors by any means confined to the Eastern traditions. The stories of many of the early Christian saints, including Saint Francis of Assisi, often include behavior that cut through the conventional minds of the day.

Saint Symeon of Emesa, a sixth-century canonized saint, was just such a "Fool for Christ." On one occasion he was employed to sell beans for an innkeeper, and instead he distributed them free to the people. He would throw nuts at people praying in church, walk about naked, throw stones at passersby, and associate with prostitutes. He had a mischievous sense of humor, but he also worked miracles. He was buried as a madman, but shortly afterward, when his coffin was reopened to grant him a decent burial, his corpse was not to be found.

The Dorje Dradul says of the master warrior,

> Most important, in every activity of his life, in every action he takes, there is always magic—always. In whatever he does, the master warrior of Shambhala guides the minds of his students into the visionary mind of the [Great Eastern Sun]. He constantly challenges his students to step beyond themselves, to step out into the vast and brilliant world of reality in which he abides. The challenge that he provides is not so much that he is always setting hurdles for his students or egging them on. Rather, his authentic presence is a constant challenge to be genuine and true.

In this chapter, I have given examples of people who have attained some degree of mastery on the path of warriorship, and who exhibit an authentic presence that has a powerful effect on their world. However, I do not want to leave you with the impression that authentic presence is only for a few, rare individuals or that authentic presence is some far-off state of being that is difficult to accomplish. Authentic presence accumulates naturally when you are kind and brave; when you see and let go of fixations about yourself and your world, and of the aggression that comes from defending these fixations; when you genuinely care for others; and when you keep your sense of humor. It accumulates gradually but inevitably in your system, little by little, as you tread the path of warriorship.

CHAPTER 13

The Dorje Dradul
and Gerald Red Elk

The Dorje Dradul is present throughout this book, but I should like here to try to convey a little more of the quality of his life and its effect on the people around him. He was a man of overwhelming authentic presence. Even before he died in 1987, his life had become almost legendary to many thousands of students in the Western world as well as throughout Asia. It will take many complete books, by many different people, before anything approaching a complete picture of the Dorje Dradul emerges. It is an impossible task for one person to convey fully the nature of such a man in one small chapter. So this can only be the merest personal sketch.

The Dorje Dradul and His Students

The Dorje Dradul was not embarrassed to live openly. He used to say with great delight that the auto accident that had changed the direction and style of his teaching in the West was a crash into a joke shop. He was not a holy man, wearing robes and preaching beautiful ideas that neither his students nor he lived up to. Outwardly, he lived an ordinary life—he married and had children; he drank and fell in love; he entered into human life with an intensity of joy and sadness that I have never seen in another person—and could not have imagined possible before I met him. Yet he was able to bring the Buddha dharma as well as the Shambhala teachings—the path of awakening in daily life—to the West with power and integrity. He led students out of their confusion. Because he lived a human life alongside his students, he was able to show them how to wake up rather than merely preach at them.

The Dorje Dradul's life was a feast of celebrations. He celebrated the dawn as well as the dusk. He did not work "hard" in the puritan sense, but he worked steadily, like an elephant walking through the jungle. He did what was necessary, sowing the seeds of many projects, and the rest unfolded because of the intense dedication that he inspired in his students whom he regarded as his friends. He said, as well, that he had some help from his drala friends.

His command of the English language went beyond mere fluency and into the subtle meanings of words. Many were the times when he would use a word in a very particular way that I would think strange—only to discover later in a dictionary that he was using the word precisely as it was meant to be used before the latest degeneration of our language.

He was physically short and overweight; he walked with a limp, as his left side was partially paralyzed by the auto accident that had changed his life. But when he entered a room, I felt a tremendous sense of power joined with humor. His love for his students could be almost too much to bear. A friend told me that once, after he had been away for a while, he went into a room where the Dorje Dradul was sitting with a few friends. My friend went up to give him a hug. "I felt so much warmth and love from the Dorje Dradul," he told me, "that I felt a physical shock and found myself closing off and pulling back. I just couldn't stand to be loved so much." Because of his radiance of love and his fierce authenticity, he was loved intensely and passionately by thousands of students.

Susan describes meeting the Dorje Dradul for the first time:

The most amazing thing I felt about him was his ability to penetrate my being—thoroughly. I had read his books and planned my trip from Chicago to Boulder for several months. I was very excited about meeting him and felt quite confident in my own right—I was a highly regarded up-and-coming actress with an active life and lots of friends. When I was finally introduced to him, I was stunned as if I had received an electric shock. He held out his hand to me, and when I took it, I felt the most unbelievable feeling of gentleness I had ever known. In contrast, my own energy felt painfully aggressive. Then I looked into his eyes. There was a softness and kindness exuding which I had never experienced before and, beyond that, a depth I could not fathom. I couldn't find the person beyond those eyes. The effect on me was tremendously powerful. It was as if this man could see through to my deepest core, and yet he accepted me. I felt I had been penetrated by loving but X-ray eyes—my masks unraveled in the light of his being so *real*. All this took a moment—just a short exchange. I didn't understand what had happened and went immediately to my own room and sat there feeling shaken. I couldn't speak to anyone. It was as if I had been in front of an uncompromising mirror that reflected every tiniest detail and hidden corner of my mind and heart. How could it be possible for someone to reflect me so clearly and yet appreciate me so completely at one glance? I guess I fell in love.

He had a mischievous and charming wit. He loved to cheer people up and play practical jokes on his students, and he loved to pun. Once, in the middle of a three-month-long retreat in which three hundred students were gathered to study and practice Vajrayana Buddhism, he initiated a battle of pea-shooters and water pistols that went on for days. His humor lay, though, not so much in his joke-telling as in his constantly pointing out the humor and foibles of the ordinary human life around him. In spite of his joyful approach to life, his humor could have a sharp edge that exposed ingenuineness mercilessly. He himself was always genuine—whether he was smiling broadly in the midst of a blistering snowstorm, or radiating black air that put everyone around him on edge. He felt and communicated tremendous sadness for the state of the world. He would end a talk on establishing genuine human society with the urgent appeal, "Let us help others, *please.*"

When I first met him in the United States in 1970, the Dorje Dradul wore cowboy shirts and jeans and he lived an ordinary life alongside his students. He would join in the parties, drinking beer and playing the bongo drums and even trying to dance rock 'n' roll to the blaring of the Rolling Stones, wearing a huge, broad, slightly quizzical grin. Yet even at those times, if you looked into his eyes, there was a feeling of tremendous openness, warmth, and uncompromising firmness—a sense of boundless intelligence and playfulness that was neither self-conscious nor manipulative yet was highly disciplined.

In 1974 the Dorje Dradul invited the sixteenth Gyalwa Karmapa to visit his students in America. The Karmapa is head of the Kagyu school of Tibetan Buddhism, and like the Dalai Lama, he is considered by many to be a living

Buddha. In preparing to host the Karmapa appropriately, the Dorje Dradul drove himself beyond the limits of any of his students' endurance. He kept them up day and night, night after night, making brocade-covered thrones, painting, preparing the house where the Karmapa was to stay, and so on. The Dorje Dradul's outpouring of devotional energy was a tremendous inspiration to his students. We saw how someone of such wisdom could be offered love with respect and dignity rather than in the casual and sloppy style to which we had been accustomed. After the Karmapa left, the students continued to treat the Dorje Dradul in the same way that they had learned and delighted in treating the Karmapa. A more formal relationship with the Dorje Dradul developed then, a relationship more like master-to-apprentice than like good ol' buddies. Yet he remained available as an intimate friend to hundreds of people.

He made it very clear that the path of warriorship had nothing to do with rejecting human society. On the contrary, the main point was to work toward building a genuinely good society. Many of his students in the 1970s had come from the hippie and drug cultures. He had attracted a rather cynical, though intelligent, bunch of educated drop-outs. But gradually, with the Dorje Dradul's encouragement, they went back to school, started businesses, got married, and reentered the flow of society. One such young woman tells of saying to him one day, in the early years, "I would do anything to serve you. Please tell me what I can do." His reply was, "Be a solid citizen."

By no means did being a student warrior apprenticed to the Dorje Dradul always mean having a good time. On the contrary, we felt a sharp edge in his presence no matter how long we had known him and no matter how well we thought we knew him. He was utterly unpredictable. He could answer a serious and solemn question with a sweet smile and a simple joke that would make me crawl with embarrassment. For example, shortly after I had met him, I approached him with a serious look on my face. "I would like to talk with you sometime about how you brought up children in Tibet," I said. I had been a schoolteacher for a while, and I suppose I thought that this would be a good way to make conversation with him. He smiled and replied, "Well, I think we used the stairs."

His simple kindness was felt not only by his students and those who knew him but also by complete strangers. Recently someone who is now a Shambhala student told this story, one of many such stories: "I had been committed to a mental hospital, but the doctors had now decided that I was well enough to be released. I could be released, however, only on condition that someone would sign that they would be responsible for me. None of my friends or family were willing to do this for me. So it seemed as if I was stuck there. Then I heard that someone whom I had never met had come to sign for me and I was released. The person who signed for me was the Dorje Dradul."

Another student tells of a time he was to drive the Dorje Dradul in a car. He opened the back door, and the Dorje Dradul, who moved slowly and somewhat awkwardly because of his limp, climbed in, reached his arm up, and put his right hand on the roof of the car to lift himself into the seat. The driver slammed the car door onto the Dorje Dradul's fingers. Panicked and mortified, the driver opened the door. The Dorje Dradul looked up at him and said, "Are you all right? You must feel awful. I am so sorry. That was a very foolish place to put my hand."

His generosity in leading his students beyond their hesitations seemed to have no bounds. One highly intelligent student, Joshua, who had a great sense of humor but was also very sharp and cynical, became very ill and wrote a long letter a few days before he died. The letter was addressed to the Dorje Dradul, but it was also intended for his fellow students. A few paragraphs of this letter here convey so well the humor and directness of the Dorje Dradul.

Dear Rinpoche,

You continue to astonish me right to the end. What amazingly good karma for me to have met you. Over the years I have not been what you would call a great student. . . . And yet you have never abandoned me—never, not for an instant. And I have somehow managed to hold you in my heart. . . .

Do you recall when you told me to "pull up your socks" I replied "I don't wear socks," and you shot back, "Then pull up your pants." That was the moment I knew I had met my teacher.

Do you recall that Sasaki Roshi gave me a "very difficult koan" to "protect my mind" at the first seminary [a three-month residential retreat introducing students to Vajrayana Buddhism], and when I arrived, without my having mentioned it, the first thing you said was, "Forget the koan."

Do you recall the time—even now thinking about it makes my heart beat—when you stood at the top of the murderous flight of stairs at 1111 Pearl and you asked me, "Are you ready?" ("ripe" you meant) and when I hesitated for a moment you plunged down the stairs! I leaped to catch you at the landing and tore my sports coat on the banister. I felt totally bewildered and dejected and said that I hoped I would someday have another chance.

"Sure," you said, and plunged down the remaining steps to my complete surprise. O Teacher—at any price, even your own body, your life.
We've really had fun together.

The Dorje Dradul was tremendously loyal to all his friends and students. He would never forget a student. He would always admonish us to pay attention to those who were having difficulties with their lives or with sitting practice, or who just seemed to be drifting off. He would ask after people who had studied with him many years previously, in England or in India, wanting to know how they were and whether they were still practicing. When the Naropa Institute began in 1974, he insisted that we try to contact several people who had been his students in England and ask them to come and teach there. If someone turned up after an absence of several years, he would welcome them like a long-lost brother or sister.

As well as being warm and benevolent, the Dorje Dradul could also be overpoweringly wrathful, berating people suddenly and unexpectedly but with piercing accuracy. He often created friction and feistiness among his students— friction that ignited a flame of power and energy—so that they could leap to another level of genuine understanding. He overflowed with stark compassion that was uncompromising with conventional niceness.

Once I was sitting in his back garden with him the day after he had conducted an empowerment of the Sadhana of Vajrayogini—a practice in the Tibetan Buddhist teaching. The empowerment was an all-day affair and had ended in the evening with a *tri*—a talk by the teacher on how to do the practice. I had been practicing the Vajrayogini Sadhana for some years and found this *tri* particularly delightful and helpful. The following afternoon, as I sat with the Dorje Dradul, during one of the long silences that often punctuated conversation between him and myself, I turned to him. "That was a *won*derful *tri* that you gave yesterday, sir," I said, with a particularly sugary emphasis on the "*won*derful." He replied, "Hm."

About an hour later we were joined by another member of his staff, and after chatting for a while the Dorje Dradul rose and walked slowly across the patio with each of us on either side of him. He stopped at a flower bed that had a clump of huge purple begonias, opened his zipper, and pissed right into the middle of the begonias. Leaning a little in my direction he said, "Jeremy, aren't they *won*derful," with exactly the same sugary intonation. Here was another lesson, as if I should have needed one by then, that the path of warriorship is not about feeling *won*derful but about discovering reality.

Conscious Drinking

The Dorje Dradul loved to drink sake. He had no embarrassment about this, and he did not try to hide it or exhibit any kind of shame or hesitation about it. Nor did his students. His senior students did, however, try to slow his drinking down out of fear for his health. His response to this was to say, "You don't understand. Don't hinder my work." In general he also made it clear that his circumstances were extraordinary, and he discouraged his students from imitating his way of drinking.

Once a visiting Tibetan teacher, also a major teacher of the Kagyu school, was asked about the Dorje Dradul's drinking. He replied, "He is an extraordinary bodhisattva." He then went on to say that great teachers often use unconventional means to show the way beyond egotism and conventional mind. Marpa, the farmer and translator who brought Buddhism from India to Tibet and thereby founded the Kagyu school, was one of many teachers of the Tibetan tradition who used alcohol in this way. In the Japanese Zen tradition, too, there are stories of great teachers, like master swordsman Yamaoka Tesshu, who enjoyed drinking in large quantities—shocking small minds and stirring the cocoon sleep of their students with their humor and wild antics.

To senior students the Dorje Dradul gave drinking lessons. These would always occur in the context of the ritual (sadhana) practice of Tibetan Buddhism. He would ask us to take a sip of sake and be mindful of the perceptual and bodily changes that we felt occurring. We would sometimes drink quite a lot at these sessions, but no one became "drunk" in the conventional sense. On the contrary, there was a sense of intensified awareness in the meditation hall at those times. The point was to learn to maintain awareness at each stage of intoxication and thereby ride the energy and raise one's windhorse further.

In an article entitled "Alcohol as Medicine or Poison," the Dorje Dradul wrote,

Whether alcohol is to be a poison or a medicine depends on one's awareness while drinking. Conscious drinking—remaining aware of one's state of mind—transmutes the effect of alcohol. Here awareness involves a tightening up of one's system as an intelligent defense mechanism. Alcohol becomes destructive when one gives in to the joviality: letting loose permits the poisons to enter one's body. . . . Alcohol's creativity begins when there is a sense of dancing with its effects—when one takes the effects of drink with a sense of humor. For the conscious drinker, or for the *yogi*, the virtue of alcohol is that it brings one down to ordinary reality, so that one does not dissolve into meditation on non-duality. . . . But naturally the ordinary drinker who tries to compete with or imitate this transcendental style of drinking will turn his alcohol into poison.

I do not recommend that anyone try the practice of conscious drinking on their own or even under the supervision of a teacher who claims to know how to work with alcohol in this way. It is too dangerous. Don't squash your skeptical mind when you approach a teacher. Does the teacher demand blind obedience or blind adherence to doctrines you do not understand or that you feel are harmful to you? In that case, it is better to stay away, no matter how charismatic he may seem. In contrast, does a teacher provide a path and a practice by which you can learn to emulate, rather than merely imitate, him or her? A teacher can really guide you only if there is mutual respect and if you are able to love him genuinely. Longing to follow in the path of a teacher and respect for that teacher are the two components of loyalty, but you have to keep your eyes wide open every step of the way. As the Dorje Dradul did, a genuine teacher shows you how to find your own profound sanity and integrity—he does not steal it from you.

The Dorje Dradul came to the West to accomplish a purpose—to establish genuine Buddha dharma here. This he fulfilled in abundance, as we can see from the thousands of students who fell in love with the dharma through his teachings both before and *after* he died. In addition, he founded a new path of secular spiritual training for the modern world—Shambhala training—which has brought to a spiritual path many thousands of people who had turned against all conventional religion. It did not matter to him how far he had to go to push *himself* in order to accomplish these purposes, and he certainly pushed his students as well as himself beyond the bounds of comfort.

Why Don't People Want to Wake Up?

The Dorje Dradul was direct and uncompromising in his dismissal of hypocrites whatever their fame, popularity, or importance. He could attend a luncheon of U.S. senators or a fund-raising dinner with the wealthy and famous and appear thoroughly drunk and uninterested. Then he could go straight to a gathering of genuine students and give a vigorous demonstration of flower arranging that was precise and overwhelmingly beautiful. When his behavior was unconventional, it was so precise and to the point that it cut right through people's habitual ideas of themselves. He had no truck with sham of any kind! His behavior weeded out the cowards, the ungenuine, the false-hearted ones claiming to be liberals. He used to say, "I am so proud of my students. They are the real thing. They are fearless and gentle and confused and sometimes awake, but *they never give up.*"

Certainly I, like all of his students, had doubts at times about the Dorje Dradul. It would not have been a genuine relationship if I had not felt doubt and irritation. His behavior sometimes seemed to be so strange—almost bizarre— that it brooked no rational explanation, it simply stopped short the conventional mind. Writing of the Dorje Dradul's teacher, Khenpo Gangshar, Reginald Ray says:

> From the time of his awakening, Khenpo Gangshar had an aura about him that frightened everyone—his disciples and detractors included— and he did things that by conventional standards seemed immoral. The question was whether one found anything profound or valuable in what the Khenpo said and did. Many people were deeply devoted to the Khenpo and found his words and actions expressions of enlightenment; others did not like him and did not want to be around him. Trungpa Rinpoche [the Dorje Dradul], as far as I can see, presents much the same configuration.

At times we all wished he would go away and leave us alone. On a few occasions my doubts became a full-blown fear for my own sanity. One day, when the Dorje Dradul had recently introduced us to the dralas, I sat at my desk thinking about these teachings and the intense and outrageous way he was manifesting at that time. He was certainly stretching our conceptions of "normal" behavior. I suddenly felt cold all over as the thought occurred, "Is this whole thing completely mad? Will I go mad if I go on with it?" My mind went numb, screaming an unspoken question, and I felt fear and doubt in my body.

Gradually, as I sat in my chair filled with doubt, I began to recollect moments of peace that I had had in my sitting practice. I began to feel again, in my body, the warmth and strength of basic goodness. Then I recalled that during my years with the Dorje Dradul, practicing as he taught, my state of being had softened from a black self-hate and anger toward the world to feeling some joy and kindness toward myself and others. I had seen others change in this way too. Finally, I began to think of the unrelenting gentleness and kindness of the Dorje Dradul himself. Gradually confidence returned to my mind and body, and a renewed joy that I had found a genuine path.

In 1977 the Dorje Dradul left for a full-year retreat. His intention was to see how well his students would handle themselves in his absence, as well as the already-large organizations that he had set up with them. Throughout his teaching, over and over again, he would throw students back on themselves. He would not allow them to treat him as their "daddy." He was there for them as a friend and as a fierce master warrior, with whom they apprenticed at their own risk. Each student was expected to live his or her own life and find his or her own genuineness.

He did not hold himself back, however, from involving himself in all aspects of his students' lives. "I could remain on my pedestal as a Buddhist teacher," he once said, "and we could have a tremendous play between each other. We would all be Buddhists. You would be great tantric practitioners and we could have a great time together. But then there is a whole other area that has been completely left out—the actual 'secular' situation, for lack of a better word. I could commit myself as a Buddhist teacher to you as Buddhist students only so far. The Shambhala vision of what we are doing is that we could actually mingle ourselves completely together, so that communication is taking place fully, thoroughly, and completely, and we have no private areas left."

In a talk to students who followed both the Buddhist and the Shambhala paths, the Dorje Dradul compared the two paths. In Shambhala terms, he said, egolessness or absence of reference point can have more spark and actually expose us more than in Buddhism, because we have to give up clutching even religious practice as a reference point for our self-centeredness. "If we are holding on to any kind of corner as a little fortress, a little capsule," he said, "we have a problem in raising windhorse. . . . The fruition of the warrior's path is the experience of primordial goodness or the complete unconditioned nature of basic goodness. This experience is the same as the complete realization of egolessness or the truth of nonreference point."

The Dorje Dradul paid tremendous attention to the details of his students' lives. He cared about how they dressed, what food they liked, and who they were dating. He even paid attention to how they ate their peas! The discovery of unconditioned basic goodness, he said, comes only from working *with* the reference points, life's ordinary conditions and situations—washing clothes, eating breakfast, drinking a cup of tea, paying bills, and so forth: "The principles of warriorship are concerned, first of all, with learning to appreciate those processes, those mundane reference points."

In his own life he was impeccable. None of his possessions, however small, was ever treated frivolously or carelessly. Each ordinary object had its place in his world, and the way he related to such objects demonstrated the sacred world more clearly than words. He even gave a name to every one of his suits. He demonstrated his respect for the world in the simple act of raising a cup, putting on a hat, or shaking someone's hand with gentleness. He had tremendous appreciation for every aspect of the ordinary world, and the dignity with which he handled everything continually demonstrated inherent goodness.

He demonstrated, too, that all these mundane aspects of our existence can become free from reference point, or personal grasping. "By relating with the ordinary conditions of your life," he wrote, "you might make a shocking discovery. While drinking your cup of tea, you might discover that you are drinking tea in a vacuum. In fact, *you* are not even drinking the tea. The hollowness of space is drinking tea. So while doing any little ordinary thing, that reference point might bring an experience of nonreference point. When you put on your pants or your skirt, you might find that you are dressing up space. When you put on your makeup, you might discover that you are putting cosmetics on space. You are beautifying space, pure nothingness. . . . The warrior fundamentally is someone who is not afraid of space. The coward lives in constant terror of space."

Two years before he died, the Dorje Dradul went away for a second retreat. During this retreat, he would sometimes stay awake continuously for several days and nights at a time. He would expect his staff of three or four, not to speak of the few guests who might be visiting, to stay awake as well. On one occasion, while I was on staff attending him, the rest of the staff were trying to catch a few hours' sleep at three o'clock in the morning. The Dorje Dradul came storming through the house banging a stick on a metal cooking pot and shouting, "Why don't people want to *wake up*?" The retreat had a profound and lasting effect on anyone who visited. We began to transcend day and night, breakfast-time, lunch-time, and dinner-time, light and dark, sleep and awake. We began to transcend the limits of our mundane perception and belief in a solid, rational world.

Meeting with Gerald Red Elk

In 1984 the Dorje Dradul had an extraordinary meeting with Gerald Red Elk, an Oglala Sioux shaman-chief, another man of great compassion and authentic presence. According to Gerald Red Elk's adopted American nephew, Roger La Borde:

Some would say that Gerald's house was cluttered; all sorts of clothes, blankets, pictures, boxes and so on were stacked around the room. His home didn't feel that way to me, though; it had a warmth to it and a feeling of a comfortable old chair that would be nice to climb into and just rest forever. . . .

Following the adoption and naming ceremonies [in which Gerald became Roger's uncle,] a big giveaway was held. Blankets, star quilts, money, food, belt buckles, and war bonnets were given away to all who attended, which was quite a few. This was my first exposure to the tremendous generosity of Gerald's family. I then knew what he did with all those things stacked in his house—he gave them away. . . .

At one time he was a very angry man. He hated the white man and all that the white man had done to his people. He was lost in alcoholism. But nearly twenty years ago, as he was near death, he prayed [to the Great Spirit] to be spared. He promised that if he was allowed to live he would change his life and help his people. . . . Gerald did keep his promise. He helped his people, and his people included everyone. He told me one day that he realized that after the Great Spirit had let him live there was only one race of people on this earth—the human race.

Gerald was deeply concerned that the bad state of mind of the present civilization was causing tremendous turmoil on the earth and that much worse was to come. Every four years he would meet with other native elders at a special place in the Rocky Mountains near Denver, Colorado, to read messages from the gods—the Star People, as he called them—etched on the rocks. The recent messages had depicted the gods weeping—warning of the terrible suffering of the earth itself. "They're telling us, for the future," he said. "Some things are going to happen, and people will have to be in a very good state of mind, so they could be strong, so they could reason without panicking, and at the same time they could learn what all those grasses and trees and (they call them weeds) what those plants are all about, because all of them are medicine and are edible."

Gerald Red Elk came to the Denver area in 1980 to read the medicine rocks, and while he was there, he asked to meet the Dorje Dradul. "I wanted to meet a Tibetan lama," he said later, "because we understand the heart of what they are. We call anybody in that state of mind a 'common man of the earth' because they live the laws of the earth, they understand, and we could communicate without talking."

Since the Dorje Dradul was not available to meet Gerald, I was asked to take his place. He came into my office one late afternoon. Tall and stooped, he wore baggy polyester pants and a short-sleeved shirt with a row of ball-point pens in the breast pocket, all clipped onto a plastic pocket guard. He looked a little like an aging truck driver. We sat down against opposite walls in my small office. Gerald began by saying that he believed that the Tibetans had knowledge about the Star People that complemented the knowledge his people had of them. Together, he felt, the two peoples could help the world in the coming bad times.

Gerald's voice was very soft and low; I could hardly understand what he was saying. I had not then heard of the Star People, though they sounded somewhat like the dralas to whom the Dorje Dradul had very recently introduced us. Yet I was completely transfixed by his presence. The room seemed filled with kindness and generosity and an almost magical enchantment. I felt, as we sat there, that he was pouring love out toward me, even as he spoke about almost incomprehensible things. As the sun set, the room grew dark, but I did not want to get out of my chair and turn on the light for fear of breaking the spell.

Eventually Gerald got up to leave, and I accompanied him downstairs. In a quiet, sad voice he again said that he would like to meet "the Tibetan." As he turned and ambled away toward the door, I felt an ache in my chest as if someone whom I had known intimately and affectionately for many years were leaving, never to return. The Dorje Dradul was still unavailable that night, and Gerald left town early the next morning. It was four years before their paths finally crossed, when Gerald Red Elk was again in Colorado to read the medicine rocks.

The meeting with the Dorje Dradul took place only a few months before Gerald died. It was on a bright summer afternoon in the Rocky Mountains at an encampment for training in Shambhala warriorship practice. At the beginning of their meeting the Dorje Dradul and Gerald talked briefly about the weather. The Dorje Dradul looked at the sky and said, "I think it is going to rain tomorrow." Gerald replied, "I think it will probably rain in a few hours." The Dorje Dradul responded, "I think it will rain tomorrow morning." Gerald said, "I think it will rain soon." Throughout the meeting thunder rumbled.

Gerald presented the Dorje Dradul with a turquoise stone that represented the nature of the universe; a red stone, the nature of the gods; a green stone, the earth; and a purple stone, medicine. They spoke together for about forty minutes, Gerald showing the Dorje Dradul drawings of the rock messages. Both commented on the similarity of some of the drawings to the animals portrayed on the Dorje Dradul's Shambhala standard: the tiger, snow lion, garuda, and dragon. "I think we can work together," the Dorje Dradul said. "It is very magical." He gave Gerald a copy of *Shambhala: The Sacred Path of the Warrior*, which had just been published. Gerald exclaimed, "The sacred path of the warrior, this is what we believe in. The honor is there. The honor is there." Later, the Dorje Dradul said, "He understood the whole book just from the cover," while Gerald commented, "We understood each other completely without needing to say anything."

The two sat quietly together for almost an hour. At the end of the meeting they embraced and the Dorje Dradul said, "I think something extraordinary will come out of this." As Gerald Red Elk walked slowly back down the valley, a slight rain began to fall. As they walked away, Roger La Borde says,

> Huge raindrops began to fall, the biggest I think I have ever seen, and I grew up where thunderstorms were common. A large electric-blue bolt of lightning struck the ground several hundred yards away. I actually saw the spot where it hit the ground. As we drove away a monsoon (or so it seemed) commenced. I said to Gerald as we were driving out to the main highway that I knew that sparks would fly during the meeting, but I didn't expect it to be lightning! Gerald's response was that the night before he had had a dream of rain and lightning during the meeting, which he took to be the gods' approval of the meeting.

As they walked away, meanwhile, the Dorje Dradul remained seated outside his tent, saying, "It's so sad, so sad." The rain fell more heavily as Red Elk continued down the road. The attendants tried to encourage the Dorje Dradul to go inside his tent, but he continued to sit outside, under the tent flap. The rain seemed to let up, and the Dorje Dradul picked up his stick and said, "Well, I guess that's enough." The rain stopped for a minute.

The Dorje Dradul and Gerald Red Elk

Then the Dorje Dradul began to shake, and he started crying, sobbing. He picked up his stick again and slammed it on his knee. At that point a torrential downpour—the heaviest rain anyone had ever experienced—flooded the valley. My nephew Carl told me, "We were standing in the center of the campground getting ready to take down the flag for the evening. It had been a beautiful warm sunny afternoon. Suddenly a big black cloud moved across the valley and seemed to stop over us. We were told to go to our tents—just forty or fifty feet away—to get our raincoats, but it started to pour and before we could even get to the tents, we were soaked. The cloud just emptied on the camp, and then moved away."

The Dorje Dradul still wouldn't go into his tent. Attendants inside and outside the tent pushed up the roof with poles to try to keep the rain from collapsing the tent. As the downpour increased to a formidable deluge the grounds were no longer visible, and a curtain of water completely surrounded the Dorje Dradul. His attendants were yelling pleas that he come inside the tent. But he shook his head. As he continued to sit, finally a rainbow formed in the valley. It was as if, in the play of the rain and hail, the lightning and sunshine, the elements had sealed a magical connection between two true master warriors.

Gerald Red Elk became ill with cancer shortly after this meeting and died a few months later. He and the Dorje Dradul never met again. When Roger went to visit Gerald in his hospital room just before he died, the first thing Gerald said was, "How's Rinpoche?"

The Dorje Dradul's
Extraordinary Legacy

The Dorje Dradul died after only sixteen years of active life in North America. When he first came to this continent, he had warned his students that he would be around for only twenty years, but we had not believed him. The last time I spoke to him, in September 1986, he said, "It seems to be happening faster than we thought." A month later, he suffered a cardiac arrest and a stroke that left him unable to speak. He died on April 4, 1987.

The Dorje Dradul's work here was recognized and praised by many of the great Tibetan Buddhist teachers and leaders who visited the West, including the head of the Kagyu school, the Gyalwa Karmapa, and Dilgo Khyentse Rinpoche, head of the Nyingma school. The Kagyu and Nyingma schools are two of the four great living lineages of Tibetan Buddhist teaching, and the Dorje Dradul was trained in both lineages. Khyentse Rinpoche was himself considered a living saint and bodhisattva during his lifetime and one of the greatest teachers of Buddhism that Tibet had known. Sogyal Rinpoche, a student of Khyentse Rinpoche, says, "To think of Dilgo Khyentse Rinpoche and of what he has done for humanity is to find gathered and displayed in one person the greatness of the gift Tibet is giving to the world."

Shortly after the Dorje Dradul's death, Khyentse Rinpoche came to the United States to preside over the cremation ceremony for the Dorje Dradul. He remarked,

> Trungpa Rinpoche is not an ordinary person. He is a being who came to this earth knowing what he was going to do, how to benefit beings according to their needs, according to their capacity. He was born in Tibet, but he spent most of his life in the West to plant the seed of his vision to create a new society.
>
> To further his vision, Trungpa Rinpoche gave many teachings in the past, and the most precious thing is to take to heart all these teachings and put them into practice. In order to create a new society which shines forth the light of great peace, it's important that each one of us develop this vision from within. The moment we can create this among us, then it will be so easy to manifest it throughout the world.

In 1993, a remarkably powerful and outspoken teacher, Khenpo Jigme Phunsok, visited North America for the first time. He is one of the few great teachers to remain in Tibet after the Chinese invasion. He escaped capture from the Chinese by hiding in caves above fourteen thousand feet. There he continued to teach the thousands of Tibetans, who risked their lives to see him in spite of the Chinese persecution. The story is told that once when the Chinese army came to capture him, Jigme Phunsok caused horrible-looking boils to appear on his body, and his students told the soldiers this was smallpox. The soldiers left without touching him. In his talks in the United States, Jigme Phunsok expressed astonishment at the extent of the Dorje Dradul's vision and accomplishment in planting the banner of Buddhism and Shambhala in the West. He commented that the work of the Dorje Dradul in the West was much harder than what he himself had done in Tibet.

Wherever students of the Dorje Dradul travel in India, Bhutan, Nepal, or Sikkim and mention the name of Trungpa Rinpoche, they are met with, "You are *so* fortunate to have met such a great teacher." Throughout Asia, the Dorje Dradul is regarded as a great bodhisattva and mahasiddha (an awakened being whose life is dedicated to the benefit of others). In the Western world we have extraordinarily narrow and romantic stereotypes of what a "spiritual" teacher should be like. We look for someone who can "save" us, who can be a kind of living god for us and save us the trouble of having to go through the nitty-gritty of our life. Furthermore, in spite of its apparent glorification of genius and of being "different," Western popular culture resents anyone who stands out powerfully as genuinely free from all stereotypes. It is not surprising, then, that the Dorje Dradul's life stirred controversy, at least among journalists, poets, and religious academics. His work continues, however, in the hearts and activities of his students and all those whose lives were altered simply by meeting someone authentic.

Elizabeth Lesser, director of the Omega Institute for Holistic Studies writes, "Chogyam Trungpa was a man whose understanding developed not only as he trained in the stillness of Buddhist monasteries, but also as he helped his people flee from the Chinese invasion of Tibet; as he left his family and culture and came to the bewildering domain of Oxford University; and again as he established himself in the United States as a preserver and teacher of Tibetan Buddhism. Here was a person who learned to trust so deeply in the messages of his own life that he turned his exile from his homeland into an enduring gift of wisdom for the world. Where he could have developed hatred and bitterness, he nurtured seeds of understanding and compassion. Where he could have given in to confusion and resignation, he worked to cultivate intelligence and courage. He sought the big picture of reality, the picture where all of the pieces of a life—the losses and the gains, the exiles and the unions—are welcomed as necessary parts of the whole."

The organizations set up under the Dorje Dradul's guidance are now led by his eldest son, the Sawang Osel Rangdrol Mukpo. In 1979 the Dorje Dradul had empowered the Sawang to be his successor in the Shambhala teachings and bear responsibility for their continued propagation and vitality. The oral transmission of empowerment, from teacher to most senior student, is an important way of preserving the living quality of the teachings. At a semiprivate ceremony in January 1986, the Dorje Dradul had also empowered the Sawang as one of two Buddhist lineage successors, along with Osel Tendzin, co-founder of the Shambhala Training Program. Osel Tendzin died in 1990, and Khyentse Rinpoche confirmed the Sawang as the Dorje Dradul's only successor. In May 1995 the Sawang was empowered as Sakyong, holder of the Shambhala lineage of spiritual warriorship, in a public ceremony conducted by Penor Rinpoche, the head of the Nyingma or Ancient Lineage of Tibet and successor to Khyentse Rinpoche.

The Dorje Dradul's accomplishments during his few years in the West would be extraordinary even for someone who had lived here a whole lifetime. In addition to establishing the international networks of Shambhala Training Programs and Buddhist meditation centers and the Naropa Institute, he wrote many thousands of poems, created hundreds of powerful calligraphies in a unique style, and founded a school of Japanese ikebana and, with Shibata Sensei, a school of kyudo. His life was a true exemplification of his teaching. He showed us how to live an ordinary but magical life so that every moment, every person, and every thing in it becomes sacred.

CHAPTER 14

Authentic Action and an Enlightened Society

A Warrior's Action Is Response, Not Reaction

Any genuinely beneficial action—personal or social—can come only from appreciating sacredness and basic goodness. Much social action today, while well meaning, only makes situations worse because it stems from guilt, depression, and aggression. We cannot bring others to an appreciation of their own basic goodness and the sacredness of our home, the earth, if our own actions do not stem from this appreciation. Genuine social action can come only from the personal discipline of being gentle and fearless, letting go of self-centered ambition, and helping others from a joyful and genuine heart. As the Dalai Lama has said on many occasions, "First practice not harming others, then perhaps you can help others."

A warrior's action is based on responding to situations, not on reacting to them. A reaction is mindless and automatic, and it always produces the same situation as the one you are reacting to. If you *react* to aggression, you will only produce more aggression. When you see a situation clearly and feel sympathy for it at the same time, you can be responsive to it and bring to it what it really needs. If it needs to be pacified, you can pacify it; if it needs to be enriched, you can enrich it; if it needs to be stopped, you can stop it.

To act in the world genuinely and responsively, you have to let go of continually manipulating your experience and elaborating what is really very simple. If someone says to you, "You made a mistake. That doesn't go here, it goes there," you could simply put it right. Or you could go through a huge upheaval: "Oh boy, he is always telling me what to do. I never seem to do things right. What is the matter with me? I'm not accomplishing anything in my life. No one thinks I'm worth very much." Or: "He's full of it—what right does he have to tell me what to do anyway?" If you look carefully and honestly, you'll probably see that a great deal of your activity comes out of such overreacting. You do not need to give up these things because they are "bad" or "sinful." You could give them up just because when you make your experience unnecessarily complicated and try to manipulate the world to fit your own picture of it, you keep yourself from living authentically.

Instead of taking everything out of proportion, you can simply touch your gentleness, see what needs to be done, do it in a straightforward way, and let go. Seeing what needs to be cultivated and what needs to be stopped is very different from scheming to manipulate a situation to your own benefit. It is not at all the same as making judgments of things as "good" or "bad." It is much more subtle than that, like knowing when to say yes and when to say no to a child. You can know when to say yes or no only if you care for her enough to feel how she feels and see what will benefit her.

The way to determine what you can best do and accept in your life is to find what wakes you up to nowness, rouses windhorse in yourself and others, and takes you toward the joy-and-sadness of genuine heart and the Great Eastern Sun vision. What you can reject is what takes you away from that, into the setting-sun cocoon. Having this vision shows you how to keep going forward along the path of warriorship toward the sun of wakefulness that radiates peaceful confidence. You do not get sidetracked and slowed by clouds or fall asleep in the darkening twilight of cowardice.

The complete action of a warrior involves the four qualities of warriorship. The warrior's action can be seen in terms of four stages, although in real situations these are subtle and overlap:

1. *Meekness: Feel the ground.* Explore the situation. Take an attitude of humbleness and inquisitiveness toward the situation before you involve yourself in it. Provide space for people to express their needs and fears, with an empty mind free from preconception about what is going on or what needs to be done. Be gentle and humble but alert.

2. *Perkiness: Show your genuine interest.* When you have clearly seen what is needed, with an uplifted, fresh attitude extend yourself out to the others. Make genuine contact with them. You are not yet ready to act but are able to appreciate their goodness. In this way they feel their own goodness and richness, and they are able to let go of their own doubts and feelings of inadequacy.

3. *Outrageousness: Act without bias.* Since you have shown interest, you are already involved. You create a gap in the situation by not being caught up in your own or in other people's expectations and fears. Since you thoroughly laid the ground in the first two stages, you can now leap right in without hesitation and without worrying about whether you are making a mistake. You can act in a way that transforms the energy of the situation rather than try to impose your own energy on top of it.

4. *Inscrutability: Let go of any preconceived outcome.* Let the drama happen— just let it evolve naturally—but stay with it with confidence in your decision and action. Cut any doubt and wandering mind that might creep in at the last moment, any attachment to what you would like the outcome of your action to be, and any self-gratification that might come from a seemingly successful result.

It is important to realize that you do not have to think deliberately, "Now I am being meek, now outrageous," and so on. In fact, such thoughts would make your action awkward and heavy-handed, like trying to read a manual on lovemaking while you are in the middle of doing it. This description of action may seem a little abstract, although those who have practiced a martial art such as aikido may already be familiar with something along these lines. The description should be regarded more as a contemplation than a manual. The key points are: Lay the ground for your action gently and thoroughly. Take a genuine interest. Don't force anything, but act when a gap naturally opens in the situation. See it through to the end without being attached to the outcome.

Let us consider some examples. Perhaps you are confronted by an angry teenager or an employee filled with resentment. First pause and give the other person some distance. You can be alert and watchful—you don't need to let yourself be taken in by any deception that is going on, but still you can be open. Listen to what they have to say with an attitude that perhaps you *don't* really know what they have on their mind.

Next, you can begin to show interest. Be inquisitive, ask questions, and really find out what is behind the display of anger or resentment, but don't get caught up in the negativity and depression of the other person or doubt whether you can handle it. The situation is sparky and full of energy. That can be uplifting and a basis for very real communication as you continue to ride your windhorse.

Be patient, and wait for a gap in their anger or resentment. There will always be a gap, a flicker of openness. At a certain point they will show that they don't quite believe their own complaint one hundred percent. At that point there is an opening for you to slip in and offer your kindness and firmness. You can be daring and direct if you wait for the gap and enter it with gentleness. You can say what needs to be said without worrying about its effect. A spark of humor is possible.

Having stuck your neck out, you don't turn around and run back into your own cocoon. You don't excuse yourself or apologize for being so direct. Nor do you try to force things to go your way. Just stay with it, and the energy will already be transformed. In this way, anger can turn into humor and resentment can soften into sadness.

In another example, perhaps you are attracted to someone. How do you go about entering a joyful relationship with them? The first stage, the stage of meekness, is to pause, wait, and feel your attraction and your interest with wide-open eyes. This stage is vital, just as in dealing with aggression. If you do not pause and feel the basic nature of the situation before you act, then your action and that of the other person will be purely reactive. Open your eyes, look at the other person, and *see* them. Is your interest stimulated by superficial attractiveness, or do you feel some genuine connection there? It does not matter which it is, as long as you know. Take an attitude of being cheerfully self-contained but inquisitive about your potential friend, and watchful.

Now you can reach out toward that person and make some gesture or word of invitation. If your interest in another comes from appreciating their goodness, showing it to them makes them feel enriched and awakened themselves, and they will respond. You have already entered a relationship with that person. Still, you do not act too soon. You wait, with the meekness of the tiger and the upliftedness of the snow lion, until there is a moment of genuine openness in your heart toward the other. Then you can express your affection without fear of how it will be received, because you know it is genuine and does not need confirmation.

Finally you let the encounter continue in its own way. Perhaps the other person does not respond to your interest. Perhaps a lasting friendship evolves.

The outcome is not yours to determine or manipulate. Stay with the new relationship without getting caught up in your expectations of how it ought to go. In that way it will be fulfilling, however it turns out. Then if it is time to end, you can end it without any regrets.

The end of an activity is the beginning of a transition. Times of transition can be dangerous, because the mind tends to wander, giving the cocoon a chance to slip back and steal our awareness and confidence. We might chalk these slips up to exhaustion or lack of concentration. But they happen in part because we always feel that we have to rush on to the next thing. We never give ourselves the opportunity to complete anything properly. You might, for example, be doing an intricate wood carving. Just as you are making the last strokes with the chisel, you think of what a good piece you have carved and what has to be done next. Your attention wavers, your hand slips, and the whole piece is ruined, not to mention that you just cut your hand—hopefully it won't need stitches. So we need to stay with an action, pay attention to the very end.

After the action is finished, we usually want to judge what we have done. Was it a success or a failure? We want to analyze it: What did I say, what did I do? Did I do it right? What do they think of me? All this prevents us from letting go and opening ourselves to the next moment. To finish an action, then, we must first complete our action properly, without losing our awareness at the last moment, then let go of it so that we are free to begin again.

This is the expression of inscrutability, how inscrutability manifests in action. The Dorje Dradul says,

> The main point is being somewhat noncommittal, but at the same time seeing a project through to its end. You are noncommittal because you are not interested in confirmation. This does not mean that you are afraid of being caught by your actions, but rather that you are not interested in being at the center of the scene. However, at the same time, you are very loyal to others, so that you always accomplish your project with sympathy for them.

This warrior's action may take place in a flash—for example, encountering an angry colleague at the office. Or it may be an action taking many months or years—for example, ruling a country. Once the Dorje Dradul asked a group of his students what they would do if they suddenly found themselves running a kingdom. After they gave their own answers, they asked what he would do. His response was, "First announce that everything would continue as usual, and then find out what people are actually doing." This is the stage of meekness.

The Dorje Dradul always knew what was going on in the organizations he had founded. He had friends everywhere. Whenever he went to a party or a reception or met people informally in any situation, he would always ask, "How are you doing? How is your work? How is your love life?" He also knew, to a degree that sometimes shocked his friends, what was going on in the world beyond these organizations. On one occasion, long before the lifting of the Iron Curtain, he described in detail the inside of a Russian tank. Sometime later someone read in a magazine the same details, as described by a Russian defector. So the stages of meekness and perkiness were always happening with him.

In the early days of the Naropa Institute, the organization reached a particularly difficult point and there was a tremendous amount of infighting among the staff. There were two executive directors, one for administration and one for academics, and they were constantly at odds with each other. I was supposed to be overseeing the Institute, acting on behalf of the Dorje Dradul, but whenever I visited, I was met by a morass of discontent that I did not know how to handle. The Dorje Dradul himself did nothing for many months, besides listen to formal and informal reports. He had the staff draw up a plan for reorganization, but that plan was complicated and did not accomplish any real change. He encouraged the board of directors, of which he was the president, to try to sort it out—he always wanted decisions to be made by consensus. However, the situation became worse and worse. No one was specifically to blame—it was as if the Institute as a whole had become caught in the trap of doubt, and all its staff members along with it.

One evening the Dorje Dradul visited the Institute to give a public talk. Before the talk began, the staff, including myself, the two executive directors, and his attendants sat in the office with him, with a feeling of black air in the room. Suddenly he said, quietly and gently but with a sharp tone, "I have been thinking that we need a change of leadership at the Institute. I think we need one person in charge and that [so-and-so] should take over." He told us to think about it and let him know what we thought. The next day he left town for three months.

We were all absolutely stunned. It was a bolt from the blue. For several months afterward people approached the Dorje Dradul, to suggest that "so-and-so" was not the right person, or to argue that one of the current executive directors should continue alone, or to present their favorite candidate. However, the Dorje Dradul had already gone through the meekness and perkiness stages—he had done all the research needed and he had talked with everyone remotely involved. His action was outrageous, slipping his vision of the Institute's needs through the gap that had been created when our own confusion, jealousy, and competitiveness had exhausted us. In the months that followed, he still listened carefully to what everyone had to say and was interested, but he remained unwavering. The staff cheered up immediately after the new leadership took office, and after a year or so the Institute entered a completely new phase of growth. His abrupt action was precisely what had been needed. Yet it had not come from his having a personal agenda, but from seeing so clearly what the Institute needed. Authentic action makes others no less important than oneself, and this is the basis for establishing an enlightened society.

What Is an Enlightened Society?

An enlightened society is not a utopia by any means. It is not a dreamland where everyone is already perfect. An enlightened society is one where people are *willing* to practice, to let go of their fear, to be genuine and kind to each other. Connecting with the energy of the dralas means nothing if people keep the discovery to themselves. We must bring that energy to earth and help other people. We can manifest windhorse in the good old solid day-to-day world of friends and society. The purpose of the Shambhala teachings is not merely to provide another path of personal spiritual development. The purpose is to provide the means by which we can begin, together, to build a community of warriors. We all need the company of fellow travelers on the path of warriorship. We need a genuine human society.

There have been enlightened societies, though never utopias, many times before all over the world, at various periods in history, in large civilizations and small tribal groups. In this book I have neither the intention nor the space to analyze how an enlightened society needs to be organized politically and socially. There is no fixed form for such a society—it evolves according to the needs of time and place. A few examples, however, might give you a sense of what our enlightened society might look like. We can find signs of it in the Kingdom of Shambhala; in the early Ming period in China; during the era of Shotoku Taishi in Japan; at times in Tibet, Thailand, Cambodia, India, Bhutan, and Bali (before tourism, of course); in the Ibo and Yoruba civilizations of West Africa; at periods in ancient Greece and Rome; in Britain at the time of Arthur; in Europe in the early Middle Ages; with many Native American tribes such as the Navajo and Huichol of Mexico; and with indigenous peoples around the world such as the Bushmen of the Kalahari and the Xavante of Brazil.

Many friends have visited the Himalayan kingdom of Bhutan and returned remarking how like a Shambhala society it is in many ways. I have not myself visited the country and this account is based on a beautiful photographic essay, *Bhutan: A Kingdom of the Eastern Himalayas,* by Guy van Strydonck, Françoise Pommaret-Imaeda, and Yoshior Imaeda.

Bhutan is a mix of various populations that live in valleys isolated from one another and cut off from the outside world by high and treacherous mountain barriers. Yet the one million inhabitants share the same pride in being Bhutanese that is rooted in a mutual respect for the cultural values of each of the peoples that make up the Bhutanese nation.

Describing the people of Bhutan, a traveler who visited the country in 1774 wrote: "The simplicity of their manners, their slight intercourse with strangers, and a strong sense of religion, preserve the Bhutanese from many vices to which more polished nations are addicted. They are strangers to falsehood and ingratitude. Theft, and every other species of dishonesty to which the lust of money gives birth, are little." By all accounts this is still true today, although Bhutan is rapidly facing obstacles caused by contact with cultures that have just those "vices of more polished nations."

The Bhutanese are striking in their simplicity of manners, common sense, uncommon consideration for others, and their quiet pride in who they are. Bhutanese society is organized in a complex hierarchy and governed by rigorous etiquette, and they behave in a formal and respectful manner toward their superiors. Yet, each individual's place in society is accepted by everyone and there is no class arrogance. They are full of good spirits, uninhibited in expressing themselves and ready for all sorts of jokes. They enjoy making the most of life and make any occasion into an excuse for dancing, singing, archery, playing darts, and stone pitching.

For 90 percent of the population, everyday life consists of working in the fields and tending animals. Agricultural equipment is very simple, and electricity and running water are still unknown in most villages. In spite of this rigorous daily existence, the irrepressible good nature of the Bhutanese is always present: Work in the fields and building houses is enlivened by singing, and mocking laughter and mischievous sarcasm punctuate their activities.

The Bhutanese live mainly in households that include several generations and different branches of one family. Men and women share the work, with women contributing to the family income. The men are not above looking after the children and showing their affection for them. The opinion of the family plays an important role in all decisions. They are in general very religious, and signs of their Buddhist faith mark their landscape: shrines, monasteries, stupas, and prayer flags. Each major event in their lives is celebrated by a religious ceremony, and even the poorest houses have at least an altar with a few pictures, books, flowers, and offerings to the dralas.

Centuries of tradition have combined harmoniously with steady but restrained economic development and social progress over the last few decades to make Bhutan a remarkable nation. Bhutanese society has experienced profound changes and undergone cultural shocks, which might have created instability or destroyed Bhutan's awareness of its heritage. This has happened surprisingly little because the government has endeavored to take account of the aspirations of the people and has taken care not to offend ancestral values.

Bhutan is not an ideal society, and in recent years changes in attitudes in Bhutan have been taking place alongside rapid modernization. The monarchy is a dynamic force that is instrumental in bringing about economic innovation and social progress. It is gentle and by no means dictatorial—any Bhutanese citizen can stop the king's car and hand him a petition as he drives through the countryside. But some chafe under the traditionalism, and there are a few who would like to abolish the monarchy altogether. There are laws requiring men and women to wear the traditional garb in public, and no one is allowed to watch television. You may own a TV set, but if you turn it on all you will get is static, and you will be fined if you are caught using a satellite dish. The government, led by the king, is very concerned about protecting the environment, but not all the people share that concern. Some Nepalese immigrant workers live in conditions very inferior to those of any Bhutanese citizens. The Nepalese minority do not want to be forced to follow traditional Bhutanese customs and are making strident demands for change.

All these are signs of the difficulty that the traditional Bhutanese society is having in preserving its traditional customs and gentleness while accommodating the pressures of the modern era and being surrounded by societies that have already succumbed to the lure of consumerism.

Indeed, each of the societies we suggested as examples of an enlightened society had not only its own color and style, determined by the culture and beliefs of the times, but its corruption and ego-centered forces. But each does, or did, recognize the fundamental goodness of humans and sought to nourish this goodness and to promote decency, dignity, elegance, and bravery in its people. Now the dralas are ready to help us establish enlightened human society again. Yet to do so, we cannot go back to a prescientific era, and even if we could, it would make no sense. We cannot forget what we have learned, our scientific discoveries and our technology. Enlightened society must be possible even within that context. We can only go forward in the vision of the Great Eastern Sun, rather then let ourselves slip into the darkness of the setting sun.

The Dorje Dradul introduced Shambhala students to the dralas for the express purpose of helping to create a good society—an enlightened society— on earth again, in the context of the modern world and modern understanding. He constantly encouraged his students to pay attention to the state of the world and to the desperate need for a society founded on basic goodness, where people know how to nourish basic goodness, where they care for each other and act genuinely toward each other.

How Can We Establish an Enlightened Society?

The way to establish an enlightened society is not complicated or difficult to understand. People can be decent and trustworthy when they recognize basic goodness in others. We don't *have* to fight and compete, make the best deals, slaughter the competition, spy on them, and cut them off. We don't have to worry about ourselves—no matter what our history. We can wake up here and now, work together, and care for others. We don't need to worry so much about our livelihood. We don't really need more food and wealth to survive, unless we live in Ethiopia or Somalia or another sad and needy part of the world. We have enough already, and we can help those needy parts. When we have the intention to help others, if we follow our passion and longing and take care of the details of our life, then our livelihood will come along. We may not be rich—even Mozart died a pauper—but we will manage.

Some form of spiritual practice is essential in an enlightened society, and in a modern society many different practices can coexist. However, an enlightened society is not merely a group of individuals who just happen to be practicing warriorship together. To nourish basic goodness and provide opportunities for people to awaken to their goodness, the enlightened society itself has to be structured according to the principles of warriorship. The structure of society begins with one-to-one relationships. Its primary relationships are modeled in the family and small community. In the personal relationships of the home, family, and friendships, we can practice creating an enlightened society. We have to begin here if it is to be genuine. The family provides a practical and immediate realm to practice the Shambhala teachings in community. When sharing and working with others in a gentle and fearless way, the most mundane activities are sacred—even cleaning the toilet bowl. We can always be working to extend our feeling of family, and we could feel ourselves as part of a larger family—the world tribe of warriors—which includes our ancestors, our neighbors, and future generations.

Being decent Shambhala citizens comes from our practice and from our tender heart. Our decency is as literal as paying our debts on time, as much as we can, and not disappointing our friends who have been kind to us. It is in relaxing in our discipline and having a natural sense of humor. It is practicing good speech—speaking gently and refraining from empty chatter. There is no benefit to be gained from slandering others. We can respect others in our society, starting with our parents who gave us life and our elders who showed us how to go forward with vision and bravery. We can appreciate everyone who ever taught us anything—including insane leaders who teach us how important it is to be sane.

Leadership is natural in a good human society. People who practice the warrior's disciplines together—the disciplines of mindfulness and awareness, gentleness and fearlessness, and raising windhorse—know who their leaders are. A leader with authentic presence raises people up—encourages them to follow the path of warriorship so that they can surpass that leader. When there is genuine leadership, based on the sanity and practice of the people, then the political setup reflects a natural hierarchy. The rule of the setting sun, in which people find the best ways to keep each other asleep in their shared cocoon, doesn't happen. Nor does authoritarian rule arise, based on confusion and greed and keeping people down, because people are willing to be fearless *and* gentle.

The natural hierarchy of an enlightened society is like a flower reaching from the solid support of earth to the open space of heaven, in contrast to a lid that keeps people squashed down. We pay attention to the natural hierarchy of the sun and the sea and the moon, the flowers and the birds, the rocks and the earth, the dust bits and the garbage bits. If we slow down, be inquisitive, and let ourselves feel, then we can make our lives a work of art. Trust basic goodness, and we can bring some joy and laughter, caring and tears to the world. We can conduct ourselves with the dignity and wholesomeness of the warrior. We can stop polluting the world with our neurosis. We can stop making war. *We* can do this. We don't have to worry about others doing it. Good society comes from this.

Many of the conventional manners in modern society originated as ritual ways for people to show respect for each other and to acknowledge each other's windhorse and invite dralas into their shared world. People used to tip their hats to each other as they passed on the street; men would not enter a restaurant without a coat and tie, or women without their shoulders covered; they would hold a door open to allow the other to go first; and so on.

Very few people now realize that the practice of shaking hands, for example, originated as a ritual in the medieval days of chivalry and knighthood. Knights would hold out their right hand to show that they held no weapon and as a gesture of peace. So now, when we meet a friend walking down the street, we hold out our open hand, our friend holds out his hand, and we join hands and shake them in a ritualistic way.

All these are expressions of decorum and decency, acknowledgments of basic human goodness. Such simple everyday rituals carry centuries of wisdom about how to bring peace into relationships. The raw wildness of being human has been tamed over thousands of years by our ancestors, who in their wisdom developed rituals for all aspects of human intercourse. *It is only because of this that there is any human society at all.* In this sense all of us practice ritual in everyday life in even the simplest interactions with one another.

Beyond these everyday patterns of behavior, ritual and ceremony play a profound role in all human societies. They bind human beings together, with each other, with the natural world, and with the dralas. You can generally feel the power of the dralas more easily when you invoke them in a group for the well-being of all. Through group ceremonies that invite the dralas to join in, a society maintains wisdom, compassion, and power.

Because of the separation between the secular and the sacred in the West, the sense of sacredness in all human intercourse depended on religion. As religion declined, social norms of behavior and ceremonies lost their heartfelt magical ritual quality and became hollow shells. In the setting-sun world the etiquette of simple decency is disdained as an expression of repression and lack of freedom, and people try to do away with it and become completely casual. Ceremony has become empty-hearted theatrics. The result is further and further depression. Of course, when windhorse and the connection with dralas is lost, it makes little difference how we behave, and such mannered ways of behaving *can* be hollow and petty. They become just another form of externally imposed morality or authoritarian rule that in the end buries genuine goodness alive.

Yet when we raise windhorse, we can feel the heart of our traditional ways. Then we *want* to treat our bodies and the world around us with modesty and respect and to behave decently to each other. When we rediscover the heart in simple codes of behavior and group ceremonies, they become part of the celebration of life and of each other's humanity, rather than rules and theatrics that are imposed on us through fear or ignorance.

Let Us Join Together

Can we imagine a genuine enlightened society where everyone trusts each other; where no one is defensive because they are genuinely who they are and they trust themselves; where they can relax and do not feel as if they need protection from each other; where people help each other and care about each other and take care of the world; where everyone is cheerful and delighted, listening to flowers and rocks and dralas, dancing with their energy? Can we live in a magical and powerful sphere of energy where we play and dance and celebrate goodness with our fellow warriors who have kind hearts and gentle natures but wide-open eyes? Does it sound like Disney Dizzy Land? It's not a fantasy. It has been done before and we can do it now, but we have to help each other. We are all here, including the dralas, and together we can do it.

The enlightened society seems far out of reach. But with the help of the dralas we can touch into enlightened energy and bring it onto earth. Establishing an enlightened society is very much a question of relating with the real earth upon which we dwell, opening to it with bravery and tenderness, and caring for it. The Dorje Dradul said,

Too often, people think that solving the world's problems is based on conquering the earth, rather than on touching the earth, touching the ground. That is one definition of the setting-sun mentality: trying to conquer the earth so that you can ward off reality. There are all kinds of deodorant sprays to keep you from smelling the real world, and all kinds of processed food to keep you from tasting raw ingredients. Shambhala vision is not trying to create a fantasy world where no one has to see blood or experience a nightmare. Shambhala vision is based on living on this earth, the real earth that grows crops, the earth that nurtures your existence. You can learn to live on this earth: how to camp, how to pitch a tent, how to ride a horse, milk a cow, build a fire. Even though you may be living in a city in the twentieth century, you can learn to experience the sacredness, the *nowness* of reality. That is the basis for creating an enlightened society.

We start from square one and take a little baby step, and then another, and then suddenly we find ourselves leaping giant steps. When we plant a tender seed, we nurture and nourish it, water it and care for it. It sprouts tender shoots, uncertain and doubtful—and maybe afraid of being trampled on or eaten by the cat. But before we know it, it has grown into a lovely, blossoming bush—very quickly. The start is slow, but then it takes off with vigor and energy. We can start slowly with patience, but we have to remember that time is running out. We have so little time to create our enlightened society. We cannot waste time in cocoon fascination. Time passes quickly—we thought it took so long for our baby to learn to walk, but oh my, she's already leaving home. When we are very young we think we have all the time in the world, but when we reach middle age we know we don't.

Yet time is also endless. When we renounce the setting-sun world, we discover we already have an enlightened society, and suddenly we *do* have all the time in the world. The time is *now*. Let's go along now with the energy of the great big glorious sacred world, strange and full of magic. Loons are magical; electricity is magical; our job is magical, and so is our lover, if we tell the truth. Let's not deny the world by planning and scheming and figuring it out. We don't have to look for a handle to hold on to for dear life; we don't need stability to play with phenomena and dance to the tune of the cha cha cha. We don't need to wait to find someone we can trust. If we trust *ourselves,* that's enough. Take the attitude that the whole world is trustworthy and good because we are trustworthy and good. Have a secret smile—we know it's true.

This is such a huge, big world—let's not constrict or limit ourselves in the name of ideals like "conventional wisdom," "political correctness," "good judgment," "science," "artistic freedom," or anything else we can think of. We can have a good time together. We can have fun—but genuine fun, which includes a good, feisty, but friendly fight. We know that good and bad, happy and sad, love and irritation are all part of the giant feast. We can let them happen in basic goodness. We can join with others who care the same way, and we and they can join with more others, and so on. Then when we look around, we'll see that we don't have to struggle or create anything—our world is already enlightened.

The Dorje Dradul's son and successor as head of the Shambhala community, Osel Rangdrol Mukpo, commented to a group of Shambhala students:

When we think about enlightened society, we often feel that we have to create something. I think it is important to realize that nothing is created; everything already exists. The enlightenment of society is pre-existent. It is a matter of tuning in to the situation. You could go to countries that are based on similar principles of compassion and teachings on how to create enlightened society, but there is still corruption and abuse, so I don't think we can imitate any examples of that kind. Rather, we are trying to communicate with one another's dignity. So enlightenment and enlightened society are self-existing. If that realization comes about, then everything is possible.

Enlightened society wouldn't mean having cars that don't touch the ground or anything like that. Enlightened society is very much right here in this room, among ourselves. If we actually acknowledge basic goodness and tender heart, if we can acknowledge our fear or whatever we may feel, then there is some kind of common ground to work with. That is what we mean by enlightened society.

We need to learn to have soft, tender, sad, and even broken hearts. We can cry together, and then we can love each other. When you love, start small then expand. Love a dog, and then you can expand to your children, your spouse, your friends, your colleagues, your government officials, the dralas, and all the rest, including the birds and the bees. Nothing need keep us from falling in love. Fall in love with whatever you can—with a frog or tree bark or an ant or your best friend. It doesn't really matter. By loving we include the world in a bigger sphere where all can be included. Buddhist teacher Joseph Goldstein describes genuine love as "a universal, nondiscriminating sense of care and connectedness. . . . Love is inclusive and powerful—not the near-enemy of attachment, but something much deeper—infusing our awareness, enabling us to open to and accept the truth of each moment; and [it is] service that feels our intimate connectedness with all things and responds to the wholeness of life."

Love—the genuine love of the sacred world—is the key, and its power shines everywhere. Indigenous peoples throughout the world know genuine love; they have always loved the earth and its beings, cared for it and protected it. The Buddhists know this; they know the way to develop *maitri*—lovingkindness. Christians know this and feel it; they realize the love of basic goodness. Some scientists know this; the best science is done when scientists have empathy with what they observe. We *all* know the power of genuine love. We can all work together to build the genuine society.

A whole underground society is happening now, at this very moment. Many decent, down-to-earth, up-to-heaven people feel this way and have taken the vow, "We will create enlightened society on earth." There are movements of many kinds—some people call it the New Age, but who cares, maybe it's the Old Age—an endless stream of good warriors being born again in the sacred world. Their warrior's cry cuts aggression and offers friendship and genuine affection.

Let's do it together—whatever path we choose. We have shown you the Shambhala path of the warrior. It is a good path, genuine and true, real and workable. We would love you to come along, but if you have another path, that's okay too. Let's all work together and have a jolly good time. We can cheer up now, love and help others, and create our enlightened society in this lifetime.

APPENDIX
The Shambhala
Training Program

Shambhala training is offered to the public in weekend programs and other formats. The programs consist of talks, group discussions, individual private interviews, instruction and guidance in mindfulness-awareness practice, and opportunities for group practice. The practices of raising windhorse and executing the stroke of confidence are taught at Warrior Assembly, an advanced residential program.

For further details, please write, phone, or fax:

Shambhala Training International
1084, Tower Road
Halifax, Nova Scotia
Canada, B3H 2Y5
Phone: (902) 423-3266
Fax: (902) 423-2750

Shambhala Training Programs, as well as other programs and events related to the Shambhala teachings, take place in Shambhala Centers. Shambhala Centers or study groups are located in the following cities:

United States
Atlanta, Georgia
Austin, Texas
Baltimore, Maryland
Barnet, Vermont
[Bay Area] California
Boise, Idaho
Boston, Massachusetts
Boulder, Colorado
Brunswick, Maine
Burlington, Vermont
Chicago, Illinois
Cincinnati, Ohio
Cleveland, Ohio
Columbia, South Carolina
Columbus, Ohio
Denver, Colorado
Durham, North Carolina
Houston, Texas
Juneau, Alaska
Kansas City, Kansas
Lexington, Kentucky
Los Angeles, California
Milwaukee, Wisconsin
Minneapolis, Minnesota
New Haven, Connecticut
New York, New York
Northampton, Massachusetts
Philadelphia, Pennsylvania
Portland, Maine
Red Feather Lakes, Colorado
San Diego, California
Sarasota, Florida
Seattle, Washington
Sun Valley, Idaho
Tyler, Texas
Washington, D.C.

Canada
Edmonton, Alberta
Fredericton, New Brunswick
Halifax, Nova Scotia
Montreal, Quebec
Nelson, British Columbia
Ottawa, Ontario
St. John's, Newfoundland
Toronto, Ontario
Vancouver, British Columbia
Victoria, British Columbia

Australia
Melbourne

Austria
Vienna

Brazil
São Paulo

Chile
Santiago

Czech Republic
Prague

Denmark
Copenhagen

England
London

France
Marseilles
Paris

Appendix

Germany
Berlin
Bremen
Frankfurt
Freiburg
Hamburg
Marburg
Munich

Greece
Athens

Holland
Amsterdam

Italy
Milan

Japan
Osaka

Mexico
Mexico City

New Zealand
Auckland

Poland
Cracow

Spain
Madrid

Sweden
Stockholm

Switzerland
Bern
Lugano

For information concerning the Naropa Institute, write or call:

The Naropa Institute
2130 Arapahoe Avenue
Boulder, Colorado 80302
Phone: (303)444-0202

References and Suggested Reading

Angelou, Maya. *I Know Why the Caged Bird Sings*. New York: Bantam, 1971.

Assagioli, Roberto. *Psychosynthesis*. London: Turnstone Press, 1975.

Bernbaum, Edwin. *The Way to Shambhala*. New York: Anchor, 1980.

Black Elk, Wallace, and William S. Lyon. *Black Elk: The Sacred Ways of a Lakota*. New York: HarperCollins, 1991.

Borysenko, Joan. *Minding the Body, Mending the Mind*. New York: Bantam, 1987.

Boyd, Doug. *Rolling Thunder*. New York: Delta, 1974.

Cheng, François. *Empty and Full: The Language of Chinese Brush Painting*. Boston: Shambhala Publications, 1994.

Chodron, Pema. *The Wisdom of No Escape and the Path of Loving Kindness*. Boston: Shambhala, 1991.

Cleary, J. C., trans. and ed. *Worldly Wisdom: Confucian Teachings of the Ming Dynasty*. Boston: Shambhala, 1991.

Coe, Stella Mathieu. *Ikebana*. Woodstock, NY: Overlook Press, 1984.

Csikszentmihalyi, Mihaly. *Flow: The Psychology of Optimal Experience*. New York: Harper and Row, 1990.

Devereux, Paul. *Symbolic Landscapes: The Dreamtime Earth and Avebury's Open Secrets*. Glastonbury: Gothic Image Publications, 1992.

250
References and Suggested Reading

Dong, Paul, and Aristide H. Esser. *Chi Gong: The Ancient Chinese Way to Health*. New York: Paragon, 1990.

Dossey, Larry. *Meaning and Medicine*. New York: Bantam, 1992.

Feuerstein, Georg. "Drukpa Kunley and the Crazy Wisdom Method of Teaching," Intro. Keith Dowman, *The Divine Madman*. Clearlake, CA: Dawn Horse Press, 1990.

Fingarette, Herbert. *Confucius—The Secular as Sacred*. New York: Harper and Row, 1972.

Forward, Nancy Wake. *The White Mouse*. Macmillan Australia, 1985.

Franck, Frederick. *The Zen of Seeing*. New York: Vintage, 1973.

———— *Zen Seeing, Zen Drawing*. New York: Bantam, 1993.

Fryba, Mirko. *The Art of Happiness: Teachings of Buddhist Psychology*. Boston: Shambhala, 1989.

Gersi, Douchan. *Faces in the Smoke*. Los Angeles: Tarcher, 1991.

Ghiselin, Brewster. *The Creative Process*. New York: Mentor, 1952.

Goldstein, Joseph, and Jack Kornfield. *Seeking the Heart of Wisdom*. Boston: Shambhala, 1987.

Grudin, Robert. *The Grace of Great Things*. New York: Ticknor and Fields, 1990.

Guteson, David. "No Place Like Home." *Harper's*, November 1992.

Halifax, Joan. *Shamanic Voices*. New York: Arkana, 1979.

Harman, Willis, and Howard Rheingold. *Higher Creativity*. Los Angeles: Tarcher, 1984.

Heinze, Ruth-Inge. *Shamans of the Twentieth Century*. New York: Irvington, 1991.

Herrigel, Eugen. *Zen in the Art of Archery*. New York: Vintage, 1971.

Isozaki, Arata. "Ma: Space-Time in Japan." *Japan Today*, no. 36.

Jahn, Robert, and Brenda Dunne. *Margins of Reality: The Role of Consciousness in the Physical World*. New York: Harcourt Brace Jovanovich, 1987.

Kabat-Zinn, Jon. *Full Catastrophe Living*. New York: Delacorte, 1990.

Katz, Nathan. *Buddhist and Western Psychology*. Boulder: Prajna Press, 1983.

Knudtson, Peter, and David Suzuki. *The Wisdom of the Elders*. New York: Bantam, 1992.

Koestler, Arthur. *The Roots of Coincidence*. New York: Vintage, 1972.

Kornfield, Jack. *A Path with Heart*. New York: Bantam, 1993.

La Borde, Roger. "Gerald Red Elk." *Vajvadhata Sun*, December 1984.

LaChapelle, Dolores. *Sacred Land, Sacred Sex*. Silverton, CO: Finn Hill Arts, 1988.

Langer, Ellen J. *Mindfulness*. Reading, MA: Addison-Wesley, 1989.

Lawlor, Robert. *Voices of the First Day*. Rochester, VT: Inner Traditions, 1991.

Liu I-Ming. *Awakening to the Tao*, trans. Thomas Cleary. Boston: Shambhala, 1988.

Maclean, Dorothy. *To Hear the Angels Sing*. Hudson, NY: Lindisfarne Press, 1990.

Mathieu, W. A. *The Listening Book*. Boston: Shambhala, 1991.

Matsuoka, Seigow. "Aspects of Kami." *Japan Today,* no. 12.

Matsuwa, don Jose. In Joan Halifax, *Shamanic Voices*. New York: Arkana, 1979.

Maybury-Lewis, David. *Millennium: Tribal Wisdom and the Modern World*. New York: Viking, 1992.

McGaa, Ed, Eagle Man. *Mother Earth Spirituality*. New York: HarperCollins, 1989.

McNeley, J. K. *Holy Wind in Navajo Philosophy*. Tucson, AZ: University of Arizona Press, 1981.

Moore, Thomas. *Care of the Soul*. New York: HarperCollins, 1992.

Morgan, Marlo. *Mutant Message*. Lees Summit, MO: MM Co., 1991.

Moyers, Bill. *Healing and the Mind*. New York: Doubleday, 1993.

Moyne, John, and Coleman Barks, trans. *Open Secret: Versions of Rumi*. Putney, VT: Threshold, 1984.

Nollman, Jim. *Dolphin Dreamtime*. New York: Bantam, 1990.

Ono, Sokyo. *Shinto: The Kami Way*. Rutland, VT: Tuttle, 1962.

Patterson, Freeman. *Photography and the Art of Seeing*. Toronto: Van Nostrand Reinhold, 1979.

Peat, F. David. *Synchronicity: The Bridge Between Matter and Mind*. New York: Bantam, 1987.

Ray, Reginald. "Gone Beyond Lhasa." *Shambhala Sun,* September 1994.

Rheingold, Howard. *They Have a Word For It*. Los Angeles: Tarcher, 1988.

Rowan, John. *Subpersonalities*. London: Routledge, 1990.

Sacks, Oliver. *The Man Who Mistook His Wife for a Hat*. New York: HarperPerennial, 1990.

Sagarn, Keith, ed. *D. H. Lawrence and New Mexico*. Salt Lake City: Gibbs Smith, 1982. Thanks to Bill Gordon for this quote.

Sen, Soshitsu. *Tea Life, Tea Mind*. New York: Weatherhill, 1981.

Seng-ts'an. "On Trust in the Heart," in *Buddhist Texts Through the Ages*. Trans. and ed. Edward Conze, I. B. Homer, David Snellgrove, and Arthur Waley. New York: Harper and Row, 1954.

Shallis, Michael. *On Time*. New York: Schocken, 1983.

Sliker, Gretchen. *Multiple Mind*. Boston: Shambhala, 1992.

Sogyal Rinpoche. *The Tibetan Book of Living and Dying*. New York: HarperCollins, 1992.

Stevens, John. *The Sword of No-Sword*. Boston: Shambhala, 1984.

Stick, Gina Etra. "Dwelling in Oriental Architecture." Unpublished M.A. thesis, University of Washington, 1989.

Suzuki, Shunryu. *Zen Mind, Beginner's Mind*. New York: Weatherhill, 1973.

Tendzin, Osel. *Buddha in the Palm of Your Hand*. Boston: Shambhala, 1982.

Thich Nhat Hanh. *Peace Is Every Step*. New York: Bantam, 1991.

Thompson, Robert Farris. *Flash of the Spirit: African and Afro-American Art and Philosophy*. New York: Vintage, 1984.

Thundup Rinpoche, Tulku. *Hidden Teachings of Tibet*. London: Wisdom, 1986.

Trungpa, Chogyam. *Glimpses of Abhidharma*. Boulder, CO: Prajna Press, 1975.

————. *The Myth of Freedom*. Boston: Shambhala, 1976.

————. *Born in Tibet*. Boulder, CO: Shambhala, 1977.

————. *Journey Without Goal: The Tantric Wisdom of the Buddha*. Boulder, CO: Prajna Press, 1981.

————. *Shambhala: The Sacred Path of the Warrior*. Boston: Shambhala, 1988.

————. *The Heart of the Buddha*. Boston: Shambhala, 1991.

————. *The Lion's Roar*. Boston: Shambhala, 1992.

Tulku Rinpoche, Ugyen. *Repeating the Words of the Buddha*. Kathmandu: Rangjung Yeshe, 1992.

van der Post, Laurens. *The Lost World of the Kalahari*. New York: Harcourt Brace Jovanovich, 1986.

van Strydonck, Guy, Françoise Pommaret-Imaeda, and Yoshiro Imaeda. *Bhutan: A Kingdom of the Eastern Himalayas*. Boston: Shambhala, 1985.

Varela, Francisco, Eleanor Rosch, and Evan Thomson. *The Embodied Mind*. Boston: MIT Press, 1992.

Walker, Susan, ed. *Speaking of Silence*. New York: Paulist Press, 1987.

Wall, Steve, and Harvey Arden. *Wisdom Keepers: Meetings with Native American Spiritual Elders*. Hillsboro, OR: Beyond Words, 1990.

Wilber, Ken. *Quantum Questions*. Boulder, CO: Shambhala, 1984.

Wilber, Ken, Jack Engler, and Daniel P. Brown. *Transformations of Consciousness*. Boston: Shambhala, 1986.

Williams, William Carlos. *The Collected Poems, Volume I*. New York: New Directions, 1985.

Zim, Joshua. "Letter to Rinpoche." *Vajvadhata Sun*, December 1985/January 1986.

Index

About the Authors

Jeremy Hayward, Ph.D., was a close friend and student of Chogyam Trungpa's, the first Tibetan Buddhist teacher in America and founder of the internationally renowned Naropa Institute in Colorado. Dr. Hayward taught with Trungpa Rinpoche and helped him develop Shambhala training in America. He was a Vice President and Trustee at the Naropa Institute for many years, is now Education Director at Shambhala Training International, and teaches Shambhala warriorship retreats around the world.

Karen Hayward, also a close friend and student of Trungpa Rinpoche's, has taught in the Shambala Training Program for many years, and was the first director of the Kalapa Ikebana school of flower arranging that was founded by Chogyam Trungpa. Jeremy and Karen live in Nova Scotia with their daughter, Vanessa.